Controlling The World With Your PC

Paul Bergsman

LLH
Technology Publishing
Eagle Rock, Virginia
www.LLH-Publishing.com

Printed in the United States of America.

Cover design: Brian McMurdo, Ventana Studio, Valley Center, CA
Acquisitions editor and project manager: Harry Helms, HighText Publications
Page design, layout, and production services: Greg Calvert, Artifax, San Diego, CA

ISBN: 1–878707–15–9
Library of Congress catalog number: 94–075298

Technology Publishing

Visit us on the web: www.LLH-Publishing.com

Table of Contents

DIGITAL INPUTS

ANALOG INPUTS

Introduction

I've been teaching electronics for over twenty years, and have been asked repeatedly since the introduction of the Apple IIe computer to interface real world devices with computers. Groups as varied as model train clubs, students developing science fair projects, actors involved with amateur stage productions, and the Cub Scouts have all requested circuits to connect a computer with a real world device. For the last four years, I have been using this knowledge to design museum and trade show exhibits.

This book is based on my experience, and is meant to be a bridge between programmers and hardware hackers. Some folks are a whiz at programming, but know little about the mechanical and electronic aspects of computers. They know how to "talk" to a standard external device, like a printer, but would be lost if asked to write a program to make a computer turn on the kitchen coffee pot at 7:00 a.m. every weekday morning. Others have expertise with a soldering iron. They can interconnect IC chips to perform incredible tasks, but have little understanding of how to get a high level computer language to control their creations.

This book is a union of these two camps. It is a sourcebook for ideas on how to control and monitor real world devices with your IBM/IBM compatible computer. Most of the circuits presented connect to the parallel printer port. This approach provides— pardon the pun—portability.

The *de facto* printer port standard is the IBM PC/ IBM compatible PC printer port (the Apple Macintosh has chosen to follow the beat of a different drummer, unfortunately). These machines currently represent 87% of the PC market. The circuits in this book can plug into any IBM PC/PC compatible printer port. The schematics all use the DB-25 (25 pin) female connector present on IBM type parallel printer ports. Full technical data on the parallel printer port can be found in the hardware reference for your computer. Appendix F of this book describes how to expand the printer port to input or output 24 bits of data. Appendix D also shows how to use the IBM

PC's game port as a data input, although this is very slow and not recommended in most circumstances. The parallel printer port does not vary greatly between different makes of PCs. Some manufacturers may elect to omit some control lines, but each parallel port pin has the same meaning on every computer. Every computer language provides routines to "talk" with the printer. This enables computers to interface to myriad electronic devices.

Most people think the printer port can only output 8-bit data. Not true! The printer port also contains nine input lines. Parallel data entry greatly reduces hardware circuit overhead because many IC chips are designed to directly interface to an 8-bit data port. Though some newer computers are being shipped with bidirectional 8-bit printer ports, most are not. Most printer ports have eight data output bits, five input control bits, and another four bidirectional control bits. This book shows you a variety of methods for inputting *and* outputting 8-bit data from any parallel printer port.

Many IC devices are advertised as "microprocessor compatible." That means they need minimal hardware to connect to a parallel data port. To use the serial port, additional circuitry would have to be added. This would require more circuit board space, increased project cost, and additional assembly time. More parts means there are more things that can go wrong, so reliability suffers. And, since the computer must convert this serial data back to its parallel format, the circuit's speed is reduced by over 500%! This book includes material explaining some special applications that justify serial port interfacing. For the majority of your needs, however, the parallel port is the most cost and time efficient way to go.

When I am asked to give a lecture, I travel to my destination with a small briefcase containing circuit boards and a disk of program listings. Upon arrival, I plug the host's printer cable into my circuit boards, connect power, and boot the software. Quick, efficient, portable—it's that simple.

How This Book Developed

I wanted to provide readers with a book of proven circuits and working software for their use. How many times have you typed in a program listing only to have it bomb, and only track down the error after hours of debugging? How many times have you read a magazine article containing an interesting circuit, only to discover in the fine print that software was available—for a price? Hopefully you will not feel short changed after reading this book. The complete source code in C, Pascal, and/or BASIC accompanies each circuit, and the source code files are contained in the disk bound into the back of this book. The disk also includes compiled, executable (.EXE) files for the software in case you don't want to compile your own versions.

A lot of time went into this book. For each circuit requiring software, I did extensive research, including a lot of reading through data manuals. I then developed a schematic of each circuit and constructed a prototype circuit. A program in Borland's Turbo Pascal was written to operate the prototype circuit. (In a corner of my workshop now sits a large box filled with all the prototype boards developed for this book.) After the Pascal program was debugged, edited, and documented, most of my Pascal source code listings were then converted to C. I prepared each schematic you see in this book myself using PADS software. I then converted most programs to BASIC and—finally!—I documented each chapter with text.

This process took a little longer than simply writing theory about an IC chip. But I think the time was well spent. You now have a resource book filled with working circuits and the code listings of working programs. In my contract with HighText, they agreed not alter or change anything in my circuits or program listings. As a result, there may be a misspelled word now and then that got past my spelling checker, but I know the programs and circuits work. In the past, I have spent hours tracking down a misplaced semicolon in a published program listing. Hopefully, because of my self-inflicted development structure, you will be spared the same grief!

Using This Book

This book is organized into stand-alone "applications." Circuits, related theory, and example software accompanies each unit. The software listings are pre-

sented in Borland's Turbo Pascal, Borland's Turbo C, and QBASIC where appropriate.

The appendices provides additional support material I felt was needed but couldn't fit neatly into any of the book's sections.

Software Selection

Pascal

This book's programs were all written in Borland's Turbo Pascal, then converted to Borland's Turbo C, and finally to Microsoft's QBASIC. I have found Pascal the most time efficient MS-DOS software development language. Pascal code is very readable, and you should find the Pascal listings easy to follow even if you're not normally a Pascal programmer.

Pascal has been described as more "restrictive" than C. Pascal does force you to use good programming techniques and the compiler catches many programming errors. For instance, Pascal will not let you assign a real value to a character type variable:

```
PROGRAM Example;
VAR X : INTEGER;
 CH : CHAR;
BEGIN
CH := X;
END.
```

The compiler will tell you something like "TYPE MISMATCH." In contrast, a C compiler would compile and run the code. The program might lock up your computer, but it would "run!"

Pascal's error checking features can be turned off after program testing and debugging by using compiler directives. The resulting compiled code is just as fast as C code. The difference is development time. When you add the debugging time to software generation time, Pascal is more efficient and the bigger the application the greater the savings.

Another issue is updating. Suppose you wrote a program three years ago and now must change one variable. How fast you find that variable, and can make a correction, is dependent on how readable your code is. Since Pascal is more readable than C or BASIC, corrections and updates take less time. Pascal forces you to write good, structured code; the safeguards are built in.

Suppose your program has one little section that gets called over and over. You want that small section to run as fast as possible. Pascal, like C, allows you to include assembly language in your program. The following example has two lines of Pascal code followed by two lines of assembly language code:

```
BEGIN
X := X + 1;
Y := 38 * C;
 ASM
 MOV AH, DH
 SHR AX, 1
 END; { asm }
END; { example }
```

For readability, debugging, and updating on an IBM/IBM compatible PCs, I feel Pascal is currently the most efficient software development language.

C

C skyrocketed in popularity after IBM announced that it would support the language on all of its products. C is marginally portable to other platforms. However, this book was written for use with an IBM/IBM clone printer port. There is nothing presented in this book that requires C's "special" features. "Special" is in quotes because no one has been able to demonstrate to me one "special" feature C has when running on an IBM/compatible machine!

BASIC

BASIC is included with PC-DOS or MS-DOS. Everyone knows some BASIC. It is most people's first exposure to programming. Because it is so user-friendly, BASIC often introduces novice programmers to bad programming habits.

For simple tasks, BASIC is fast and efficient. If you need to write a "quick-and-dirty" routine, BASIC might be the way to go. However, many programs are not practical in BASIC (try writing a terminate and stay resident—TSR—program in BASIC). In addition, large BASIC program listings are hard to follow. New versions of BASIC have added Pascal and C type functions. Unfortunately, doing away with line numbers and adding *WHILE* loops did not eradicate BASIC's shortcomings. And BASIC programs run slower since a compiler is not part of the PC-DOS/MS-DOS package—QBASIC is interpreted line-by-line during program execution. If you're going to invest in a compiler, you might as well invest in a language designed for large applications.

Instead of learning BASIC's patchwork of upgrade enhancements, you will find it far more time efficient to learn Pascal from the beginning.

I Recommend Pascal!

Pascal is part of most high school computer literacy programs. It logically follows LOGO, taught in many elementary and middle schools. BASIC was taught in years past because it came packaged with most computers. Schools are always short of money, and BASIC was a "quick and dirty" fix.

By contrast, Pascal was developed to teach good programming skills and techniques. It might have died a slow death if not for Borland International. They have expanded the language and continually added procedures that exploit the features of new generations of Intel microprocessors. A measure of Pascal's acceptance in education can be seen in the questions relating to Pascal found on SAT and advanced placement examinations.

Over the years BASIC has also undergone some changes. Many of its newer commands mirror ones found in Pascal. Despite these changes, BASIC is NOT Pascal and is still NOT a good language for learning sound programming skills. BASIC does only minimal code checking before running (as does C). And BASIC, like C, encourages you to write poor code. If you really try, you can write good BASIC code. But it takes a lot of work.

If your local high school is still teaching BASIC, your children (or maybe you!) are being shortchanged. Picket your school board and demand curriculum improvements, starting with a switch to Pascal!

With that off my chest, I hope you find the circuits and software in this book to be fun as well as useful.

Paul Bergsman

About the Author

For 21 years, Paul Bergsman has taught high school technology education and mathematics in the Philadelphia public schools. He attended Temple University to study electronics technology and later received a Bachelor of Arts in secondary education from Temple.

Paul's interests include computers, chess, bike riding, folk dancing, folk music, amateur radio (his station call sign is N3PSO), live theater, and going to the movies. He is an active member of the Philadelphia Area Computer Society (PACS), where he chairs the Engineering and Robotics Special Interest Group.

Dedication

To Oliver Cheney, my teacher, mentor, and friend.

Credits

All circuits were drawn PADS PCB (PADS Software, Inc., 119 Russell St., Littleton, MA; 800–255–7814).

All Pascal programs were written in Turbo Pascal. Turbo Pascal is a registered trademark of Borland International, Inc.

All C++ programs were using Borland's C++ compiler. Turbo C++ is a registered trademark of Borland International, Inc.

All BASIC listings were written with QBASIC. QBASIC and "QuickBasic" are trademarks of Microsoft Corporation.

Borland's SideKick, version 1, was used to write this book's text. This program is still a gem. The compact little editor proved very time-efficient for the author, since Borland provides basically the same text editor in SideKick, Turbo Pascal, and Turbo C++. Borland's Turbo Lightning was used to check text spelling.

Webster's New World On-Line Thesaurus 2, by Simon & Schuster Software, was used to find synonyms.

A Word from the Author

There will undoubtedly be future revisions and updates of this book. I would like to see it grow in size and depth. You can help. I want to hear your comments. If you know of an IC device that should be included in the next addition, let me know. If there is something in the book you do not like, I want to know that too. I will give a personal reply to any reasonable correspondence that includes a stamped, self addressed envelope.

I have developed printed circuit boards for many of the circuits in this book. I also maintain an inventory of all the IC chips used in this book, and have put together "kits" with parts and circuit boards for the major circuits. Send a stamped, self addressed envelope for a complete catalog of boards and kits..

Address all correspondence to:

Paul Bergsman
521 E. Wynnewood Rd.
Merion Station, Penna., 19066-1345

I look forward to hearing from you, and thanks!

A Note For BASIC Users

Some versions of BASIC insist on sending a carriage return and line feed out the printer port when the printer buffer is filled. The action takes place even if every LPRINT statement ends in a semicolon. If your version of BASIC insists on sending unwanted characters, you can correct the problem by opening an output file of width 255 to the printer. By using a width of 255, you are instructing the PC to treat the printer port as a communications device, not maintain a character count. It will never send a carriage return or line feed signals. The following program opens LPT1 as a communication device, and then sends every combination of eight bits out the LPT1 printer port:

```
10   OPEN "LPT1:"   FOR OUTPUT AS #1
20   WIDTH #1,   255
30   FOR N = 0 TO 255
40   PRINT #1,   CHR$(N) ;   : REM you still need the trailing semicolon
50   FOR X = 1 TO 1000 : NEXT X :   REM delay loop
60   NEXT   N
70   END
```

Controlling Light Emitting Diodes with Source Current

Circuit Theory

By design, TTL logic can sink up to 15 mA. Since most LEDs operate on 1.4 volts at 15 mA, they can be directly driven by the printer port's TTL logic. Figure 1 shows a circuit to do this.

Resistors R9 and R10 are "pull-up" resistors for the ACK and ERROR lines. By tying the ACK and ERROR lines to logic high, while securing the BUSY and PAPER-END lines to logic low, the computer is fooled into thinking it is connected to an on-line printer ready to receive data.

Each diode has a limiting resistor in series with it. The resistor keeps the current flowing through an LED to a safe level. An LED is "lit" when the corresponding data bit is high.

For many applications, I stay clear of using the computer's power supply to power external equipment. Power hungry projects, those with inductive loads, or circuits susceptible to static discharge are best powered by external power supplies. In some cases, you will even want to optocouple your circuits from the computer. If there is any chance your circuit can unintentionally send out spikes, noise, or static discharges, or short circuit the computer power supply, then use a stand-alone power source. In addition, you may want to use opto-couplers to completely isolate your computer from outside signals. It is always best to err on the side of conservatism. I always prototype a design with an external power supply and then *sometimes* tap into the computer to power the final and well-packaged product.

All that said, this circuit CAN be powered from your PC if—that's a big IF—you follow safe wiring practices. There are three possibilities:

• an unused disk drive cable
• the game port
• the keyboard connector.

To use a disk drive cable, you will need to build an extension to bring the cable beyond the computer case. To use the keyboard connector, you will have to

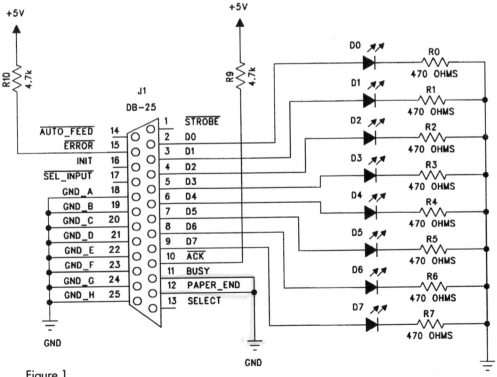

Figure 1

build a Y-adaptor so your project and keyboard can function simultaneously. You can get the necessary DIN connectors from electronics parts suppliers. For small, non-power hungry projects, the easiest solution is to use a game port. You can also get the DB-15 connectors you'll need from electronics parts suppliers.

Software

The programs LED_SRCE.BAS, LED_SRCE.PAS, and LED_SRCE.C demonstrate how to sequentially turn on each LED.

The computer has programming instructions buried in BIOS that tell the computer how to talk to a printer. One of the things the code does is to count the number of characters sent out the parallel port. Whenever the number reaches 80, the computer automatically sends out carriage return and line feed instructions. Just as every computer language has commands for talking to a printer, they also have commands for telling the computer to ignore the character count and never send a carriage return or line feed instruction.

In BASIC, placing a semicolon, (" ; "), at the end of an LPRINT instruction does the trick. In PASCAL, using WRITE instead of WRITELN yields the same results. The C language does not suffer from this problem, as C won't do anything without explicit instructions. You must add code for C to force a carriage return or line feed.

BASIC Source Code Listing

```
100 REM    FILE = LED_SRCE.BAS
110 REM
120 REM    SOURCE CURRENT control LEDs connected to parallel printer port.
130 REM    LEDs are "lit" when data logic is HIGH.
140 REM    Written in QBASIC
150  T = 1
500 REM
510 REM   begin program
520 REM   REPEAT
530 GOSUB 1000
540 LPRINT CHR$(255);
550 IF INKEY$ = CHR$(27) THEN STOP
560 GOSUB 2000
570 IF INKEY$ = CHR$(27) THEN STOP
580 GOTO 510
590 stop
1000 REM
1010 REM -=[ subuoutine,   Output_All_Combinations_Of_Bits ]=-
1020 REM   just a check to be sure all LEDs are working
1030 REM
1040 FOR e = 0 TO 255
1050 PRINT e: LPRINT CHR$(e);
1060 IF INKEY$ <> "" THEN STOP
1070 NEXT e
1080 RETURN
2000 REM
2010 REM   -=[ subroutine,   Run_Up_And_Down_The_Bits }
2030 REM   turn each printer port data bit on, and then off.
2040 DIM Two(8)
2050 A = 0: e = 0
2060 REM
2090 Two(0) = 2^0:  Two(1) = 2^1:  Two(2) = 2^2:  Two(3) = 2^3:
2100 Two(4) = 2^4: Two(5) = 2^5: Two(6) = 2^6: Two(7) = 2^7:
2110 FOR A = 1 TO 10
2120 FOR e = 0 TO 7
```

```
2130 PRINT Two(e):  LPRINT CHR$(Two(e));
2135 SLEEP (T)
2140 IF INKEY$ <> "" THEN STOP
2150 NEXT e
2160 REM
2170 FOR e = 7 TO 0 STEP -1
2180 PRINT Two(e): LPRINT CHR$(Two(e));
2190 SLEEP (T)
2200 IF INKEY$ <> "" THEN STOP
2210 NEXT e
2220 NEXT A
2230 RETURN
```

Pascal Source Code Listing

```pascal
PROGRAM LED_SRCE;
{
  SOURCE CURRENT control LEDs connected to parallel printer port.
  LEDs are "lit" when data logic is HIGH.
  Written in Borland's Turbo Pascal, 6.0
}
USES CRT, Printer;
VAR Temp : Char;

PROCEDURE Output_All_Combinations_Of_Bits;
{ just a check to be sure all LEDs are working }
BEGIN
FOR E := 0 TO 255 DO
   BEGIN WRITELN(E); WRITE(LST, CHAR(e)); IF KEYPRESSED THEN EXIT;END;
END; { output all bit combinations }

PROCEDURE Run_Up_And_Down_The_Bits;
  { turn each printer port data bit on, and then off. }
VAR TWO  : ARRAY[0..7] OF INTEGER;
    A, E : INTEGER;
BEGIN
{  PASCAL does not have a powers function. It takes far less space to just }
{  asign some values here, than write out a power function.                }
TWO[0] := 1;  TWO[1] := 2;  TWO[2] := 4;  TWO[3] := 8;
TWO[4] := 16; TWO[5] := 32; TWO[6] := 64; TWO[7] := 128;
FOR A := 1 TO 10 DO
 BEGIN { for a }
 FOR E := 0 TO 7 DO
   BEGIN
   WRITELN(Two[E]); WRITE(LST, CHAR(Two[e]));
   delay(100);
   IF KEYPRESSED THEN EXIT;
   END;
 FOR E := 7 DOWNTO 0 DO
   BEGIN
   WRITELN(Two[E]); WRITE(LST, CHAR(Two[e]));
   delay(100);
   IF KEYPRESSED THEN EXIT;
```

```
      END;
    END; { for a }
  END; { run up and down the bits }

BEGIN { main, led srce }
  REPEAT
  Output_All_Combinations_Of_Bits;
  WRITE(LST, CHAR(255)); delay(1500);
  IF KeyPressed THEN Temp := ReadKey;
  IF Temp = CHAR(27) THEN EXIT;
  Run_Up_And_Down_The_Bits;
  If KeyPressed THEN Temp := ReadKey;
  UNTIL Temp = CHAR(27);
END. { main, led srce }
```

C Source Code Listing

```
/*                        PROGRAM LED_SRCE
                   Code conversion by Eugene Klein


   Source current control LEDs connected to parallel printer port.
   LEDs are "lit" when printer port data logic is High.
   Written in Borland's Turbo Pascal, 6.0
 */

#include <dos.h>
#include <stdio.h>
#include <conio.h>
#include <stdlib.h>
#include <string.h>
#include <bios.h>
#include "My_TPU.h"
#include <math.h>

char Temp;
int E, A, Value;

void Output_All_Combinations_Of_Bits(void)
// just a check to be sure all LEDs are working
{
 for(E=0;E<=255;E++)
 {
  printf("%d\n",E);
  putc(E,stdprn);
  if(kbhit())
   exit(0);
 }
}

void Run_Up_And_Down_The_Bits(void)
  // turn each printer port data bit on, and then off.
{
```

```c
for(A=1;A<=10;A++)
{
 for(E=0;E<=7;E++)
 {
  Value = pow(2,E);
  printf("%d\n",Value);
  putc(Value,stdprn);
  delay(100);
  if(kbhit())
   exit(0);
 }
 for(E=7;E>0;E--)
 {
  Value = pow(2,E);
  printf("%d\n",Value);
  putc(Value,stdprn);
  delay(100);
  if(kbhit())
   exit(0);
 }
 }
}

void main()
{
 do
 {
  Output_All_Combinations_Of_Bits();
  putc((char)0,stdprn);
  delay(1500);
  if(kbhit())
   Temp = getch();
  if(Temp==27)
   exit(0);
  Run_Up_And_Down_The_Bits();
  if(kbhit())
   Temp = getch();
 }while(Temp !=27);
}
```

Controlling Light Emitting Diodes with Sink Current

Circuit Theory

The printer port of IBM/compatible PCs uses TTL logic. By definition, TTL logic can sink more current than it can source. The circuit in Figure 1 shows how to wire LEDs for sink current operation. Sink current is the preferred method of supplying control power. The problem is in understanding the control logic; LEDs are "lit" when the control logic is low.

Each LED is in series with a 330Ω limiting resistor. This resistor is smaller than the one used in Figure 2. This means more current will flow through the circuit and the LED will be brighter than an LED operated by TTL source current.

Resistors R9 and R10 are "pull-up" resistors for the ACK and ERROR lines. By tying the ACK and ERROR lines to logic high, while securing the BUSY and PAPER-END lines to logic low, the computer is fooled into thinking it is connected to an on-line printer ready to receive data.

Software

The programs LED_SINK.BAS, LED_SINK.PAS, and LED_SINK.C demonstrate how to sequentially turn on each LED.

The computer has programming instructions buried in BIOS that tell the computer how to talk to a printer. One of the things the code does is to count the number of characters sent out the parallel port. Whenever the number reaches 80, the computer automatically sends out carriage return and line feed instructions. Just as every computer language has commands for talking to a printer, they also have commands for telling the computer to ignore the character count and never send a carriage return or line feed instruction.

In BASIC, placing a semicolon, (" ; "), at the end of a LPRINT instruction does the trick. In Pascal, using WRITE instead of WRITELN yields the same results. The C language does not suffer from this problem, as C will not do anything without explicit instructions. You must add code for C to force a carriage return or line feed.

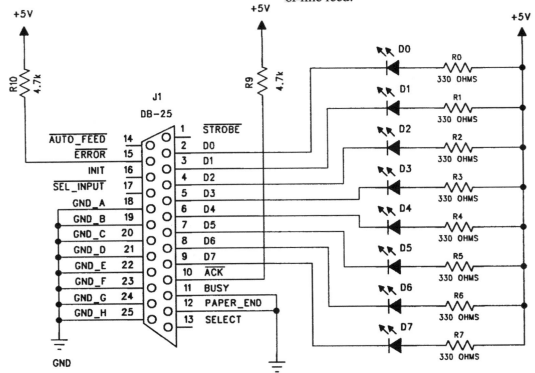

Figure 2

BASIC Source Code Listing

```
100 REM PROGRAM LED_SINK.BAS
105 REM
110 REM SINK CURRENT control of LEDs connected to parallel printer port.
120 REM LEDs are "lit" when printer port data logic is LOW.
130 REM Written in QBASIC
140 REM
150 t = 1
210 REM
220 GOSUB 1000
230 LPRINT CHR$(0); : SLEEP (t)
240 IF INKEY$ = CHR$(27) THEN STOP
250 GOSUB 1070: REM    Run_Up_And_Down_The_Bits;
260 IF INKEY$ = CHR$(27) THEN STOP
270 GOTO 210
280 STOP
1000 REM -=[ subroutine, Output_All_Combinations_Of_Bits ]=
1010 REM    just a check to be sure all LEDs are working
1020 FOR E = 0 TO 255
1030 PRINT E: LPRINT CHR$(E); : IF INKEY$ <> "" THEN STOP
1035 NEXT E
1040 RETURN
1050 REM
1060 REM    -=[ subroutine,  Run_Up_And_Down_The_Bits ]=
1070 REM    turn each printer port data bit on, and then off.
1080 DIM Two(8)
1090 A = 0:  E = 0: VALUE = 0
1100 REM
1110 Two(0) = 2^0:  Two(1) = 2^1:  Two(2) = 2^2:  Two(3) = 2^3
1120 Two(4) = 2^4: Two(5) = 2^5: Two(6) = 2^6: Two(7) = 2^7
1130 FOR A = 1 TO 10
1140 FOR E = 0 TO 7
1150 VALUE = Two(E)
1160 VALUE = (255 - VALUE): REM    get the compliment
1170 PRINT VALUE: LPRINT CHR$(VALUE);
1180 SLEEP (t)
1190 IF INKEY$ <> "" THEN STOP
1200 NEXT E
1210 FOR E = 7 TO 0 STEP -1
1220 VALUE = Two(E)
1230 VALUE = (255 - VALUE): REM    get the compliment
1240 PRINT VALUE: LPRINT CHR$(VALUE);
1250 SLEEP (t)
1260 IF INKEY$ <> "" THEN STOP
1270 NEXT E
1280 NEXT A
1290 RETURN
1300 END
```

Pascal Source Code Listing

```
PROGRAM LED_SINK;
{
   SINK CURRENT control LEDs connected to parallel printer port.
   LEDs are "lit" when printer port data logic is LOW.
   Written in Borland's Turbo Pascal, 6.0
}
USES CRT, Printer;
VAR Temp : Char;

PROCEDURE Output_All_Combinations_Of_Bits;
{ just a check to be sure all LEDs are working }
BEGIN
FOR E := 0 TO 255 DO
   BEGIN WRITELN(E); WRITE(LST, CHAR(e)); IF KEYPRESSED THEN EXIT;END;
END; { output all bit combinations }

PROCEDURE Run_Up_And_Down_The_Bits;
   { turn each printer port data bit on, and then off. }
VAR TWO   : ARRAY[0..7] OF INTEGER;
     A, E, Value : INTEGER;
BEGIN
{  PASCAL does not have a powers function. It takes far less space to just }
{  asign some values here, than write out a power function.               }
TWO[0] := 1;  TWO[1] := 2;  TWO[2] := 4;  TWO[3] := 8;
TWO[4] := 16; TWO[5] := 32; TWO[6] := 64; TWO[7] := 128;
FOR A := 1 TO 10 DO
 BEGIN { for a }
 FOR E := 0 TO 7 DO
    BEGIN
    Value := Two[E];
    Value := 255 - Value;    { get the compliment }
    WRITELN(value); WRITE(LST, CHAR(Value));
    delay(100);
    IF KEYPRESSED THEN EXIT;
    END;
 FOR E := 7 DOWNTO 0 DO
    BEGIN
    Value := Two[E];
    Value := 255 - Value;    { get the compliment }
    WRITELN(value); WRITE(LST, CHAR(Value));
    DELAY(100);
    IF KEYPRESSED THEN EXIT;
    END; { for e }
 END; { for a }
END; { run up and down the bits }

BEGIN { led sink  }
  REPEAT
  Output_All_Combinations_Of_Bits;
  WRITE(LST, CHAR(0)); delay(1500);
  IF KeyPressed THEN Temp := ReadKey;
  IF Temp = CHAR(27) THEN EXIT;
  Run_Up_And_Down_The_Bits;
  If KeyPressed THEN Temp := ReadKey;
  UNTIL Temp = CHAR(27);
END. { led sink }
```

C Source Code Listing

```
/*                        PROGRAM LED_SINK
                    Code conversion by Eugene Klein


     SINK CURRENT control LEDs connected to parallel printer port.
     LEDs are "lit" when printer port data logic is LOW.
     Written in Borland's Turbo Pascal, 6.0
  */

#include <dos.h>
#include <stdio.h>
#include <conio.h>
#include <stdlib.h>
#include <string.h>
#include <bios.h>
#include "My_TPU.h"
#include <math.h>

char Temp;
int E, A, Value;

void Output_All_Combinations_Of_Bits(void)
// just a check to be sure all LEDs are working
{
 for(E=0;E<=255;E++)
  {
   printf("%d\n",E);
   putc(E,stdprn);
   if(kbhit())
     exit(0);
  }
}


void Run_Up_And_Down_The_Bits(void)
   // turn each printer port data bit on, and then off.
{
 for(A=1;A<=10;A++)
  {
   for(E=0;E<=7;E++)
    {
     Value = pow(2,E);
     Value = 255 - Value;    // get the compliment
     printf("%d\n",Value);
     putc(Value,stdprn);
     delay(100);
     if(kbhit())
       exit(0);
    }
   for(E=7;E>=0;E—)
    {
     Value = pow(2,E);
     Value = 255 - Value;    // get the compliment
     printf("%d\n",Value);
```

```
      putc(Value,stdprn);
      delay(100);
      if(kbhit())
       exit(0);
    }
  }
}

void main()
{
 do
 {
  Output_All_Combinations_Of_Bits();
  putc(NULL,stdprn);
  delay(1500);
  if(kbhit())
   Temp = getch();
  if(Temp==27)
   exit(0);
  Run_Up_And_Down_The_Bits();
  if(kbhit())
   Temp = getch();
 }while(Temp !=27);
}
```

Latched Control of Light Emitting Diodes with Correct Reading Logic

Circuit Theory

Software is easier to understand and follow if printer port data does not have to be inverted before transmission. The most straightforward method of using active high logic to control active low devices is by adding a buffer to the circuit. Figure 3 shows how to accomplish this. The 74LS563 octal latch not only inverts each data bit, but it also latches the signal. If you disconnect the computer, the 74LS563 will still maintain its last value. If a 74LS563 were added to each of your projects, they could be *multiplexed*, meaning that several devices could share the same data lines.

The 74LS563 inputs data from the printer ports data lines. The 74LS563's output is inverted. Low inputs are output high, and high inputs are output low. Each diode has a limiting resistor in series with it. The resistor keeps the current flowing through an LED to a safe level. The LEDs are wired to sink current from the 74LS563. Therefore, an LED is "lit" when the printer port data bit is high.

Resistors R9 and R10 are "pull-up" resistors for the ACK and ERROR lines. By tying the ACK and ERROR lines to logic high, while securing the BUSY and PAPER-END lines to logic low, the computer is fooled into thinking it is connected to an on-line printer ready to receive data.

The printer port's strobe is an inactive high strobe. The 74LS563 expects an active high strobe. A 7404 inverter/buffer solves the problem. The printer port puts the data on the data line and then strobes the strobe line. The 74LS563 ignores any printer port signals until it reads the strobe signal. It then latches the input data. The 74LS563 continually outputs the data until another strobe tells it to read new data. The output is continually active, since the inactive high OUTPUT ENABLE line is tied to ground.

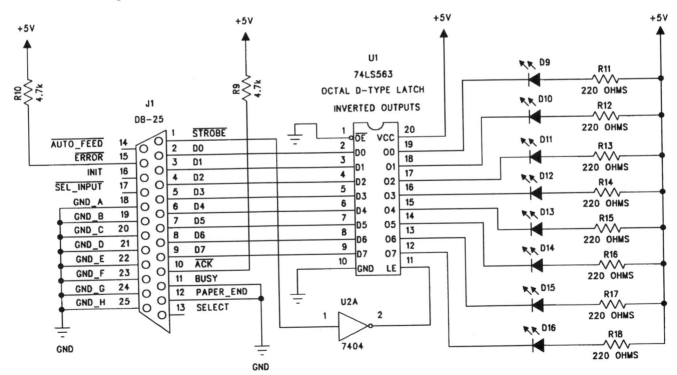

Figure 3

Software

The programs LED_SRCE.BAS, LED_SRCE.PAS, and LED_SRCE.C from the previous Application 1 circuit description demonstrate how to sequentially turn on each LED.

The computer has programming instructions buried in BIOS that tell it how to talk to a printer. One of the things the code does is to count the number of characters sent out the parallel port. Whenever the number reaches 80, the computer automatically sends out carriage return and line feed instructions. Just as every computer language has commands for talking to a printer, they also have commands for telling the computer to ignore the character count and never send a carriage return or line feed instruction.

In BASIC, placing a semicolon, (" ; "), at the end of an LPRINT instruction does the trick. In PASCAL, using WRITE instead of WRITELN yields the same results. The C language does not suffer from this problem, as C will not do anything without explicit instructions. You must add code for C to force a carriage return or line feed.

Controlling 7-Segment LED Displays from a Parallel Printer Port

Circuit Theory

A 7-segment LED display is a group of seven bar-shaped LEDs housed in a single IC package, usually in the shape of a slanted figure-8. By powering selected LED elements, numbers and letters can be formed. One side of all seven LEDs are tied together. Some displays also contain a decimal point (DP). While many LED displays look similar, pin assignments can vary widely between different devices. In spite of advances in display technology, LED displays are still widely used. There are many applications where they are cost-effective, and they are easier to read in direct daylight or in darkness than other display types. Often several displays will be housed in a single package. This arrangement simplifies wiring for such applications as digital meter, clock, and calculator displays.

If the positive (anode) leads of the LEDs are all tied together, the package is called an common anode 7-segment display. If the negative (cathode) leads of the LEDs are all tied together, the package is called a common cathode 7-segment display. Both types of displays are widely available in various packages and pin assignments from electronics parts dealers. The

components used here are the H.P. E101-3351 (common anode) and H.P. E103-3353 (common cathode) displays.

Since it is best to have TTL logic use sink current, a buffer/driver is usually inserted between the display and control logic. Figure 4-A shows the preferred method of controlling common cathode displays while Figure 4-B shows how to drive common anode displays. The 74LS563 in Figure 4-B inverts the printer port's control logic. When a control signal is high, the 74LS563's output is low, sinking LED current. This arrangement allows for straightforward programming code. A high data bit results in a corresponding LED being lit.

Less common is the arrangement in Figure 4-B. Here the LEDs will light when the input is **low**. We still need a buffer, but this time it is non-inverting. The LEDs now have a larger series limiting resistor, so they will be a little dimmer when lit.

Both the 74LS573 and 74LS563 have a latch to lock data when the strobe line receives an active high pulse. This arrangement allows you to multiplex several displays interfaced to one printer port. (In future circuits, you will see some displays with the latch/drivers built into the display chip.)

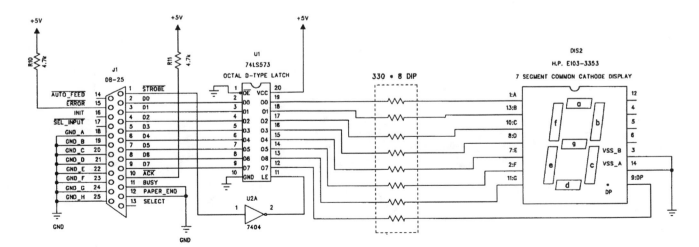

Figure 4-A

Resistors R10 and R11 are pull-up resistors for the ACK and ERROR lines. By tying the ACK and ERROR lines to logic high, while securing the BUSY and PAPER-END lines to logic low, the computer is fooled into thinking it is connected to an on-line printer ready to receive data.

While this method is simple and straightforward, it is not the best method of driving LEDs. Future applications will showcase chips designed specifically for driver applications. This method is presented mainly because the 74LS573 and 74LS563 are readily available at low cost.

Software

Inasmuch as 7-segment displays are just ordinary LEDs, you can control them using the LED software. LED_SRCE.BAS, LED_SRCE.PAS, and LED_SRCE.C from Application 2 can be used with both circuits since the circuit hardware configures both as an active high load.

Programs 7_SEG.PAS, 7_SEG.BAS, and 7_SEG.C. will operate the circuits in Figures 4-A and 4-B. Both circuits will display all hex numbers (0 to 9) and the letters A to F.

Each LED element, labeled "A" to "G," is controlled by a printer port data bit. The program assigns each constant to the value of its corresponding data bit. To light an LED, you simply output its number out the parallel port. To light more than one LED at the same time, you add the value of needed LEDs together and output the resulting number. Rather than repeatedly computing the numbers needed to form the characters shown on the 7-segment display, the program forms look-up tables for the appropriate values. Selected values are then output to the printer port.

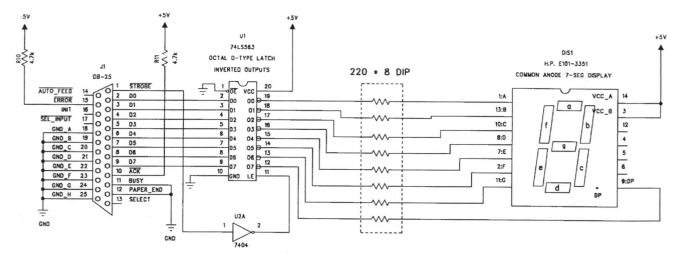

Figure 4-B

BCD to Decimal Display Using a Common Anode LED Display Driver

Circuit Theory

This circuit fully decodes a 4-bit (*nibble*) binary-coded decimal (BCD) input into a decimal number from 0 through 9 in the standard 7-segment display format and directly drives a 7-segment display. Uses for this circuit include counters, timers, multimeters, and other numeric displays.

A nibble is half of a byte, or four bits. The nibble is input to a special IC, the 7447, which is designed to decode the nibble's first ten combinations, convert them to 7-bit logic needed to drive a 7-segment display, and also provide the power to directly drive the 7-segment display. The 7447 is designed to drive an active-low common anode 7-segment display. This workhorse device has been around for a long time and is widely available. The 7447 combines several IC operations into one chip, conserving circuit board space and reducing the chip count. This results in a smaller board size and a less expensive product. Since the chip only uses 4 data bits, two chips can operate from a single printer port.

The 7447 outputs a unique character for each of the 16 input combinations. That means the 7447 will also display a unique (strange) character for each input value above 9 (10 to 15). For most applications, you will never want to see these strange characters. Therefore, you must make sure that your software does not generate numbers between 10 and 15.

In addition, the 7447 "blanks" leading or trailing zeros. That means that if the leading or trailing digit is a zero, the 7447 can be hard-wired to blank it out. This feature is disabled by leaving pins 4 and 5 unconnected.

The 7447 is designed to provide drive power for an active low (common anode) 7-segment LED display. Direct drive means the IC can supply the needed drive current. HOWEVER, YOU MUST STILL ADD CURRENT LIMITING RESISTORS IN SERIES WITH THE LEDs.

Figure 5 shows two 7447s decoding a byte of information. The two chips are hard-wired for leading zero suppression. Resistors R1 and R2 are pull-

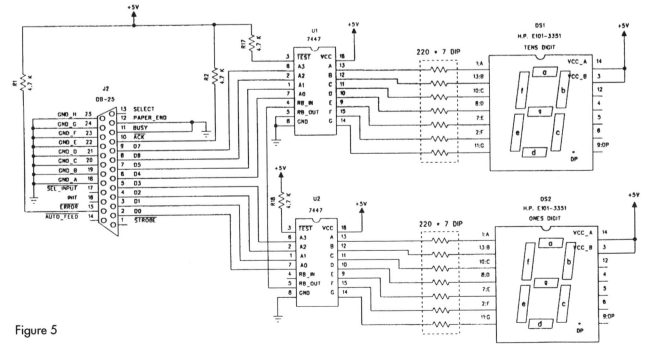

Figure 5

up resistors for the ACK and ERROR lines. By tying the ACK and ERROR lines to logic high while securing the BUSY and PAPER-END lines to logic low, the computer is fooled into thinking it is connected to an on-line printer ready to receive data. Thus, BASIC's LPRINT and PASCAL's WRITE statements can easily output data.

Software

The programs DSP_DEC.PAS, DSP_DEC.BAS, and DSP_DEC.C turn your computer into a count-down/count-up counter. Since the circuit is hard-wired for leading zero suppression, the number "09" is displayed as "9". The leading zero is blanked out.

BASIC Source Code Listing

```
100 REM   FILE DSP_DEC.BAS
110 REM
120 REM   Demonstrate how to send decimal numbers out the parallel printer
130 REM   port to two BCD to 7-segment displays
140 REM
150 REM   Display is connected to LPT1
160 REM
170 REM   Written in QBasic by Paul Bergsman
180 REM
190 SEC = 100 : REM { deley time in milli-seconds, dependent on your machine }
200 TENS = 0 : ONES = 0 : DATA = 0
210 REM
220 REM
230 FOR TENS := 0 to 9
240 FOR ONES := 0 to 9 DO
250 DATA := 16 * TENS : REM      { move Tens value to HI Nibble    }
260 DATA := DATA + ONES;         { add Ones digit                 }
270 PRINT "TENS = ";Tens;"   ONES = ";Ones;";        DATA = ";Data
280 LPRINT CHR$(DATA);
290 IF INKEY$ <> "" THEN 1000    { end program if a key is pressed }
300 FOR X = 1 TO SEC : NEXT X
310 NEXT ONES
320 NEXT TENS
340 IF INKEY$ = "" THEN GOTO 180 : REM { repeat until a key is pressed }
1000 END
```

Pascal Source Code Listing

```
PROGRAM DSP_DEC; { .PAS }
{
 Demonstrate how to send decimal numbers out the parallel printer
 port to two BCD to 7-segment displays
 Display is connected to LPT1
 Written in Borland's Turbo Pascal 6.0 by Paul Bergsman
}
USES CRT, PRINTER;
CONST Sec = 100;  { deley time in milli-seconds, dependent on your machine } VAR Tens,
Ones, Data : BYTE;
BEGIN
CLRSCR;
    REPEAT
    FOR Tens := 0 to 9 DO
        FOR Ones := 0 to 9 DO
            BEGIN
```

```
                Data := 16 * Tens;{ move Tens value to HI Nibble }
                Data := Data + Ones;    { add Ones digit              }
WRITELN('TENS = ',Tens:2,'    ONES = ',Ones:2,';         DATA = ',Data:4); WRITE(LST,
CHAR(DATA));
                IF KEYPRESSED THEN HALT;  { end program if keypressed }
                DELAY(Sec);
                END; { for ones }
        UNTIL KEYPRESSED;
END. { dsp_dec }
```

C Source Code Listing

```
/*                      PROGRAM DSP_DEC
            Code conversion by Eugene Klein

Demonstrate how to send decimal numbers out the parallel printer
port to two BCD to 7-segment displays

Display is connected to LPT1

Original written in Borland's Turbo Pascal 6.0 by Paul Bergsman

*/


#include <dos.h>
#include <stdio.h>
#include <conio.h>
#include <stdlib.h>
#include <string.h>
#include <bios.h>
#include "My_TPU.h"


const int Sec = 100;  // deley time in milli-seconds, dependent on your machine
unsigned int  Tens, Ones, Data;

void main()
{
 clrscr();
 do
 {
  for(Tens=0;Tens<=9;Tens++)
  {
   for(Ones=0;Ones<=9;Ones++)
   {
    Data = 16 * Tens;            // move Tens value to HI Nibble
    Data += Ones;                // add Ones digit
    printf("TENS = %2i    ONES =  %2i    DATA = %4i\n",Tens,Ones,Data);
    putc(Data,stdprn);
    if(kbhit())
     exit(0);
    delay(Sec);
   }
  }
 }while(!kbhit());
}
```

Common Cathode
Display Driver

Circuit Theory

This circuit is similar to that in Application 5. The 7448 is used to drive common cathode 7-segment displays. It is pin compatible and functionally identical to the 7447 except for one detail: the 7448 is designed to supply source current (the 7447 supplies sink current).

Figure 6 details how to connect two 7448s to a IBM/IBM compatible parallel printer port. Note that the two chips are wired for trailing zero suppression. If your software output "90" in hex, the display would show "9", blanking out the trailing zero.

Software

Program listings DSP_DEC.PAS, DSP_DEC.BAS, and DSP_DEC.C are used with this circuit. These are given in Application 5.

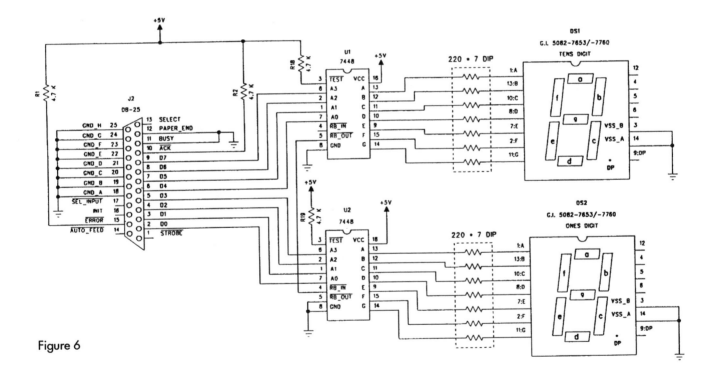

Figure 6

BCD to Decimal Display Using a Common Cathode/ Common Anode Display Driver

Circuit Theory

This circuit fully decodes a 4-bit (nibble) binary-coded decimal (BCD) input into a number from 0 through 9 in the standard 7-segment display format and directly drives a 7-segment display. It is based on the CD4543B, a very versatile CMOS device. It can operate from 5 to 20 volts DC, drives LCD and/or 7-segment LED displays, contains an input data latch, and can sink or source drive current. Since the CD4543B is a CMOS device, pull-up resistors are required to interface it with a printer port's TTL logic.

Tying pin 6 to ground configures the chip to sink current for common anode 7-segment displays. Tying pin 6 to Vcc configures the chip to source current for common cathode 7-segment displays. The CD4543B has automatic character blanking. If the input data is not between 0 and 9, the output is automatically blanked. The input data latch allows this chip to be multiplexed with other devices that can share the parallel printer port.

Figure 7-A shows the CD4543B wired to sink current for an active low, common anode display. Figure 7-B shows the CD4543B wired to source current for an active high, common cathode display. Resistors R8 and R9 are pull-up resistors for the ACK and ERROR lines. By tying the ACK and ERROR lines to logic high, while securing the BUSY and PAPER-END lines to logic low, the computer is fooled into thinking it is connected to an on line printer ready to receive data. This means BASIC's LPRINT and PASCAL's WRITE statements can easily output data.

Pull-up resistors are required to interface the printer port's TTL signals with the CD4543B's CMOS inputs. The printer port's STROBE line is inverted by one section of a 7404 inverter/buffer. The inverted strobe is then sent to the CD4543B's "latch disable" line at pin 1. In spite of the awkward name, the latch disable line functions as a standard active high latch enable line. When the chip detects positive going strobe pulse it reads the code on the data lines. With a strobe transition from active high to inactive low, the input code is latched.

Even though the CD4543B contains driver circuitry, you must still include current limiting resistors for proper operation. Since the chip is designed to sink or source current, 220 resistors are used in both circuits.

Software

The listings DSP_DEC.PAS, DSP_DEC.BAS, and DSP_DEC.C turn your computer into a count-down/count-up counter. These listings can be used with either circuit. These listings are given with the preceding Application 5.

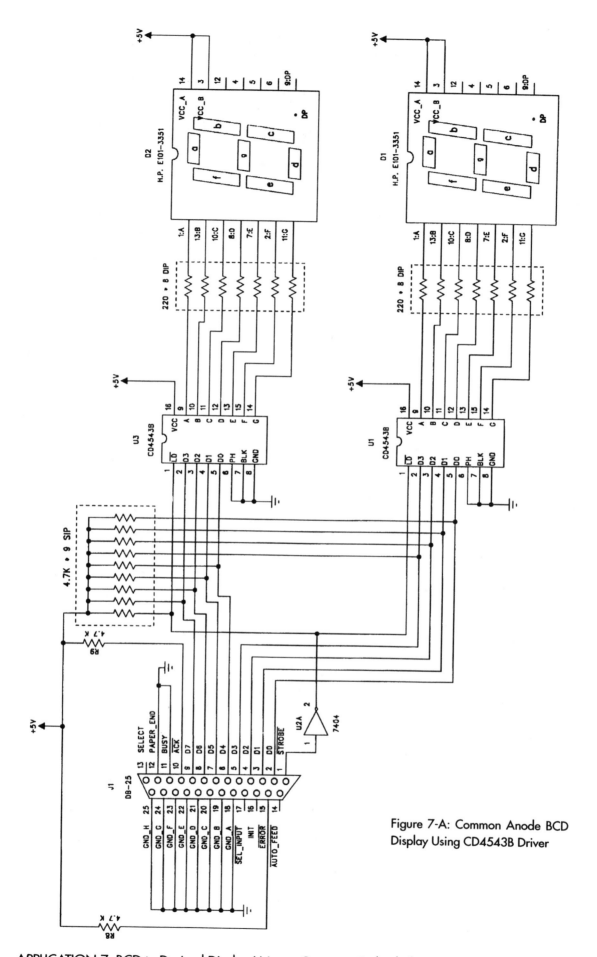

Figure 7-A: Common Anode BCD
Display Using CD4543B Driver

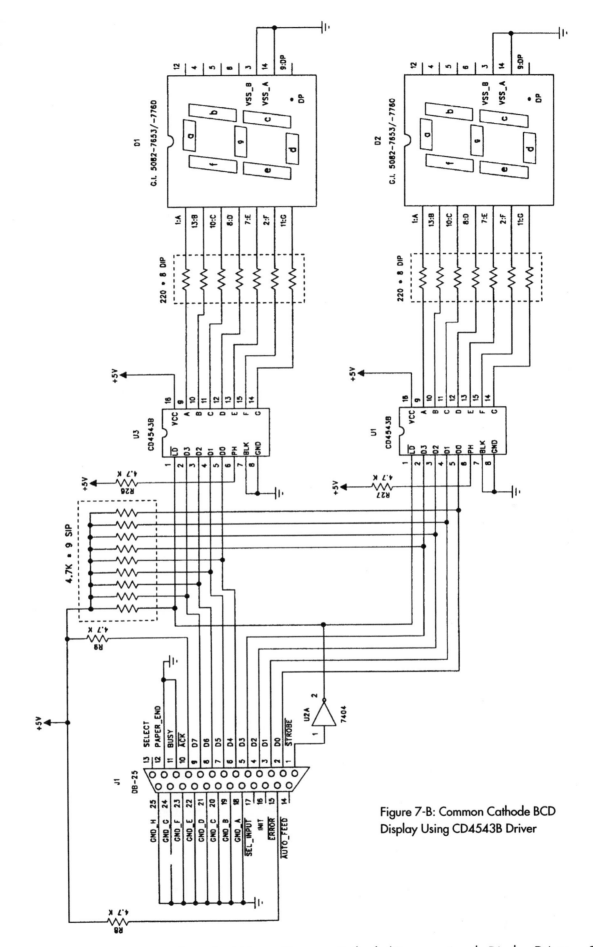

Figure 7-B: Common Cathode BCD
Display Using CD4543B Driver

BCD to Decimal Display Using a Common Cathode/Common Anode Display Driver   25

Displaying a Data Byte in Hexadecimal Form

Circuit Theory

Programmers and hardware hackers may need a constant, visible display of a data byte in hexadecimal form. Several chips are on the market that input a binary nibble (4 bits), convert it to 7-segment display logic, and provide the driver power for a 7-segment LED display. Two such devices are the DM9368N amd DM9374N, both from National Semiconductor.

The DM9368N is a TTL chip designed to supply source current for an active high, common cathode 7-segment display. Since it has built-in current-limiting resistors, it can directly drive LED displays rated at 20 mA at 1.7 volts. A typical application is shown in Figure 8-A. The circuit uses two DM9368N devices to drive two H.P. E103-3353 common cathode 7-segment displays, and has hexadecimal decode for-

mat which produces numbers "0" through "9" and alphabetical codes "A" through "F" using upper and lower case fonts. The DM9368N has on-board logic to suppress leading or trailing zeros.

Its pin compatible "brother," the DM9374N, is designed to supply sink current for an active low common anode 7-segment display. Figure 8-B shows how two can be used to drive two H.P. E101-3351 common anode 7-segment displays. Note the resistors between each DM9374N and the display it drives. The DM9374N does not have internal current limiting resistors, but is otherwise feature compatible with the DM9368N. For additional information on the DM9368N and DM9374N, consult National Semiconductor's *LS/S/TTL Logic Databook*.

Figure 8-A shows how to monitor the output of a printer port in hex. The inactive high strobe signal is

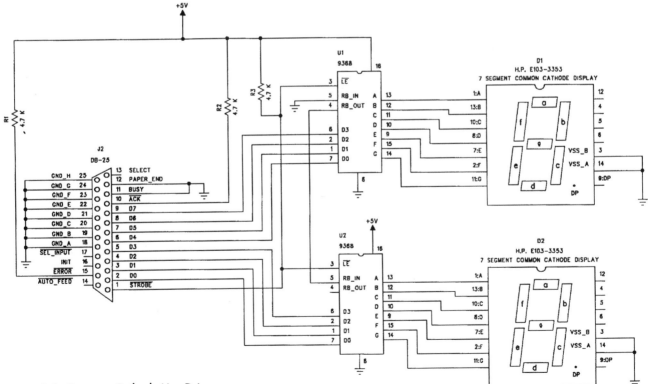

Figure 8-A: Common Cathode Hex Driver

fed to DM9368N's latch enable pin 3. If you want to continually monitor a data byte without a strobe signal, tie the latch enable line, pin 3, to ground. Since the DM9368N contains driver limiting resistors, the driver outputs are directly connected to the active high, common cathode 7-segment display. While the H.P. E103-3353 is used in Figure 8-A, any LED display rated at 20 ma. at 1.7 volts can be used. The DM9368Ns are hard-wired to blank leading zeros. If you want to see the leading zeros, then leave pins 4 and 5 of both ICs unconnected.

Figure 8-B performs the same functions for active high, common anode 7-segment displays using the DM9374N.

Software

The circuits in Figure 8-A and 8-B need no software. Both will automatically decode, latch, and display any strobed data byte.

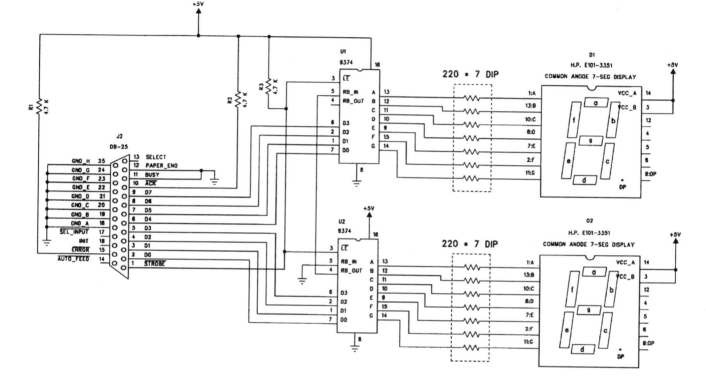

Figure 8-B: Common Anode Byte to Hex Converter/Latch/Display Driver

Decode, Latch, and Display a Data Byte in Hexadecimal

Circuit Theory

Hewlett-Packard has a line of LED displays that have on-board latch and decoder logic. Some, like the 5082-7300 and 7302, display numeric values "0" through "9". The 5082-7340 displays nibble hexadecimal values "0" through "9" and "A" through "F." Both displays are made up of 20 small LEDs arranged in a figure-8. The on-board logic reads a binary nibble, decodes it, and displays the hex value. This display method is a little more expensive than the previous display circuits in this book. However, since the latch, decoder, driver, and display are in one package, it is a real space saver.

Figure 9 shows how simple it is to use these devices. To operate correctly from a parallel printer port, the inverted strobe line must be reinverted to active high logic. A single section of a 7404 inverter/buffer does the job. The H.P. devices accept TTL logic inputs so pull-up resistors are not required. R3 and R4 are optional. If you want to continually monitor a data byte without a strobe, tie each latch enable line, pin 5, to Vcc through a 1K to 4.7K resistor.

Software

This circuit requires no software. The 5082-7340 devices will automatically decode, latch, and display any strobed data byte.

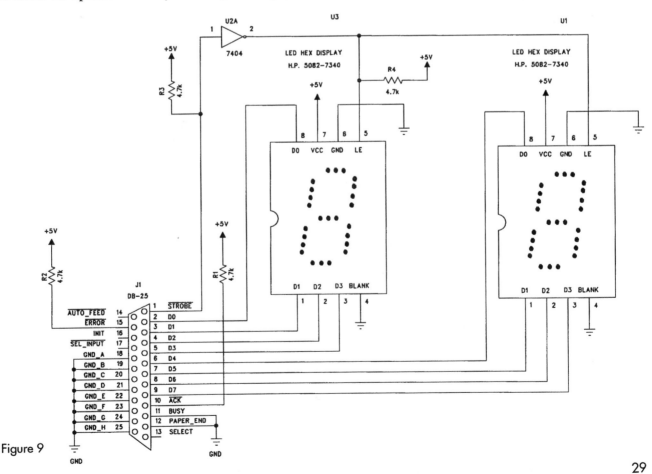

Figure 9

Controlling a LCD Display from an 8-Bit Data Port

Circuit Theory

One very popular controller IC for use with liquid crystal displays (LCDs) is the HD44780. This chip can be programmed to control all formats of LCDs of up to two lines and 40 characters. In the application we'll discuss here, all necessary multiplexing, control, driver, and display hardware are included on one circuit board. Several manufacturers package the HD44780 together with drivers and appropriate LCD display. For more details on a specific HD44780 device, consult the data sheet from the device's manufacturer.

Before the LCD display can accept data, it must know if the display is one or two lines, how many characters are on a line, and what to do with the cursor. This information is sent during initialization. The HD44780 wants the control word sent three times. Additional control words can be used to define your own characters or to tell the HD44780 to use its internally stored special characters. After the initial set-up, any ASCII characters placed on the data lines will be read when a strobe pulse is received.

Figure 10 shows the simplicity of interfacing an LCD display to your parallel printer port. All HD44780

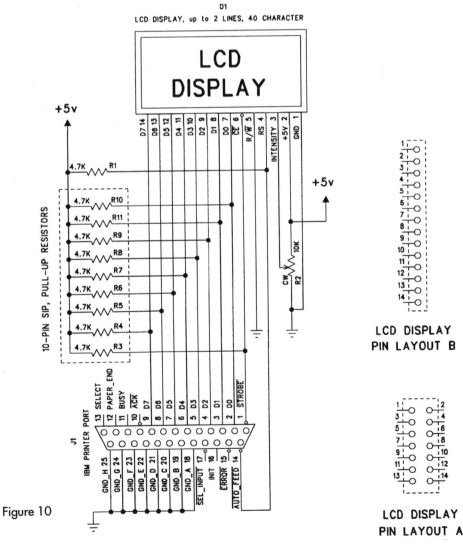

Figure 10

LCD DISPLAY
PIN LAYOUT B

LCD DISPLAY
PIN LAYOUT A

type displays use a 14-pin interface. Each pin has a specific function. However, manufacturers select board connector schemes based on their own needs. This results in boards with two types of connectors. The layouts of these two connectors are shown on Figure 10.

The circuit requires two control lines: one for a data strobe and one to tell the display that a control byte is being sent. The HD44780 looks at the RS signal, at pin 4, for an instruction. If the RS pin is high, the data on the control lines is a control word; if the RS pin is low, the data on the control lines is a display character.

The printer port's strobe line, at pin 1, supplies the strobe signal. The printer port's auto feed line, at pin 14, supplies the RS signal. You can't just use the Pascal WRITELN or BASIC LPRINT commands. Instead, you must write software to turn the strobe and auto feed lines high and low at will.

Many of these displays uses CMOS logic. The pull-up resistors interface the printer port's TTL logic to the CMOS display. Even if the display uses TTL logic, the pull-up resistors are still a good idea because they help provide good, clean, TTL signals to the display.

Software

The HD44780 has internal fonts to form large letters. In other words, if you want a small case "g" to extend below the line, you must tell the chip to use large letters. You can also redefine up to three characters for display. The program listing LCD_DEMO.PAS controls three types of displays: straight ASCII, large letters, and user-defined characters. There is no BASIC listing; it's just not practical.

Pascal Source Code Listing

```
{$D+,L+} { to be sure complete debug information is generated }
PROGRAM LCD_Demo;
{   Demonstrates how to control an LCD device from your parallel printer port.
You can control any LCD display using an Hatachi 44780 controller chip. Demonstrates
how to generate 5 by 7 graphics, 5 by 10 graphics, and use display's internal 5 by 10
character set.
      Written in Turbo Pascal 6.0.
}
USES DOS, CRT, My_Tpu;
TYPE String30 = String[80];
CONST
T    = 1;
All_High = 4;      { 00000100, all control line outputs HIGH, inverted or not }
All_Low = 11;      { 00001011, all control line outputs LOW, inverted or not   }
Strobe = $FF01;   { 11110001,   strobe = D0, Base + 2, bit 1            } AutoFeed
= $FF02; { 00000010, AutoFeed = D1, Base + 2, bit 2              }
VAR                    Temp : INTEGER;
Tab, Dàta : BYTE; Use_Large_Letters : BOOLEAN;
Message : String30;
RS, Lpt_Num, Lpt_Port_Address : WORD;
Regs : REGISTERS;
PROCEDURE Pulse_Strobe_Line(Strobe : WORD);
{   provide the LCD module with an ACTIVE LOW strobe                           }
{   in other words, pulse inverted strobe line so output goes HIGH, then LOW  }
BEGIN
Strobe := LO(Strobe);
{   pulse strobe line HIGH }
 PORT[ Lpt_Port_Address + 2] :=
        (255 - Strobe ) AND PORT[ Lpt_Port_Address + 2];
{   pulse strobe line LOW }
PORT[ Lpt_Port_Address + 2] := Strobe OR PORT[ Lpt_Port_Address + 2]; delay(t); {
turn strobe LOW }
END; { pulse strobe }
```

```
PROCEDURE Set_Control_Bit(Lpt_Port_Address, Bit : WORD);
BEGIN
IF Hi(Bit) = $FF THEN { process inverted bit }
    BEGIN
    Bit := LO(Bit);
PORT[Lpt_Port_Address + 2] := All_Low; DELAY(T); { clear I/O lines,00000100 } IF Bit
= 2 THEN{ turn RS, ( = D1, inverted AutoFeed line) HIGH        }
          Temp := PORT[ Lpt_Port_Address + 2] AND (255 - Bit)
    ELSE    { turn RS, ( = D1, inverted AutoFeed line ) LOW         }
          Temp := PORT[ Lpt_Port_Address + 2] OR Bit;
PORT[Lpt_Port_Address + 2] := Temp; delay(t);        { read value at Lpt1 + 2 }
    END; { if HI bit }
END; { send control bit }
PROCEDURE Transmit_Byte(Lpt_Port_Address, Bit : WORD; Data : Byte);
{   RS = AutoFeed = Bit 2 of Base + 2.  This is an INVERTED bit                    }
VAR Temp : BYTE;
BEGIN
Set_Control_Bit(Lpt_Port_Address, RS);
PORT[ Lpt_Port_Address ] := Data; delay(t);        { put data on data lines }
Pulse_Strobe_Line(Strobe);
END;
PROCEDURE Write_Character(VAR Lpt_Port_Address : WORD; Data : BYTE);
{   RS must be high to send LCD display character data }
BEGIN
RS := $FF02;
Transmit_Byte( Lpt_Port_Address, RS, Data);
END;
PROCEDURE Write_Instruction(VAR Lpt_Port_Address : WORD; Data : BYTE); {RS must be
LOW to to send LCD display control instruction }
VAR E : INTEGER;
BEGIN
RS := $FF00; Transmit_Byte(Lpt_Port_Address, Rs, Data); END;
PROCEDURE Init_LCD_Module(Lpt_Port_Address : WORD);
{   Transmit Control Word three times to tell module you are initializing set-up.}
{   Just follow sequence set forth in LCD's data manual: to initialize module:}
{     -send control number three times with small delay between transmissions.}
{     -Delay provids time for LCD chip to digest information.  Delay is }
{      usually not required for PASCAL, C, or BASIC compiled programs, BUT,  }
{     -Delay is a must for Embedded controller / LCD module control.      }
VAR E : INTEGER;
BEGIN
PORT[ Lpt_Port_Address + 2] := All_Low; Delay(T); { set all control lines LOW  } Data
:= $34;       { 30hex = 48dec,  set for 8-bit interface, one display line }
PORT[ Lpt_Port_Address] := Data; delay(T);
FOR E := 1 to 3 do                              { set 8 bit interface 3 times  }
    BEGIN
    Pulse_Strobe_Line(Strobe);
    DELAY(T);
    END; { for e }
END; { init LCD module }
PROCEDURE Set_Desired_Configuration(Large_Letters : BOOLEAN);
{   all options are listed in LCD data manual    }
BEGIN
{   Set 8 bit interface, 1 line display, & 5 by 10 character set = $34   }
IF  Large_Letters  =  TRUE  THEN  Data  :=  $34  ELSE  Data  :=  $30;
Write_Instruction(Lpt_Port_Address, DATA);
```

```
{   display on, cursor off  }
    Data := $0C; Write_Instruction(Lpt_Port_Address, DATA);
{   clear display }
    Data := $01; Write_Instruction(Lpt_Port_Address, DATA);
{   move cursor to beginning of line }  { for beginning of 2ed line, use $40  }
    Data := $02; Write_Instruction(Lpt_Port_Address, DATA);
{   increment addr counter after each write, to keep cursor moving to right }
    Data := $06; Write_Instruction(Lpt_Port_Address, DATA);
END; { set configuration }
PROCEDURE Send_Message(Tab : BYTE; Message : String30);
{       For each byte of data sent:                                          }
{       1) Tell module you are going to write to CG memory                    }
{       2) Send data to that address                                          }
VAR E : BYTE;
BEGIN
{   clear display }
        Data := $01; Write_Instruction(Lpt_Port_Address, DATA);
{   move cursor to beginning of line }
        Data := $02; Write_Instruction(Lpt_Port_Address, DATA);
{   tab to center text }
        Data := 127 + Tab; Write_Instruction(Lpt_Port_Address, DATA);
{   send message }
FOR E := 1 to LENGTH(Message)  DO
        BEGIN
        Data := ORD(Message[E]);
Write_Character(Lpt_Port_Address, Data); END;
Delay(1500);
END; { send message }
PROCEDURE Load_User_Defined_Character(Redefined_Character : String30);
{   Send redefined character info to CG memory }
VAR        Instr, E : BYTE;
BEGIN
Instr := $40;
FOR E := 1 TO   LENGTH(Redefined_Character)  DO
        BEGIN
{   tell LCD module you are going to write to CG memory, at address Instr }
        Write_Instruction(Lpt_Port_Address, Instr);
{   write character definition BYTE to CG memory }
Data := ORD(Redefined_Character[E]); Write_Character(Lpt_Port_Address, DATA);
        Instr := Instr + 1;
        END; {  for e }
END; { load user defined character }
PROCEDURE Define_And_Load_Airplane;
{   Define airplane.  This is one case where BASIC had a better idea.  DATA
    statement support would be very useful here.
}
VAR Instr, E : BYTE;
Char_0, Char_A, Char_B, Char_C : String[10];
            Airplane : String[80];
BEGIN
Char_C := ConCat( CHAR($00),
CHAR($00),
CHAR($00),
                CHAR($1C),     { 000* **00 }
                CHAR($1F),     { 000* **** }
CHAR($00),
```

```
CHAR($00),
CHAR($00));
 char_B  := Concat(CHAR($10),  { 000* 0000 } CHAR($0C),  { 0000 **00 } Char($06),
0000 *0*0 } CHAR($1F),  { 000* **** } char($1F),  { 000* **** } Char($06),  { 0000 *0*
} Char($0C),   { 0000 **OO } char($10)); { 000* 0000 }
 char_A   := Concat(CHAR($18),  { 000* *000 } CHAR($18),  { 000* *000 } CHAR($18),
000* *000 } CHAR($1F),  { 000* **** } CHAR($1F),  { 000* **** } Char($00),
                      CHAR($00),
                      CHAR($00));
 Char_0   := Concat(CHAR($00),
                    CHAR($00),
                    CHAR($00),
                    CHAR($00),
                    CHAR($00),
                    Char($00),
                    CHAR($00),
                    char($00));
Airplane :=  concat(Char_0 + Char_A + Char_B + Char_C);
Load_User_Defined_Character(Airplane);
END; { define airplane }


PROCEDURE Define_And_Load_Happy_Face;
VAR Happy_Face : String[80];
BEGIN
{   this is the closest thing to BASIC's DATA statement }
Happy_Face := CONCAT(
            { char A }  CHAR($03),  { 0000 00** }
CHAR($08),    { 0000 *000 } CHAR($10),   { 000* 0000 } CHAR($12),   { 000* 00*0 }
CHAR($10),    { 000* 0000 } CHAR($10),   { 000* 0000 } CHAR($14),   { 000* 0*00 }
CHAR($03),    { 0000 00** } CHAR($08),   { 0000 *000 } CHAR($03),   { 0000 00** }
CHAR($00),    { 0000 0000 }
            { spaces }  CHAR($00),CHAR($00), CHAR($00), CHAR($00), CHAR($00),
            { char B }  CHAR($18),  { 000* *000 }
CHAR($02),    { 0000 00*0 } CHAR($01),   { 0000 000* } CHAR($09),   { 0000 *00* }
CHAR($01),    { 0000 000* } CHAR($01),   { 0000 000* } CHAR($05),   { 0000 0*0* }
CHAR($18),    { 000* *000 } CHAR($02),   { 0000 00*0 } CHAR($18),   { 000* *000 }
CHAR($00)); { 0000 0000 }
Load_User_Defined_Character(Happy_Face); END; { load happy face }
BEGIN   { main }
Select_Printer_Port( Lpt_Num, Lpt_Port_Address); { in My_Tpu } Init_Printer_Port(Lpt_Num
Lpt_Port_Address);
    REPEAT
writeln('-=[ 5 by 10 characters with user defined happy face ]=-');
    Init_LCD_Module(Lpt_Port_Address);
Use_large_Letters  :=  TRUE;  Set_Desired_Configuration(Use_Large_Letters);
Define_And_Load_Happy_Face;
Message := CONCAT(CHAR($01), CHAR($02),           { happy smile  pattern } ' HELLO! ',
            { ASCII characters      }
          CHAR($01), CHAR($02));                  { happy smile  pattern } Tab := 3;
Send_Message(Tab, Message);
    IF KEYPRESSED THEN EXIT;
    WRITELN('-=[ send  ASCII  using  5  by  10  character  set  ]=-');
Init_LCD_Module(Lpt_Port_Address);
Use_Large_Letters := TRUE; Set_Desired_Configuration(Use_Large_Letters);
    Message := ConCat('Paul Ber', CHAR($E7), 'sman');
    Tab := 2; Send_Message(Tab, Message);
```

```pascal
    WRITELN;
Writeln('-=[ 5 by 7 characters with user defined airplane ]=-');
    Init_LCD_Module(Lpt_Port_Address);
Use_large_Letters  :=  FALSE;  Set_Desired_Configuration(Use_Large_Letters);
Define_And_Load_Airplane;
Message :=  CHAR($01) + CHAR($02) + CHAR($03)  + { airplane characters  } ' HELLO! '
+                       { normal ASCII letters }
             CHAR($01) + CHAR($02) + char($03);    { airplane characters  } Tab :=
2; Send_Message(Tab, Message);
    IF KEYPRESSED THEN EXIT;
WRITELN('-=[ send ASCII using 5 by 10 character set ]=-');
    Init_LCD_Module(Lpt_Port_Address);
Use_Large_Letters := TRUE; Set_Desired_Configuration(Use_Large_Letters);
    Message := ConCat('Paul Ber', CHAR($E7), 'sman');
    Tab := 2; Send_Message(Tab, Message);
    WRITELN;
    UNTIL KEYPRESSED;
END. { main }
```

Controlling Large Loads with Optically Isolated Solid State Relays

Circuit Theory

A solid state relay is the safest way to control a large AC or DC load from your computer. Solid state relays are optically coupled switches. They allow a printer port's TTL signal to safely control high voltage AC and DC loads.

A solid state relay (SSR) is a pre-packaged device containing an LED sealed inside a plastic case along with an optosensor and other circuitry needed to control a large AC or DC load. With no input applied, the optocoupler's optosensor is in its off, or high impedance, state and no power is supplied to the load.

The only thing between the LED and the optosensor is air. That means that the SSR's load could experience spikes, surges, or shorts but still protect your computer. Your computer is *optically isolated* from the load. However, the internal load circuitry is different for AC and DC SSRs. You must select an appropriate SSR for your application.

Most SSRs will accept an input of 3 to 32 volts at 5 mA. SSRs get their power from the load's power supply. The output rating is the MAXIMUM power handling capability. If the SSR is rated for 117 volts AC at 5 amps, it can probably operate a 12 volt AC load just as well.

When compared to mechanical relays, SSRs have many advantages. They have very long life, no moving parts, no contact bounce, are immune to acoustical noise, and provide design flexibility. A very good book which describes everything you ever wanted to know about solid state relays is *Solid-State Relay Handbook With Applications* by Anthony Bishop, published by Howard W. Sams in 1986.

The mechanical relays which SSRs replace are not computer compatible. With additional circuitry you can add mechanical relays to your projects. Relays do offer some advantages. They cost less than SSRs, do not require heat sinks, can control AC or DC circuits, and can include multiple contacts.

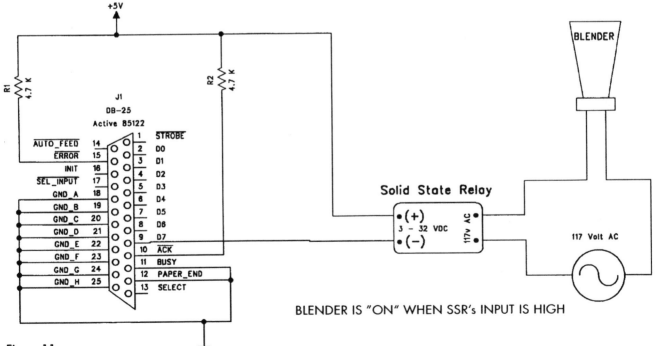

Figure 11

Since most SSRs only require 3 volts at 5 mA for proper operation, they can operate directly from the parallel port's TTL data pins. Figure 11 shows an SSR connected to D0, pin 1, of an IBM/clone printer port to switch a blender motor off and on. Since SSRs contain their own internal current limiting circuit, no additional parts are required. However, you may still want to add a 220Ω series resistor in the input circuit as printer port logic "insurance." When the signal applied to D0 goes high, the LED inside the SSR will go out and optocoupled circuitry will close an internal electronic switch. The switch will remain closed until the signal on D0 goes low or is removed.

Now look at the DB-25 connector. All IBM compatible computers use a female DB-25 connector. Resistors R1 and R2 hold the printer port's ERROR line (pin 15) and ACK line (pin 10) high. PAPER-END, Pin 12, and BUSY, Pin 11, are tied to ground. These logic levels make the computer think it is talk-ing to a printer that is on-line and ready to receive data.

Software

Normally, the computer sends data out the printer port with a carriage return (ASCII 13) and line feed (ASCII 10) added to the end of each line. The added codes tell the printer to move it's print head to the beginning of the next line. BASIC's LPRINT, with a trailing semicolon, or PASCAL'S WRITE commands can be used to send data out the parallel port without the trailing carriage return and line feed signals. Listings SSR_DEMO.PAS, SSR_DEMO.BAS, and SSR_DEMO.C illustrate this concept. Once a character is sent, the printer port data remains latched until another data byte is received. That means you can set D0 high, then have the computer do something else. D0 will remain high until you send the printer port more data.

BASIC Source Code Listing

```
10 REM    -=[ BASIC  Program to control Solid State Relay
20 REM
25 REM PRINT(CHR$(0)); : REM set all parallel port bits to LOW
30 FOR A = 1 TO 150
40 LPRINT(CHR$(1); :   GOSUB 1000 :   REM turn relay on
50 LPRINT(CHR$(0); :   GOSUB 1000 :   REM turn relay off
60 NEXT A
70 END
80 REM
1000 REM
1010 REM -=[ DELAY SUBROUTINE ]=-
1020 REM
1030 CT = 0
1040 FOR T = 1 TO 1000
1050 CT = CT + 1
1060 NEXT T
1070 RETURN
```

Pascal Source Code Listing

```
PROGRAM SSR_DEMO; { Written in Borland's Turbo Pascal                    } {re-
peatedly turn solid state relay on and off                          }
{   SSR is connected between D0 and +5 volts                             }
{   Written in Turbo Pascal 6. However, any version of Pascal should work.  }
USES CRT, Printer;
VAR A : INTEGER;
BEGIN
WRITE(LST, char(0));   { set all parallel port bits to LOW }
FOR A := 1 TO 150
```

```
DO BEGIN
    { turn solid state relay off }
WRITE(LST, char(1)); delay(500);  { turn bit 3, OFF, in binary = 00000000 }
WRITE(LST, char(0)); delay(500); { turn bit 3, ON,  in binary = 00000100 }
END; { for a }
END.
```

C Source Code Listing

```c
/*                    PROGRAM SSR_DEMO
          Code conversion by Eugene Klein
   Repeatedly turn solid state relay on and off.
   SSR is connected between D0 and +5 volts
   Written in Turbo Pascal 6. However, any version of Pascal should work.
*/

#include <dos.h>
#include <stdio.h>
#include <conio.h>
#include <stdlib.h>
#include <string.h>
#include <bios.h>
#include "My_TPU.h"


void main()                //SSR_DEMO
{
 int A;

 fprintf(stdprn,"\x00");  // set all parallel port bits to LOW
 for(A = 1;A <=150;A++)
 {
  // turn solid state relay off
  fprintf(stdprn,"\x01"); delay(500); // turn bit 3, OFF, in binary = 00000000
  fprintf(stdprn,"\x00"); delay(500); // turn bit 3, ON,  in binary = 00000100
 }
}
```

Using Optocouplers for Isolation

Circuit Theory

An optocoupler is a device consisting of an LED positioned near photo-sensitive silicone. There is a space between the two parts, and the whole thing is sealed in plastic. An optocoupler allows you to send digital signals between two circuits with different grounds. Since the digital signal is transmitted on a light beam, the two circuits are 100% electrically isolated. This inexpensive device provides low cost insurance that protects your computer from static electricity, relay and motor back-EMF, and ground loop damage. It is imperative that you include optocouplers in AC controlled projects.

Optosensors are arranged with all input pins on one side of the chip and all output pins on the opposite side. This creates a physical separation between input and output circuitry capable of providing up to 7500 volt isolation between input and output (ratings vary widely between products). Circuit board layout should be designed to maintain this separation. Input and output circuits should use separate ground planes, power supplies, and a physical separation at least equal to the distance between the optosensor's input and output pins, (usually .300").

Not all optocouplers are created equal. Manufacturers select different photo-sensitive devices for different applications. You must select an optocoupler that meets your electrical needs. Manufacturers of optocouplers do supply data sheets that give full specifications of their devices, and you should consult these before deciding on a specific optocoupler.

Figure 12 depicts four different types of optosensors. All circuits use the printer port's TTL signals to provide sink current control. Circuit design was chosen so output logic follows input logic. In other words, when an input to the optosensor goes high, the output will be high, and when the input goes low, the output will go low.

U1 is a photo-transistor optocoupler used to provide an isolated TTL signal. The output is read between the opto-sensor and the 4.7K pull-up resistor.

U2 is a silicon controlled rectifier (SCR) optocoupler used to control large DC loads. Bringing U2's pin 2 input to an active high will result in secondary current flow. Once the SCR starts conducting, it is no longer affected by its internal LED. To remove power from the load, you must break the current path. The normally closed (NC) momentary action switch stops the current flow when pressed. However, when the switch is released power will again flow in the load circuit if the optosensor's input has not been returned to an inactive high. Therefore, to stop load current, you must first bring the optocoupler's input low and then press the momentary switch.

U3 is a triac optocoupler. Triacs are designed to control large AC voltages. Unlike an SCR, the input logic can turn the output current on or off.

U4, a solid state relay, is a special class of optosensor. It contains internal circuitry to accept a wide range of of input voltages. Different models provide AC or DC control of varying amperage. The whole package is equipped with a heat sink.

Software

The program listings OPTOS.PAS and OPTOS.C show how to turn each device on and off.

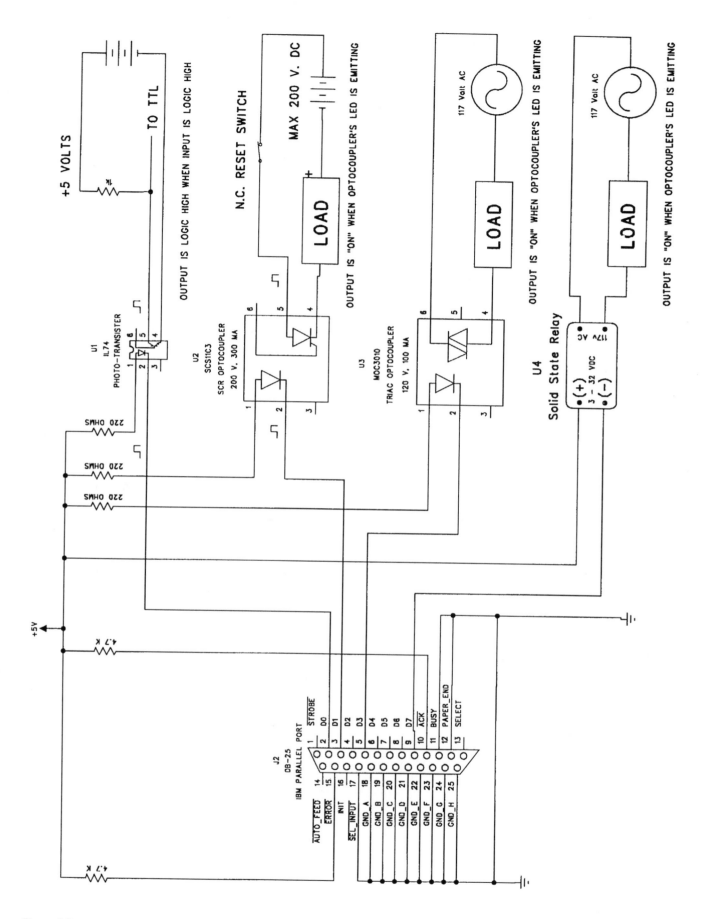

Figure 12

Pascal Source Code Listing

```pascal
PROGRAM Optos;
USES CRT, Printer;
{
Repeatedly turn each opto-coupler in FIGURE OPTOS high and low until any key is
pressed
}
CONST  D0_High = 1;  { photo-transistor opto-coupler } D0_Low  = 0;
D1_High = 2;  { SCR opto-coupler                }
        D1_Low  = 0;
D3_High = 8;  { triac opto-coupler              }
        D3_Low  = 0;
D5_High = 0;  { SSR, solid state relay          }
        D5_Low  = 32;
        Time = 500;
VAR E : INTEGER;
PROCEDURE Transmit_Data(High_Bit_Value, Low_Bit_Value : BYTE);
{
Send data out LPT1, parallel printer port.
Sequence:
    set bit to active high
    delay
    set bit ti active low
    delay
}
BEGIN
WRITE(LST, CHAR(High_Bit_Value));
DELAY(Time);
WRITE(LST, CHAR(Low_Bit_Value));
DELAY(Time);
END; { transmit data }
BEGIN { main, opto }
    REPEAT
Transmit_Data(D0_High, D0_Low);  { photo-transistor opto-coupler } Transmit_Data(D1_High,
D1_Low);  { SCR opto-coupler                } Transmit_Data(D3_High, D3_Low);  { triac
opto-coupler               } Transmit_Data(D5_High, D5_Low);   { SSR opto-coupler
} UNTIL KEYPRESSED
END. { main, optos }
```

C Source Code Listing

```c
/*                      PROGRAM Optos
        Code conversion by Eugene Klein
    Repeatedly turn each opto-coupler in FIGURE OPTOS high and low
    until any key is pressed
*/

#include <dos.h>
#include <stdio.h>
#include <conio.h>
#include <stdlib.h>
#include <string.h>
#include <bios.h>
#include "My_TPU.h"
```

```c
const int D0_High = 1;    // photo-transistor opto-coupler
const int D0_Low  = 0;
const int D1_High = 2;    // SCR opto-coupler
const int D1_Low  = 0;
const int D3_High = 8;    // triac opto-coupler
const int D3_Low  = 0;
const int D5_High = 32;   // SSR, solid state relay
const int D5_Low  = 0;
const int Time = 500;
int E;

void Transmit_Data(unsigned char High_Bit_Value,unsigned char Low_Bit_Value)

/* Send data out LPT1, parallel printer port.
   Sequence:
     set bit to active high
     delay
     set bit ti active low
     delay
*/
{
 putc(High_Bit_Value,stdprn);
 delay(Time);
 putc(Low_Bit_Value,stdprn);
 delay(Time);
}

void main()
{
 do
 {
  Transmit_Data(D0_High, D0_Low);   //{ photo-transistor opto-coupler
  Transmit_Data(D1_High, D1_Low);   //{ SCR opto-coupler
  Transmit_Data(D3_High, D3_Low);   //{ triac opto-coupler
  Transmit_Data(D5_High, D5_Low);   //{ SSR opto-coupler
 }while(!kbhit());
}
```

Driving High Power Loads and DC Relays

Circuit Theory

A buffer driver circuit is necessary if you want to use a printer port's TTL logic to control high power resistive and inductive loads. By definition, each TTL output can only sink only 15 mA and source 7 mA of current. If you want to control larger loads, you must add a buffer designed for the job. The ULN2803 is suitable for driving relays, solenoids, lamps, and stepping motors.

The ULN2803 octal driver is designed as an interface between low-level TTL/CMOS circuitry and high-power DC loads. The chip contains eight high voltage, high current driver amps. The physical arrangement of the pins places each driver's input opposite its output. D0 is input on pin 1 and output on pin 18, D2 is input on pin 2 and output on pin 17, and so forth. This arrangement makes circuit board design logical and straightforward.

The ULN2803 accepts TTL or CMOS inputs. Each output is rated at 50 volts, 500 mA continuous and 600 mA intermittent. Its big brother, the ULN2813, can drive 600 mA loads continuously. It can safely control inductive loads since each driver contains transient protection diodes. Silicon logic does not take well to heat. Place a heat sink on the IC if you are driving larger loads.

Figure 13-A shows a basic high power load driver circuit. The printer port's TTL data pins, D0 to D7, drive the ULN2803's eight inputs on pins 1 through 8. The pull-up resistors help ensure clean logic signals. Resistors R9 and R10 keep the printer port's ACK and ERROR lines at logic high. The PAPER-END and BUSY lines are tied to logic low. The computer "thinks" it is talking to an on-line printer, ready to receive data. The ULN2803 is designed to sink a load. Since outputs are inverted from inputs, a load is "on" when the input logic is high.

Figure 13-B shows the ULN2803 used to drive a DC relay. The relay is energized whenever the input logic is high.

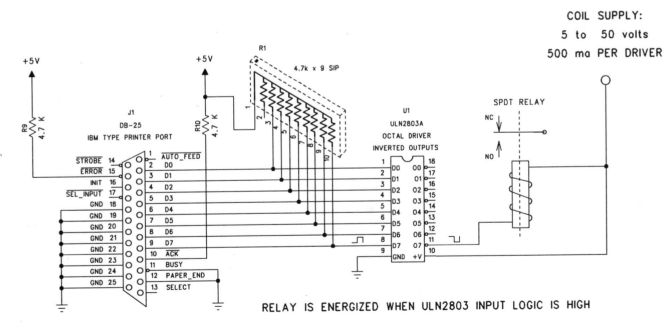

RELAY IS ENERGIZED WHEN ULN2803 INPUT LOGIC IS HIGH

Software

Program listings DRIVER.BAS, DRIVER.PAS, and DRIVER.C are used with the circuit in Figure 13-A.

The listings DRV_RLY.BAS, DRV_RLY.C, and DRV_RLY.PAS are used with the circuit in Figure 13-B. When executed, these programs will keep energizing and de-energizing the relay connected to D7, at pin 9, until any keyboard key is pressed.

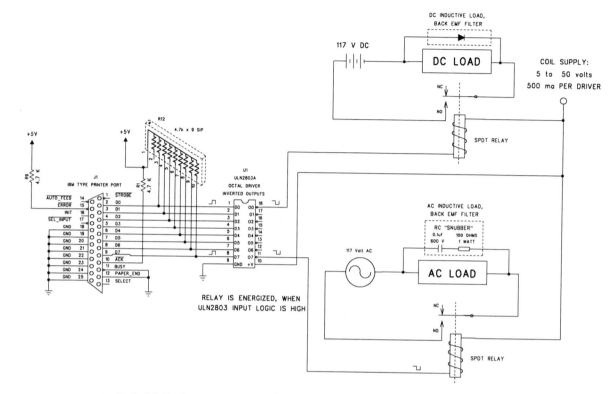

BASIC Source Code Listing for Figure 13-A

```
100 REM DRIVER.BAS
110 REM
120 REM   Repeatedly turn each data bit, D0 - D7 on and off.
130 REM   Pressing any key will end the program
140 REM
150 t = 1: D = 128
160 REM
170 REM   -=[  main, driver  ]=-
180 REM
190 D = 1
200 REM  REPEAT
210 LPRINT CHR$(D);
220 SLEEP (t)
230 LPRINT CHR$(0);
240 SLEEP (t)
250 D = D + D
260 IF D < 129 THEN GOTO 200
270 IF INKEY$ = "" THEN GOTO 180
280 END
```

Pascal Source Code Listing for Figure 13-A

```
PROGRAM DRIVER;
{
Repeatedly turn each data bit, D0 - D7 on and off.
    Pressing any key will end the program
}
USES CRT, PRINTER;
CONST t = 5;
VAR D : INTEGER;
BEGIN { main, driver }
REPEAT
D    := 1;
    REPEAT
    WRITE(LST,CHAR(D));
    Delay(t);
    WRITE(LST,CHAR(0));
    Delay(t);
    D := D + D;
    UNTIL D > 128;
UNTIL KEYPRESSED;
END. { main, driver }
```

C Source Code Listing for Figure 13-A

```
/*                      PROGRAM DRIVER
              Code conversion by Eugene Klein

  Repeatedly turn each data bit, D0 - D7 on and off.
  Pressing any key will end program
*/

#include <dos.h>
#include <stdio.h>
#include <conio.h>
#include <stdlib.h>
#include <string.h>
#include <bios.h>
#include "My_TPU.h"

unsigned char D;

void Delay(int T)
// provide a delay proportional to T.
{
 int X, Y;
 Y = 0;
 for(X=1;X<=T;X++)
  Y+=T;
}

void main()
{
```

```
  D=1;
  do
  {
   do
   {
    putc(D,stdprn);
    delay(1000);
    putc(NULL,stdprn);
    delay(1000);
    D+=D;
   }while(D > 128);
  }while(!kbhit());
 }
```

BASIC Source Code Listing for Figure 13-B

```
100 REM FILE: DRV_RLY.BAS
110 REM
120 REM  Repeatedly turn a relay interfaced to a printer port's D7, pin 9,
130 REM  on and off.
140 REM
150 D7 = 128: T = 1000
160 REM
170 REM REPEAT
180 LPRINT CHR$(D7);
190 FOR A = 1 TO T: NEXT A
200 LPRINT CHR$(0);
210 FOR A = 1 TO T: NEXT A
220 IF INKEY$ = "" THEN 170
230 END
```

Pascal Source Code Listing for Figure 13-B

```
PROGRAM DRV_RLY;
{
Repeatedly turn a relay interfaced to a printer port's D7, pin 9,
    on and off.
}
USES CRT, PRINTER;
CONST D7 = 128; t = 5;
BEGIN
REPEAT
WRITE(LST, D7);
DELAY(t);
WRITE(LST, 0 );
DELAY(t);
UNTIL KEYPRESSED;
END.
```

C Source Code Listing for Figure 13-B

```
/*                          PROGRAM DRV_RLY
                      Code conversion by Eugene Klein


   Repeatedly turn a relay interfaced to a printer port's D7, pin 9,
    on and off.
*/


#include <dos.h>
#include <stdio.h>
#include <conio.h>
#include <stdlib.h>
#include <string.h>
#include <bios.h>
#include "My_TPU.h"

const int D7 = 128;
const int t = 5;

void main()
{
 do
  {
   putc(D7,stdprn);
   delay(t);
   putc(0,stdprn);
   delay(t);
  }while(!kbhit());
}
```

Speech Output from a Parallel Printer Port

Circuit Theory

There are several speech cards that require only a single slot in your IBM-compatible computer and produce very realistic speech. If you have the need, and physical space, then one of these commercial boards, like the *de facto* standard SoundBlaster card, may be for you. However, if you want your project to interact with the user by saying a few pre-defined phrases, then this circuit can be a very cost effective alternative.

The project relies on a General Instruments SPO256 speech synthesizer IC. The English language is made up of 59 distinct sounds, and the SPO256 knows how to generate all 59 of them. The SPO256 data sheets identify each sound by codes familiar to linguistic scholars. The data sheets also includes English usage examples of each sound as well as a small dictionary "sounding out" some common words.

Figure 14 shows a working application of the SPO256. The computer sends data with data bits D0 through D5. The SPO256 knows when data should be read when its ALD line, at pin 20, is pulsed with an active low strobe. If the chip is not ready to receive new data, its LRQ line, pin 9, is pulled to an active low.

On the printer port connector J1, resistors R1 and R2 are pull-up resistors for the printer port's ERROR and ACK lines. By tying the ACK and ERROR lines to logic high, while securing the PAPER-END and BUSY lines to logic low, the computer is fooled into thinking it is connected to an on-line printer ready to receive data. Therefore, BASIC's LPRINT (with a trailing semicolon) and PASCAL's WRITE statements can output data with a minimum of software code.

Rather than grounding the printer port's BUSY line, the circuit routes it to the SPO256's LRQ line, pin 9. When the SPO256 pulls its LRQ line low, the computer thinks it has a printer that is out of paper and stops sending data. When the BUSY line returns to high, the computer will start sending more data. The entire process is handled by ROM BIOS and hidden from your software. The SPO256's audio output is then filtered and ready for connection to your audio power amp.

Software

The program listings SPEECH.PAS and SPEECH.C demonstrate how to generate words from the parallel printer port.

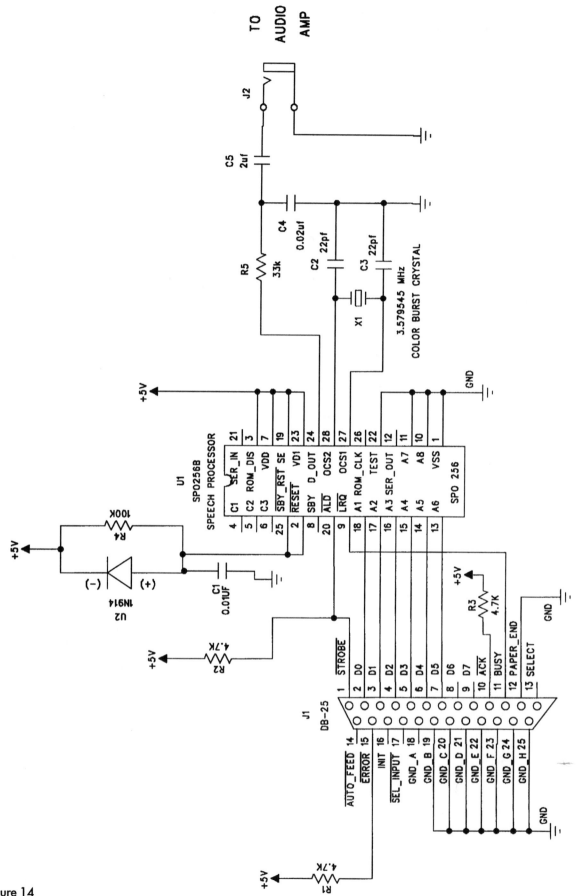

Figure 14

```
PROGRAM SPEECH;
{
Produce speech using General Instrument's SPO256 Speech Processor.  The chip has 64 address
locations each identifying instructions for sounding an allophone.  The chip's output should be
fed to an audio amplifier.
}
USES CRT, PRINTER, My_Tpu;
TYPE        String80 = STRING[80];
            Set_Of_Char = SET OF CHAR;
{
NOTE: The pound sign, "#", in front of a number, tells the Turbo Pascal compiler that the
number is an ASCII value to be assigned to the character variable in front of the equal sign.
}
CONST
{
 Allophone information based on General Instruments' Data Sheets,
and Radio Shack Data sheet packaged with item 276-1784.
}
{              DATA SHEET    DICTIONARY                          }
{              ALLOPHONE      PRONUNCIATION                      }
{              SYMBOL      SYMBOL              NOTES       }
{*}        AA =  #24;    {   Ñ    }
{*}        AE =  #26;    {   a    }
{*}        AO =  #23;    {   É    }
           AR =  #59;    {   Ñr   }
{*}        AW =  #32;    {   ou   }
{*}        AX =  #15;    {   u    }
           AY =  #6;{    ç    }
           BB1 = #28;    {   b    final position }
                        {   b    between vowels, or in clusters }
           BB2 = #63;    {   b    initial position before a vowel }
           CH =  #50;    {   ch   }
           DD1 = #21;    {   d    final position }
           DD2 = #33;    {   d    initial positin }
           DH1 = #18;    {   th   word's initial position }
           DH2 = #54;    {   th   word's final position    }
                        {   th   between vowels            }
{*}        EH =  #7;{    e    }
           EL =  #62;    {   l    }
           ER1 = #51;    {   ar   }
           ER2 = #52;    {   ur   }
           EY =  #20;    {   Ö    }
{*}        FF =  #40;    {            silent, use singly in final position }
           GG1 = #36;    {   g        before high front vowels: ir, ä, i, Ö, e, er }
           GG2 = #61;    {   g        before high back vowels: ïï, oo, ï, oi, u    }
                        {   g        before clusters }
           GG3 = #34;    {   g        before low vowels: a, ou, ç, Ñr, Ñ, É, ìr, ar, ur }
                        {            medical clusters }
                        {   g        final position }
           HH1 = #27;    {   h        before front vowels: ir, ä, i, ä, e, er, a }
           HH2 = #57;    {   h        before back vowels: ïï, oo, ï, oi, É, ìr, Ñr }
{*}        IH =  #12;    {   i    }
           IY =  #19;    {   ä    }
           JH =  #10;    {   j    }
           KK1 = #42;    {   k        before front vowels
                               ir, ä, i, Ö, e, er, ç, a, ar, ur, u }
                        {   k        initial clusters }
           KK2 = #41;    {   k        final position }
           KK3 = #8;{    k        before back vowel:ïï, oo, ï, oi, ìr, Ñr, É }
```

```
                    LL  = #45;    {    L    }
              MM  = #16;    {    m    }
              NG  = #44;    {    ng   }
              NN1 = #11;    {    n          before front and central vowels:
                    ir, ä, i, Ö, e, er, a, ar, ur, u, ou, ç, ï } {    n          final clus-
ters }
              NN2 = #56;    {    n          before back vowels: oo, ï, oi, ìr, Ñr, É }
              ORR = #58;    {    ìr   }
              OW  = #53;    {    ï    }
              OY  = #5;{    oi   }
              PP1 =  #9;    {    P    }
              RR1 = #14;    {    _R         initial position = beginning of word }
              RR2 = #39;    {    r          initial cluster                      }
              SH  = #37;    {    sh   }
(*)   SS  =  #55;  { silent }
(*)   TH  =  #29;  { silent }
              TT1 = #17;    {    t          final cluster before SS }
              TT2 = #13;    {    t          all other positions }
{*}   UH  =  #30;  {    oo        }
              UW1= #22;     {    ïï         after y }
              UW2 = #31;    {    ïï         in one syllable words }
              VV  = #35;    {    V          }
              WH  = #48;    {    hW         }
              WW  = #46;    {    W          }
              XR  = #47;    {    er         }
              YR  = #60;    {    ir         }
              YY1 = #49;    {    y          clusters         }
              YY2 = #25;    {    Y          initial position }
              ZH  = #38;    {    Zh         }
              ZZ  = #43;    {    z          }
PA1 = #0; { pause 10 ms, before BB, DD, GG, and JH                } PA2 = #1; { pause 30 ms,
before BB, DD, GG, and JH                     } PA3 = #2; { pause 50 ms, before PP, TT, KK, and
CH, and between words } PA4 = #3; { pause 100 ms, between clauses and sentences           }
PA5 = #4; { pause 200 ms, between clauses and sentences                    }
{    allophones proceeded by "*", can be doubled }
VAR                                       E : BYTE;
Computer, Talking, Hello, Phrase : String80; Lpt_Num, Lpt_Port_Address : WORD;
Ok_Set : Set_Of_Char;
PROCEDURE Speak(Phrase : String80);
{
Transmit each allophone byte of phrase to SPO256.
    Procedure will only transmit to LPT1.
}
CONST D6 = 64;
VAR    N : BYTE;
BEGIN { speek }
FOR N := 1 TO Length(Phrase) DO
    BEGIN { for n }
    WRITE(LST, CHR(ORD(Phrase[N]))
    );
    delay(30);                            { put data on data lines              }
    END; { for n }
END; { speek }
PROCEDURE Say(Phrase : String80);
{
Transmit each allophone byte of phrase to SPO256.
    Will transmit on LPT1, LPT2, or LPT3.
}
CONST D7 = 128;
VAR N, Temp : Byte;
BEGIN { say }
FOR N := 1 TO Length(Phrase) DO
```

```
      BEGIN { for n }
{     Check speech chip's standby line, LRQ, ( D7, at pin 10 on printer port    }
{     When LRQ is logic high, chip can accept new data}
      REPEAT UNTIL ( PORT[Lpt_Port_Address + 1] AND D7 ) = D7; { ok to transmit? }
{     DO set HIGH = 0. Why? Because you have to account for inverteed logic}
{     All four control lines, at LPT Port Address + 2, are set to inactive }
{        logic levels by sending 10, binary 00001010.    }
{     Remember, Storbe line is inverted. High is 0, Low is 1.    }
PORT[Lpt_Port_Address + 2] := 10;                   { set all control bits to inactive }
PORT[Lpt_Port_Address] := ORD(Phrase[N]); { put data on data lines }
      PORT[Lpt_Port_Address + 2] := 11;            { set strobe, D0, to active LOW   }
PORT[Lpt_Port_Address + 2] := 10 ;          { set strobe, D0, to inactive HIGH }
END; { for n }
END; { say }
BEGIN { main, speech }
 { define words by allophone sounds }
Computer := CONCAT(KK1, AX, pa1, MM, PP1, YY1, UW1, TT2, ER1, PA3);
Talking := CONCAT(TT2, AO, AO, PA3, KK1, IH, NG, PA3);
Hello := CONCAT(HH1, EH, LL, AX, OW, PA5);
 { transmit speech allophones via LPT1 }
Speak(Computer);
Speak(Talking);
DELAY(250);
Speak(Hello);
 { alternete method of sending speech allophones to LPT1, LPT2, or LPT3        }
Select_Printer_Port(Lpt_Num, Lpt_Port_Address);
Say(Computer);
Say(Talking);
DELAY(250);
Say(Hello);
END. { main, speech }
```

C Source Code Listing

```
/*                        PROGRAM SPEECH
                 Code conversion by Eugene Klein

    Produce speech using General Instrument's SPO256 Speech Processor.  The
    chip has 64 address locations each identifying instructions for sounding
    an allophone.  The chip's output should be fed to an audio amplifier.
*/


#include <dos.h>
#include <stdio.h>
#include <conio.h>
#include <stdlib.h>
#include <string.h>
#include <bios.h>
#include "My_TPU.h"



/*
    NOTE: The pound sign, "#", in front of a number, tells the Turbo
        Pascal compiler that the number is an ASCII value to be
        assigned to the character variable in front of the equal sign.

    Allophone information based on General Instruments' Data Sheets,
    and Radio Shack Data sheet packaged with item 276-1784.
```

```
                DATA SHEET      DICTIONARY
                ALLOPHONE       PRONUNCIATION
                  SYMBOL          SYMBOL                    NOTES
 */

    #define AA    24      //     _
    #define AE    26      //     a
    #define AO    23      //     _
    #define AR    59      //     _r
    #define AW    32      //     ou
    #define AX    15      //     u
    #define AY    6       //     _
    #define BB1   28      //     b    final position
                  //   b    between vowels, or in clusters
    #define BB2   63      //     b    initial position before a vowel
    #define CH    50      //     ch
    #define DD1   21      //     d    final position
    #define DD2   33      //     d    initial positin
    #define DH1   18      //     th   word's initial position
    #define DH2   54      //     th   word's final position
                  //  th    between vowels
    #define EH    7       //     e
    #define EL    62      //     l
    #define ER1   51      //     ar
    #define ER2   52      //     ur
    #define EY    20      //     _
    #define FF    40      //          silent, use singly in final position
    #define GG1   36      //     g    before high front vowels: ir, _, i, _, e, er
    #define GG2   61      //     g    before high back vowels: ••, oo, •, oi, u
                  //   g    before clusters
    #define GG3   34      //     g    before low vowels: a, ou, _, _r, _, _, "r, ar, ur

                  //          medical clusters
                  //   g    final position
    #define HH1   27      //     h    before front vowels: ir, _, i, _, e, er, a
    #define HH2   57      //     h    before back vowels: ••, oo, •, oi, _, "r, _r
    #define IH    12      //     i
    #define IY    19      //     _
    #define JH    10      //     j
    #define KK1   42      //     k    before front vowels
                  //   ir, _, i, _, e, er, _, a, ar, ur, u
                  //   k    initial clusters
    #define KK2   41      //     k    final position
    #define KK3   8       //     k    before back vowel:••, oo, •, oi, "r, _r, _
    #define LL    45      //     L
    #define MM    16      //     m
    #define NG    44      //     ng
    #define NN1   11      //     n    before front and central vowels:
                  //   ir, _, i, _, e, er, a, ar, ur, u, ou, _, •
                  //   n    final clusters
    #define NN2   56      //     n    before back vowels: oo, •, oi, "r, _r, _
    #define ORR   58      //     "r
    #define OW    53      //     •
    #define OY    5       //     oi
    #define PP1   9       //     P
    #define RR1   14      //     _R   initial position    beginning of word
    #define RR2   39      //     r    initial cluster
    #define SH    37      //     sh
    #define SS    55      //  silent
    #define TH    29      //  silent
    #define TT1   17      //     t    final cluster before SS
```

```
#define TT2   13    //   t      all other positions
#define UH    30    //   oo
#define UW1   22    //   ••      after y
#define UW2   31    //   ••      in one syllable words
#define VV    35    //   V
#define WH    48    //   hW
#define WW    46    //   W
#define XR    47    //   er
#define YR    60    //   ir
#define YY1   49    //   y       clusters
#define YY2   25    //   Y       initial position
#define ZH    38    //   Zh
#define ZZ    43    //   z

#define PA1   0 // pause 10 ms, before BB, DD, GG, and JH
#define PA2   1 // pause 30 ms, before BB, DD, GG, and JH
#define PA3   2 // pause 50 ms, before PP, TT, KK, and CH, and between words
#define PA4   3 // pause 100 ms, between clauses and sentences
#define PA5   4 // pause 200 ms, between clauses and sentences

        // allophones proceeded by "", can be doubled

unsigned  char E;
unsigned int Lpt_Num, Lpt_Port_Address;

void Speak(char *Phrase,int Size)
{
/*
  Transmit each allophone byte of phrase to SPO256.
  Procedure will only transmit to LPT1.
  Similar to using BASIC'S LPRINT, or Pascal's WRITE commands
*/

 unsigned char N;

 for(N=0;N<Size;N++)
 {
     putc(Phrase[N],stdprn);
  delay(30);                                  // put data on data lines
 }
}

void Say(char *Phrase,int Size)
{
/*
  Transmit each allophone byte of phrase to SPO256.
  Will transmit on LPT1, LPT2, or LPT3.
*/
 const int D7 = 128;
 unsigned char N, Temp;

 for(N=0;N<Size;N++)
 {
 /*  Check speech chip's standby line, LRQ, ( D7, at pin 10 on printer port
     When LRQ is logic high, chip can accept new data.
 */
  while(( inport(Lpt_Port_Address + 1) & D7 ) == 0); // ok to transmit?
  {
 /* D0 set HIGH = 0. Why? Because you have to account for inverteed logic
    All four control lines, at LPT Port Address + 2, are set to inactive
       logic levels by sending 10, binary 00001010.
```

```
         Remember, Storbe line is inverted. High is 0, Low is 1.
   */
      outport(Lpt_Port_Address + 2,10);           // set all control bits to inactive
      outport(Lpt_Port_Address,Phrase[N]);        // put data on data lines
      outport(Lpt_Port_Address + 2,11);           // set strobe, D0, to active LOW
      outport(Lpt_Port_Address + 2,10);            // set strobe, D0, to inactive HIGH
    }
  }
}


void main()
{
 // define words by allophone sounds
 char Computer[]= {KK1,AX,PA1,MM,PP1,YY1,UW1,TT2,ER1,PA3};
 char  Talking[]= {TT2,AO,AO,PA3,KK1,IH,NG,PA3};
 char Hello[]= {HH1,EH,LL,AX,OW,PA5};

 // transmit speech allophones via LPT1

 Speak(Computer,sizeof(Computer));
 Speak(Talking,sizeof(Talking));
 delay(250);
 Speak(Hello,sizeof(Hello));

 // alternete method of sending speech allophones to LPT1, LPT2, or LPT3
 Lpt_Num = Select_Printer_Port();
 Lpt_Port_Address = Init_Printer_Port(Lpt_Num);
 Say(Computer,sizeof(Computer));
 Say(Talking,sizeof(Talking));
 delay(250);
 Say(Hello,sizeof(Hello));
}
```

Generating Audio Tones from a Printer Port

Circuit Theory

The PCD3311 tone generator IC can generate three octaves of musical, dual tone multi-frequency (DTMF), and 300-1200-2400 baud modem tones. The PCD3311 contains an internal array of audio tones. Each time you send the chip a number, it generates the tone(s) identified by that number. On-board logic divides the color burst crystal's frequency to the musical, DTMF, or modem tone requested. The tone continues until it is turned off, or replaced, by new data. Notes are turned off by sending a 1, 2, or 3. A more in depth discription can be found in Volume 1, "Communications," of the *Signetics Linear Data Manual.*

As you can see in Figure 15, very few external parts are used. Q1, R1, and R5 invert the strobe line

because the PCD3311 requires an active high strobe. Resistors R1 and R3 are pull-up resistors for the ACK and ERROR lines. By tying the ACK and ERROR lines to logic high, while tying the BUSY and PAPER-END lines to logic low, the computer is fooled into thinking it is connected to an on-line printer ready to receive data. R2 ties PCD331's chip select line, CS, high. That means the PCD331 is always waiting for new data from the printer port. It knows it has valid data on its data input lines, D0–D5, when the strobe line on pin 5 goes to an active high. You could multiplex this device with other devices connected to the parallel printer port by adding an active high chip select pulse to pin 7, CS. The CS line must be high before pulsing the STROBE line, and remain high until after the completion of the last STROBE signal.

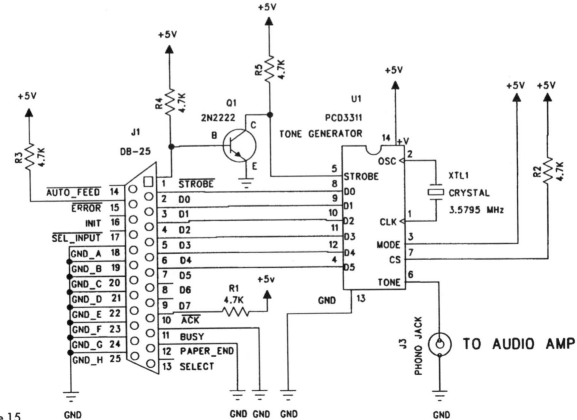

Figure 15

Software

Using BASIC's LPRINT command or PASCAL's WRITELN command will send data to the PCD3311. Both these commands were designed to send data to a printer. Both commands place the data on the LPT1's data lines and generate a strobe signal.

The programs PCD3311.PAS and PCD3311.C demonstrate how to generate a musical scale, modem, and DTMF and signals. I just let the notes play, but you can turn off a note by transmitting the number 1, 2, or 3.

The programs MUSIC.PAS and MUSIC.C demonstrate how to play music from your PC's parallel port. I transcribed the melody "Dill Rag Pickel" by Charles L. Johnson note for note from sheet music. Each note was replaced by a number the PCD331 associates with that note. Since the sheet music went down three notes below the PCD3311's tonal "range," I used negative numbers to represent them. The program adds 3 to each number before it outputs the value. This transposes the music up three tones and places all the notes within the PCD331's tonal range. Today's electronic keyboards use a similar technique to transpose notes.

Irving Berlin did a similar thing with his personal piano. Berlin always played in C. He had a piano constructed with the keyboard on tracks. A lever under the keyboard was used to move the keyboard left or right, by indexed amounts, in relation to the piano's body. Each click of the levered index moved the keyboard by one note. This allowed Berlin to generate music in any key while fingering the piano in C.

Pascal Source Code Listing for PCD3311.PAS

```
PROGRAM PCD3311; { Signetics PCD3311 }
{
FILE: PCD3311.PAS, by Paul Bergsman 11/10/1992
Generate modem, musical, and DTMF telephone tones,  from printer port LPT2 on my machine is a
third party printer card used for experimentation }
USES CRT;
CONST T : ARRAY[0..25] OF INTEGER =                 { define musical tone values }
 ($30, $31, $32, $33, $34, $35, $36, $37, $38, $39, $3A, $29, $3B,
$3C, $3D, $0E, $3E, $2C, $3F, $04, $05, $25, $2F, $06, $07, $00);
VAR Printer : TEXT;
PROCEDURE  Play_Scale;
VAR A, E : INTEGER;
BEGIN { play scale }
FOR A := 1 TO 2 DO
    BEGIN { for a }
FOR E := 0  TO 24 DO                       {   -=[ GO UP THE SCALE  ]=-        }
        BEGIN { for e }
        WRITELN ('T(',E,') = ', T[E]);
        WRITE(PRINTER,  CHAR(T[E]));
        DELAY(100);
        END; { for e }
FOR E := 24 DOWNTO 0 DO                    {   -=[ GO DOWN THE SCALE ]=-       }
        BEGIN { for e }
        WRITELN ('T(',E,') = ', T[E]);
        WRITE(PRINTER,  CHAR(T[E]));
        DELAY(100);
        END; { for e }
    WRITELN;
    END; { for a }
END;  { play scale }
PROCEDURE Output_DTMF_Tones;
VAR  A, E : INTEGER;
BEGIN { dtmf }
FOR A := 1 TO 2 DO
    BEGIN { for a }
    FOR E := 16 TO 31 DO
```

```
         BEGIN { for e }
WRITELN('DTMF TONE ',E - 15, ' = ',E); WRITE(PRINTER, CHAR(E));
         DELAY(200);
         END; { for e }
    WRITELN;
    END; { for a }
END; { dtmf }
BEGIN { main }
ASSIGN(Printer, 'LPT2'); REWRITE (Printer);
    REPEAT
    Play_Scale;
    Output_DTMF_Tones;
    UNTIL KEYPRESSED;
WRITE(Printer, CHAR(3));                    {  -=[ turn off oscillator  ]=-  } DELAY(1500);
END. { main }
```

C Source Code Listing for PCD3311.C

```c
/*             PROGRAM PCD3311; { Signetics PCD3311 }
        Code conversion by Eugene Klein

        by Paul Bergsman 11/10/1992
Generate modem, musical, and DTMF telephone tones,  from printer port
LPT2 on my machine is a third party printer card used for experimentation.
*/


#include <dos.h>
#include <stdio.h>
#include <conio.h>
#include <stdlib.h>
#include <string.h>
#include <bios.h>
#include "My_TPU.h"

unsigned int LPTx, Lpt_Num;

const int T[]=                 // define musical tone values
  {0x30, 0x31, 0x32, 0x33, 0x34, 0x35, 0x36, 0x37, 0x38, 0x39, 0x3A, 0x29, 0x3B,
   0x3C, 0x3D, 0x0E, 0x3E, 0x2C, 0x3F, 0x04, 0x05, 0x25, 0x2F, 0x06, 0x07, 0x00};


void Play_Scale(void)
{
 int  A, E;
 for(A=1;A<=2;A++)
 {
  for(E=0;E<=24;E++)              //   -=[ GO UP THE SCALE  ]=-
  {
   printf("T %i =  %i\n",E, T[E]);
   outport(LPTx,T[E]);
   delay(100);
  }
  for(E=24;E>=0;E—)                //   -=[ GO DOWN THE SCALE ]=-
  {
   printf("T %i =  %i\n",E, T[E]);
   outport(LPTx,T[E]);
   delay(100);
  }
  printf("\n");
```

```
 }
}

void Output_DTMF_Tones(void)
{
 int A, E;
 for(A=1;A<=2;A++)
 {
  for(E=16;E<=31;E++)
  {
   printf("DTMF TONE %i = %i\n",E - 15,E);
   outport(LPTx,'\E');
   delay(200);
  }
  printf("\n");
 }
}

void main()
{

 Lpt_Num = Select_Printer_Port();
 LPTx = Init_Printer_Port(Lpt_Num);
 do
 {
  Play_Scale();
  Output_DTMF_Tones();
 }while(!kbhit());
 outport(LPTx,'\3');                     // -=[ turn off oscillator  ]=-
 delay(1500);
}
```

Pascal Source Code Listing for MUSIC.PAS

```
PROGRAM Music; { Signetics PCD3311 }
{
FILE: Music.PAS, by Paul Bergsman 11/10/199
Play Dill Pickle Rag via PCD331 Tone Generator
}
USES CRT;
CONST
T : ARRAY[1..26] OF INTEGER =              { define musical tone values }
($30, $31, $32, $33, $34, $35, $36, $37, $38, $39, $3A, $29, $3B, $3C, $3D, $0E, $3E, $2C, $3F,
$04, $05, $25, $2F, $06, $07, $00);
{    Define music to be played.  Byte[0] continues number of bytes in array  }
{    smallest note is a 16th, so all notes are defined as 16th notes.         }
{    Music was transcribed by listing the ordinal value of T[n] over sheet    }
{    music notes,  then recording values into constant arrays below.          }
{    First number in array = number of active elements in array               }
    Intro : ARRAY[0 .. 6] OF INTEGER = (6,9,9,10,10,11,11);
  Line_1  :   ARRAY[0  .. 32] OF  INTEGER  =  (32,12,14,17,12,14,17,12,14,
17,12,14,17,17,14,12,12,5,7,9,5,7,9,5,7,9,5,7,9,9,7,5,5);
  End_A1  :   ARRAY[0  .. 32] OF  INTEGER  =  (32,0,2,4,0,2,4,0,2,4,0,2,4,
4,2,0,0,5,4,5,2,2,4,5,6,7,6,7,12,12,9,10,11);
  End_A2  :   ARRAY[0  .. 32] OF  INTEGER  =  (32,0,2,4,0,2,4,0,2,4,0,2,4,
4,2,0,0,7,6,7,12,12,9,7,7,5,5,5,5,5,7,3,2);
   Line_2   :    ARRAY[0   ..   32]  OF   INTEGER   =   (32,0,0,1,1,2,2,4,4,
5,5,14,12,12,14,12,12,4,4,14,12,12,14,12,12,5,5,14,12,12,14,12,12);
     End_B1   :   ARRAY[0   ..  32]  OF   INTEGER   =   (32,0,7,2,7,3,7,4,7,
```

```pascal
5,5,14,12,12,14,12,12,7,9,11,7,9,11,11,11,12,12,12,12,12,5,3,2);
 End_B2 : ARRAY[0 .. 32] OF INTEGER = (32,0,7,2,7,3,7,4,7, 5,5,14,12,12,14,12,12,13,14,16,
12,14,16,16,16,17,17,17,17,17,17,17,17);
 Line_3 : ARRAY[0 .. 32] OF INTEGER = (32,10,7,5,10,7,5,2,3, 5,2,5,7,7,5,2,0,-1,0,5,5,2,0,0,
-2,-2,-2,-2,7,7,9,9);
   Line_4  :  ARRAY[0  ..  32]  OF  INTEGER  =  (32,10,7,5,10,7,5,2,3,
5,2,5,7,7,5,2,2,7,6,7,12,12,9,7,7,5,5,5,5,7,7,9,9);
 Line_5 : ARRAY[0 .. 32] OF INTEGER = (32,10,7,5,10,7,5,2,3, 5,2,5,7,7,5,2,2,0,-1,0,5,5,2,0,0,-
2,-2,-2,-2,10,10,9,9);
   Line_6  :  ARRAY[0  ..  32]  OF  INTEGER  =  (32,7,5,7,9,10,9,10,12,
14,13,14,19,19,17,14,14,12,11,12,17,17,14,12,12,10,10,10,10,10,10,7,9);
   Line_7  :  ARRAY[0  ..  32]  OF  INTEGER  =  (32,7,5,7,9,10,9,10,12,
14,13,14,19,19,17,14,14,12,11,12,17,17,14,12,12,10,10,10,10,5,5,5,5);
VAR Printer : TEXT;
             A, C, E : INTEGER;
PROCEDURE Play_Note(Note : INTEGER);
BEGIN
{    all notes transposed up three tones because chip starts at D# not C        }
WRITE(Printer, CHAR(T[Note + 3]));
DELAY(150);
If KEYPRESSED THEN HALT;                          { exit program when keypressed } END;
PROCEDURE Display_Music;
BEGIN
CLrScr;
GOTOXY(10,2); WRITELN('-=[ DILL PICKEL RAG ]=-  by Charles L. Johnson '); gotoxy(10,4);
writeln('    transcribed by Paul Bergsman, 11/10/1992 '); GoToXY(1,7);
Writeln
('                                                                                  O');
WRITELN  ('/ƒƒƒƒƒƒƒƒƒƒƒƒƒƒƒƒƒƒƒƒƒƒƒƒƒƒƒƒƒƒƒƒƒƒƒƒƒƒƒƒƒƒƒƒƒƒƒƒƒƒƒƒƒƒƒƒƒƒÈƒƒ#Èƒƒƒƒƒ');
WRITELN
('≥                                                                                O');
WRITELN  ('√ƒƒƒƒƒƒƒƒƒƒƒƒƒƒƒƒƒƒƒƒƒƒƒƒƒƒƒƒƒƒƒƒƒƒƒƒƒƒƒƒƒƒƒƒƒƒƒƒÈƒƒ#Èƒƒƒƒƒƒƒƒƒƒƒƒƒƒƒƒ');
WRITELN
('≥                                              O  #O');
WRITELN  ('√ƒƒƒƒƒƒƒƒƒƒƒƒƒƒƒƒƒƒƒƒƒƒƒƒƒƒƒƒƒƒƒƒƒƒƒƒƒƒƒÈƒƒƒƒƒƒƒƒƒƒƒƒƒƒƒƒƒƒƒƒƒƒƒƒƒƒƒƒƒƒƒƒ');
WRITELN
('≥                             O  #O');
WRITELN  ('√ƒƒƒƒƒƒƒƒƒƒƒƒƒƒƒƒƒƒƒƒƒƒƒƒƒÈƒƒ#Èƒƒƒƒƒƒƒƒƒƒƒƒƒƒƒƒƒƒƒƒƒƒƒƒƒƒƒƒƒƒƒƒƒƒƒƒƒƒƒƒƒ');
WRITELN
('≥                    O #O');
WRITELN  ('¿ƒƒƒƒƒƒƒƒƒƒƒƒƒƒƒƒƒƒƒÈƒƒƒƒƒƒƒƒƒƒƒƒƒƒƒƒƒƒƒƒƒƒƒƒƒƒƒƒƒƒƒƒƒƒƒƒƒƒƒƒƒƒƒƒƒƒƒƒƒƒ');
writeln
('             O #O');
writeln
(' -È- #-È-');
WRITELN;
Writeln
('  -3  -2  -1    1   2   3   4   5   6   7   8   9  10  11  12  13  14  15  16  17'); END; { displa
music }
BEGIN { main }
{    my third party printer card used for development work is at LPT2 }
ASSIGN(Printer, 'LPT2'); REWRITE (Printer);
Display_Music;
REPEAT
GOTOXY(5,24); WRITE('PLAYING PART A                            '); FOR E := 1 TO Intro[0
do Play_Note(Intro[E]);
For E := 1 to Line_1[0] do Play_Note(LINE_1[E]);
For E := 1 to End_A1[0] do Play_Note(End_A1[E]); For E := 1 to Line_1[0] do Play_Note(LINE_1[E])
For E := 1 to End_A2[0] do Play_Note(End_A2[E]);
GOTOXY(5,24); WRITE('                      PLAYING PART B       '); For E := 1 to Line_2[0] d
Play_Note(LINE_2[E]);
```

```
For E := 1 to End_B1[0] do Play_Note(End_B1[E]);
For E := 1 to Line_2[0] do Play_Note(LINE_2[E]); For E := 1 to End_B2[0] do Play_Note(End_B2[E]);
GOTOXY(5,24); WRITE('                                    PLAYING PART C'); For A := 1 to 2 do
            BEGIN
            For E := 1 to Line_3[0] do Play_Note(Line_3[E]);
For E := 1 to Line_4[0] do Play_Note(Line_4[E]); For E := 1 to Line_5[0] do Play_Note(Line_5[E]);
IF A = 1 THEN For E := 1 to Line_6[0] do Play_Note(Line_6[E])
             ELSE For E := 1 to Line_7[0] do Play_Note(Line_7[E]);
            END; { for a }
UNTIL KEYPRESSED;                                        { just keep playing the song }
END. { main }
```

C Source Code Listing for MUSIC.C

```
    /*                PROGRAM Music; { Signetics PCD3311 }
                   Code conversion by Eugene Klein

      FILE: Music.PAS, by Paul Bergsman 11/10/199

      Play Dill Pickle Rag via PCD331 Tone Generator
    */


#include <dos.h>
#include <stdio.h>
#include <conio.h>
#include <stdlib.h>
#include <string.h>
#include <bios.h>
#include "My_TPU.h"




    // define musical tone values
const int   T[]=
      {0x30, 0x31, 0x32, 0x33, 0x34, 0x35, 0x36, 0x37, 0x38, 0x39, 0x3A, 0x29, 0x3B,
       0x3C, 0x3D, 0x0E, 0x3E, 0x2C, 0x3F, 0x04, 0x05, 0x25, 0x2F, 0x06, 0x07, 0x00};

/* Define music to be played.  Byte[0] contains number of bytes in array
   smallest note is a 16th, so all notes are defined as 16th notes.
   Music was transcribed by listing the ordinal value of T[n] over sheet
   music notes,  then recording values into constant arrays below.
   First number in array = number of active elements in array
*/

int Intro[] = {6,9,9,10,10,11,11};
int Line_1[] = {32,12,14,17,12,14,17,12,14,
   17,12,14,17,17,14,12,12,5,7,9,5,7,9,5,7,9,5,7,9,9,7,5,5};
int End_A1[] = {32,0,2,4,0,2,4,0,2,4,0,2,4,
   4,2,0,0,5,4,5,2,2,4,5,6,7,6,7,12,12,9,10,11};
int End_A2[] = {32,0,2,4,0,2,4,0,2,4,0,2,4,
   4,2,0,0,7,6,7,12,12,9,7,7,5,5,5,5,5,7,3,2};
int Line_2[] = {32,0,0,1,1,2,2,4,4,
   5,5,14,12,12,14,12,12,4,4,14,12,12,14,12,12,5,5,14,12,12,14,12,12};
int End_B1[] = {32,0,7,2,7,3,7,4,7,
   5,5,14,12,12,14,12,12,7,9,11,7,9,11,11,11,12,12,12,12,12,5,3,2};
int End_B2[] = {32,0,7,2,7,3,7,4,7,
   5,5,14,12,12,14,12,12,13,14,16, 12,14,16,16,16,17,17,17,17,17,17,17,17};
int Line_3[] = {32,10,7,5,10,7,5,2,3,
   5,2,5,7,7,5,2,2,0,-1,0,5,5,2,0,0, -2,-2,-2,-2,7,7,9,9};
```

```c
int Line_4[] = {32,10,7,5,10,7,5,2,3,
   5,2,5,7,7,5,2,2,7,6,7,12,12,9,7,7,5,5,5,5,7,7,9,9};
int Line_5[] = {32,10,7,5,10,7,5,2,3,
   5,2,5,7,7,5,2,2,0,-1,0,5,5,2,0,0,-2,-2,-2,-2,10,10,9,9};
int Line_6[] = {32,7,5,7,9,10,9,10,12,
   14,13,14,19,19,17,14,14,12,11,12,17,17,14,12,12,10,10,10,10,10,10,7,9};
int Line_7[] = {32,7,5,7,9,10,9,10,12,
   14,13,14,19,19,17,14,14,12,11,12,17,17,14,12,12,10,10,10,10,5,5,5,5};


int A, C, E,Lpt_Num, LPTx;

void Play_Note(int Note)
{
// all notes transposed up three tones because chip starts at D# not C       }
 outport(LPTx,T[Note + 3]);
 delay(150);
 if(kbhit())
  exit(0);                        // exit program when key pressed
}

void Display_Music(void)
{

 clrscr();
 gotoxy(10,2); printf("-=[ DILL PICKLE RAG ]=-  by Charles L. Johnson ");
 gotoxy(10,4); printf("    transcribed by Paul Bergsman, 11/10/1992 ");
 gotoxy(75,7);
 printf
 ("O\n");
 printf
 ("ÚÄÄÄÄÄÄÄÄÄÄÄÄÄÄÄÄÄÄÄÄÄÄÄÄÄÄÄÄÄÄÄÄÄÄÄÄÄÄÄÄÄÄÄÄÄÄÄÄÄÄÄÄÄÄÄÄÄÄÄÄÄÄéÄÄ#éÄÄÄÄ\n");
 printf
 ("3                                                 O             \n");
 printf
 ("ÃÄÄÄÄÄÄÄÄÄÄÄÄÄÄÄÄÄÄÄÄÄÄÄÄÄÄÄÄÄÄÄÄÄÄÄÄÄÄÄÄÄÄÄÄÄéÄÄ#éÄÄÄÄÄÄÄÄÄÄÄÄÄÄÄÄÄ\n");
 printf
 ("3                                      O  #O\n");
 printf
 ("ÃÄÄÄÄÄÄÄÄÄÄÄÄÄÄÄÄÄÄÄÄÄÄÄÄÄÄÄÄÄÄÄÄÄÄÄÄÄÄÄéÄÄÄÄÄÄÄÄÄÄÄÄÄÄÄÄÄÄÄÄÄÄÄÄÄÄÄÄÄÄÄ\n");
 printf
 ("3                O  #O\n");
 printf
 ("ÃÄÄÄÄÄÄÄÄÄÄÄÄÄÄÄÄÄÄÄÄÄÄÄÄÄÄÄéÄÄ#éÄÄÄÄÄÄÄÄÄÄÄÄÄÄÄÄÄÄÄÄÄÄÄÄÄÄÄÄÄÄÄÄÄÄÄÄÄÄÄ\n");
 printf
 ("3                O  #O\n");
 printf
 ("ÀÄÄÄÄÄÄÄÄÄÄÄÄÄÄÄÄÄÄéÄÄÄÄÄÄÄÄÄÄÄÄÄÄÄÄÄÄÄÄÄÄÄÄÄÄÄÄÄÄÄÄÄÄÄÄÄÄÄÄÄÄÄÄÄÄÄÄÄÄÄÄÄÄ\n");
 printf
 ("         O  #O\n");
 printf
 ("-é- #-é-\n\n");
 printf
 ("-3  -2  -1   1   2   3   4   5   6   7   8   9  10  11  12  13  14  15  16  17\n");
}

void main()
// my third party printer card used for development work is at LPT2
{
 Lpt_Num = Select_Printer_Port();
 LPTx = Init_Printer_Port(Lpt_Num);
 Display_Music();
```

```
     do
     {
       gotoxy(5,24); printf("PLAYING PART A");
       for (E=1;E<=Intro[0];E++)
        Play_Note(Intro[E]);
       for(E=1;E<=Line_1[0];E++)
        Play_Note(Line_1[E]);
       for(E=1;E<=End_A1[0];E++)
        Play_Note(End_A1[E]);
       for(E=1;E<=Line_1[0];E++)
        Play_Note(Line_1[E]);
       for(E=1;E<=End_A2[0];E++)
        Play_Note(End_A2[E]);
       gotoxy(5,24); printf("                    PLAYING PART B    ");
       for(E=1;E<=Line_2[0];E++)
        Play_Note(Line_2[E]);
       for(E=1;E<=End_B1[0];E++)
        Play_Note(End_B1[E]);
       for(E=1;E<=Line_2[0];E++)
        Play_Note(Line_2[E]);
       for(E=1;E<=End_B2[0];E++)
        Play_Note(End_B2[E]);
       gotoxy(5,24); printf("                    PLAYING PART C");
       for(A=1;A<=2;A++)
       {
        for(E=1;E<=Line_3[0];E++)
         Play_Note(Line_3[E]);
        for(E=1;E<=Line_4[0];E++)
         Play_Note(Line_4[E]);
        for(E=1;E<=Line_5[0];E++)
         Play_Note(Line_5[E]);
        if(A==1)
        {
         for(E=1;E<=Line_6[0];E++)
          Play_Note(Line_6[E]);
        }
        else
        {
         for(E=1;E<=Line_7[0];E++)
         Play_Note(Line_7[E]);
        }                           //just keep playing the song
       }
     }while(!kbhit);
}
```

Generating a Variable Analog Voltage from a Parallel Printer Port

Circuit Theory

A digital-to-analog converter (DAC) converts a computer's binary output to a continuous voltage or current. The analog output is proportional to the digital logic input. The DAC0832 is an 8-bit converter, meaning it divides a reference voltage into 255 divisions and outputs a voltage, or current, proportional to a reference division and the binary data input logic.

Here's an example. If the reference is set to 5 volts, the DAC0832 will divide that reference into 255 equal steps of (5v / 256) or 0.0195 volts. We say the DAC has a *step size* of 0.0195 volts. The binary input byte tells the DAC which step size to output.

D/A converters are a basic building block whose applications include computer directed volume controls, motor speed controls, frequency generators, speech synthesizers, and automated feedback circuits.

Figure 16 demonstrates how to interface a DAC0832 to an IBM type parallel printer port. The DAC0832 is a double buffered 8-bit digital to analog converter. It is designed to input an 8-bit binary value, and output a voltage proportional to that binary value. Input data is placed on the data input lines, D0–D7. Data is read when the WRITE LINE, at pin 2, sees an active low strobe signal. The LM336 provides a 2.5 volt reference voltage. The DAC0832's output voltage is amplified by the optional LM358 op amp. Resistors R4 and R5 are pull-up resistors for the printer port's ACK and ERROR lines. By tying the ACK and ERROR lines to logic high, while securing the BUSY and PAPER-END lines to logic low, the computer is fooled into thinking it is connected to an on-line printer ready to receive data. This lets BASIC's LPRINT and PASCAL's WRITE statements output data with a minimum of software code.

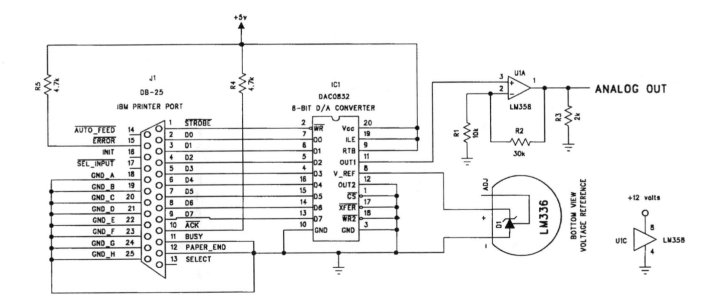

Figure 16

Software

Listings DAC0832.BAS, DAC0832.C, and DAC0832.PAS generate a sine wave. The programs divide a circle, of 360 degrees, or two radians, into 256 equal parts. The sine value for each part is computed. adjusted to yield a number between 0 and 255, and then stored in the array `Time_Slice`

The remainder of the program outputs the stored numbers to the printer port. It takes some time for the computer to compute the 256 sine values. By storing the values in an array, and then repeatedly using the array as a look-up table, fairly high audio frequencies can be generated from your parallel printer port. The actual maximum frequency will be dependent on the software time delay variable, `t`, and the efficiency of code generated by your compiler.

BASIC Source Code Listing

```
1 REM   -=[ DIGITAL TO ANALOG  ]=- ,   FILE: DAC0832.BAS
2 REM
3 REM   generate a sine wave using a DAC0832 interfaced to an 1MB PRINTER PORT
4 REM
10 DIM TimeSlice(256)
20 Pi = 3.141593: t = 1
30 byte = 256
90 CLS
95 PRINT "-=[ generating angular values ]=-": PRINT
100 FOR e = 0 TO 255
110 TimeSlice(e) = INT(((SIN(e * (2 * Pi / byte)) + 1) * 127.5) + .5)
113 REM SLEEP t
115 NEXT e
120 REM
125 PRINT "-=[ display array ]=-": PRINT
130 FOR e = 0 TO 255
140 LPRINT CHR$(TimeSlice(e));
150 REM PRINT TimeSlice(e);
160 REM SLEEP t
170 NEXT e
```

Pascal Source Code Listing

```
PROGRAM DAC0832;
USES CRT, PRINTER;
{
Digital to Analog conversion using a DAC00832 D/A interfaced to an
    IBM type parallel printer port
generate a sine wave using a DAC0832 interfaced to an IMB PRINTER PORT
}
CONST Pi = 3.141593;
            t = 50;
        Bite = 256;
VAR Time_Slice : ARRAY[0..256] OF BYTE;
              e : BYTE;
BEGIN { main }
CLRSCR;
WRITELN('-=[ generating angular values ]=-'); WRITELN; FOR e := 0 TO 255 DO
    BEGIN { for e }
Time_Slice[e] := ROUND(((SIN(e * (2 * Pi / bite)) + 1) * 127.5) + 0.5);
```

```
        END; { for e }
WRITELN('-=[ display array ]=-');   WRITELN;
FOR e := 0 TO 255 DO
    BEGIN { for e }
    WRITELN( Time_Slice[e]);
    WRITE(LST, CHR(Time_Slice[e]));
    DELAY(t)
    END; { for e }
END.
```

C Source Code Listing

```
/*                      PROGRAM DAC08302
                   Code conversion by Eugene Klein
*/

#include <dos.h>
#include <stdio.h>
#include <conio.h>
#include <stdlib.h>
#include <string.h>
#include <bios.h>
#include "My_TPU.h"
#include <math.h>

/*
   Digital to Analog conversion using a DAC00832 D/A interfaced to an
   IBM type parallel printer port

   generate a sine wave using a DAC0832 interfaced to an IMB PRINTER PORT
*/

const float Pi = 3.141593;
const int t = 50;
const int Bite = 256;
unsigned int Time_Slice[256];
int e;

void main()
{
 clrscr();
 printf("-=[ generating angular values ]=-\n");
 for(e=0;e<=255;e++)
 {
  //Time_Slice[e] := ROUND(((SIN(e * (2 * Pi / bite)) + 1) * 127.5) + 0.5);
  Time_Slice[e] = (((sin(e * (2 * Pi / Bite)) + 1) * 127.5) + 0.5);
 }
 printf("-=[ display array ]=-\n");
 for(e=0;e<=255;e++)
 {
  printf("%i\n",Time_Slice[e]);
  putc(Time_Slice[e],stdprn);
  delay(t);
 }
}
```

Sending Data Bits Via a Printer Port's Control Bit Pins

Circuit Theory

In addition to the basic data bit output pins, the IBM/IBM clone machines support four additional data bits address Base + 2: pin 1 STROBE, pin 14 AUTO-FEED, pin 16 INIT, and pin 17 SELECT-INPUT. These extra pins permit you to directly multiplex up to 16 devices from a single parallel port. These control signals can also be used to provide control signals to more sophisticated IC chips. Many of the IC circuits that follow require control logic.

The simplest things to control are LEDs, so we'll use them in our example. Figure 17 illustrates how to control four LEDs. The buffers drawn with dashed lines are part of the printer port circuitry; they are drawn here to make it easier for you to visualize the logic involved. Current will flow through the LEDs and their series resistors when printer port logic is low. In other words, the LEDs are wired to light by sink current.

Software

The programs CTRL_TST.PAS and CTRL_TST.C demonstrate how to control LEDs connected to the printer port's control pins. Constants are assigned to each control bit. If you want to turn on two or more bits at once, simply OR the two bits together, and output the resultant byte.

The program repeatedly turns on one lamp after another until any key is pressed. Without the delay loop between each output, the action would be so fast that your eyes would deceive you into thinking all four lights were on at the same time.

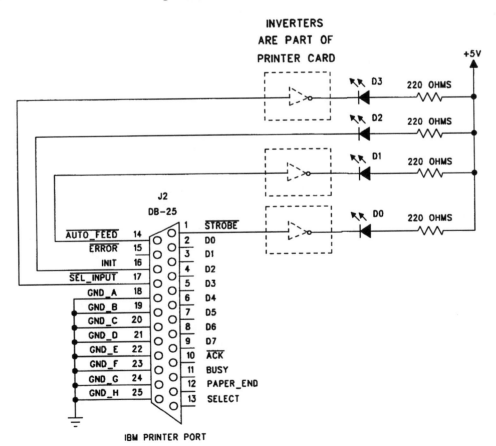

Figure 17

Pascal Source Code Listing

```pascal
PROGRAM Ctrl_Tst;
{       Sequencally send out signals on control pins.  Signals sent are:        }
{       pin 1, STROBE; pin 14, AUTO-FEED; pin 31, INIT; and pin 36, SELECT      }
USES CRT;
CONST
     All_Off = 4;{ 00000100 }
     Strobe_ON = 5;   { 00000101 }
     Auto_Feed_ON = 6; { 00000110 }
     Init_ON = 0;{ 00000000 }
     Select_ON = 12; { 00001100 }
     Time = 500; { value determined by computer model and speed }
VAR Strobe, Base, Lpt1_Base_Address : INTEGER;
PROCEDURE Find_Lpt1(VAR Lpt1_Base_Address : INTEGER);
CONST Base_Address = 1024;        Offset = 8;
     { use 8 for LPT1, use 10 to find LPT2, and 12 to find LPT3 }
BEGIN
Lpt1_Base_Address := MemW[0: Base_Address + Offset];
END;
BEGIN { main, ctrl_tst }
CLRSCR; WRITELN('PRESS ANY KEY TO END');
Find_Lpt1(Lpt1_Base_Address);
     REPEAT
     PORT[Lpt1_Base_Address + 2] := All_Off{ 00000100 }
     Port[Lpt1_Base_Address + 2] := Strobe_ON;   { 00000101 } DELAY(Time);
     Port[Lpt1_Base_Address + 2] := All_Off{ 00000100 }
Port[Lpt1_Base_Address  + 2]  := Auto_Feed_On;  {  00000110  }  DELAY(Time);
Port[Lpt1_Base_Address + 2] := All_Off;   { 00000100 }
     Port[Lpt1_Base_Address + 2] := Init_ON{ 00000000 } DELAY(Time);
     Port[Lpt1_Base_Address + 2] := All_Off{ 00000100 }
     Port[Lpt1_Base_Address + 2] := Select_ON;   { 00001100 } DELAY(Time);
     Port[Lpt1_Base_Address + 2] := All_Off{ 00000100 }
     UNTIL KEYPRESSED;
END. { main, ctrl_tst }
```

C Source Code Listing

```c
 /*                       PROGRAM Ctrl_Tst
                   Code conversion by Eugene Klein
    Sends out control pin signals.  Signals sent are:
     Pin 1, STROBE; pin 14, AUTO-FEED; pin 31, INIT; and pin 36, SELECT;
 */

#include <dos.h>
#include <stdio.h>
#include <conio.h>
#include <stdlib.h>
#include <string.h>
#include <bios.h>
#include "My_TPU.h"
```

```c
const unsigned char        Strobe_On = 1;
const unsigned char        Strobe_Off = 254;
const unsigned char        Auto_Feed_On = 2;
const unsigned char        Auto_Feed_Off = 253;
const unsigned char        Init_On = 4;
const unsigned char        Init_Off = 251;
const unsigned char        Select_On = 8;
const unsigned char        Select_Off = 247;

int LPTx, Strobe, Base, Lpt_Num;


void main()
{
 Lpt_Num = Select_Printer_Port();
 LPTx = Init_Printer_Port(Lpt_Num);
 clrscr();
 do
 {
  outport(LPTx + 2,0);   // clear control lines
  outport(LPTx + 2,Strobe_On);
  outport(LPTx + 2,0);
  outport(LPTx + 2,Auto_Feed_On);
  outport(LPTx + 2,0);
  outport(LPTx + 2,Init_On);
  outport(LPTx + 2,0);
  outport(LPTx + 2,Select_On);
  outport(LPTx + 2,0);
 }while(!kbhit());
}
```

Variable Square Wave Generator Using the Printer Port

Circuit Theory

Intel's 8253 is a small dedicated computer in a 24-pin package. An in-depth discussion of this chip is far beyond the scope of this book; other authors have written entire books dedicated to the 8253. The following discussion is meant only as a "flowchart" to chip operation. For a detailed description of the 8253 and its operation, consult volume 1 of Intel's *Microprocessor And Peripheral Handbook*.

The 8253 contains three independent counters. You tell the chip how to use the counters by sending it a control word. Each counter has five different modes of operation. One of the modes allows the chip to generate a square wave. The chip is loaded with a 16-bit number, N. The 8253 divides that number in half. It then counts N/2 clock pulses. During this time the output at pin 10, OUT0, is high. At the end of N/2 clock pulses, the 8283 inverts the output at pin 10 to high. The 8253 then counts N/2 clock pulses, whereupon the output is again inverted to low. The process is repeated until a new control word provides the 8253 with new instructions.

The circut uses a quartz crystal oscillator for the external clock. They are very reliable; when power is applied, quartz crystal oscillators always generate a square wave. Other types of oscillators, such as those designed around logic gates, are not as reliable. I used a 5 MHz pre-packaged crystal oscillator that only cost about $4.00 for the circuit in Figure 18. If you have the time and test equipment, you may want to save some money and "roll your own." See Appendix B for more details.

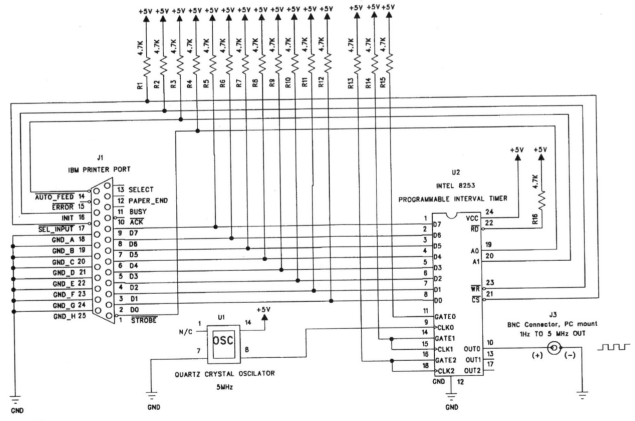

Figure 18

Software

Program listings OSC.PAS, and OSC.C demonstrate how to generate a square-wave from your computer's parallel printer port. First a control word is sent, setting up counter 0 for mode 3 square wave generator operation. Second, a midpoint number is sent. This allows the 8253 to start generating square waves. Third, the computer monitors the keyboard for input. If you press the up arrow, the frequency will increase because of making N smaller. If you press the down arrow, the frequency will decrease because of making N larger.

Pascal Source Code Listing

```
PROGRAM OSC_8253; { Produce a square wave on Intel's 8253          }
                  { file = 8253_OSC.PAS                            }


USES CRT, PRINTER, My_Tpu;
CONST    A0 = 1; { D0, Bit 1, = Strbe at Base-Address + 2          }
         A1 = 2; { D1, Bit 2, = Auto-Feed at Base-Address + 2      }
         WR = 4; { D2, Bit 3, = Initialize at Base-Address + 2     }
         CS = 8; { D3, Bit 4, = Select-Input at Base-Address + 2   }
VAR Control_Word, Data, Control_Lines : BYTE;
                  Lptx, Data_Word : WORD;
                         Num, E : INTEGER;
                            Ch : CHAR;


PROCEDURE Send_Control_Word;
BEGIN    { set up Counter 0 to Mode 3, Square Wave Generator                     }
         {                         D7  D6  D5  D4    D3  D2  D1  D0              }
         {                         Sc1 Sc0 RL1 RL0   M2  M1  M0  BCD            }
         {         select counter   0   0                                      }
         {      Load LSB then MSB            1   1                              }
         {            Select Mode 3                    0   1   1               }
         { No Binary Coded Decimal                                  0          }
         {                         _____       }
Control_Word := $36; {             0   0   1   1     0   1   1   0             }
PORT[Lptx] := Control_Word; { place control word on printer port's data lines }

                    {                    INTEL 8253 PINS:  CS   WR   A1   A0   }
                    {                                      __        __   __   }
                    {                    PRINTER PORT PINS: D3   D2   D1   D0  }
PORT[Lptx + 2] := $4; { Set ALL  control lines HIGH;        0   1    0    0   }
PORT[Lptx + 2] := $C; { set CS line to active LOW           1   1    0    0   }
PORT[Lptx + 2] := $8; { set WR line to active LOW           1   0    0    0   }
PORT[Lptx + 2] := $C; { set WR line to inactive HIGH        1   1    0    0   }
PORT[Lptx + 2] := $4; { set CS line to inactive HIGH        0   1    0    0   }
END; { send control word }


PROCEDURE Send_Data(Data : BYTE);
BEGIN
PORT[Lptx] := Data;
                    {                    INTEL 8253 PINS:  CS   WR   A1   A0   }
                    {                                      __        __   __   }
                    {                    PRINTER PORT PINS: D3   D2   D1   D0  }
PORT[Lptx + 2] := $4; { turn ALL lines to inactive HIGHs    0   1    0    0   }
```

```
PORT[Lptx + 2] := $7;  { Set A0 and A1 to LOW              0   1   1   1  }
PORT[Lptx + 2] := $F;  { set CS line to active LOW         1   1   1   1  }
PORT[Lptx + 2] := $B;  { set WR line to active LOW         1   0   1   1  }
PORT[Lptx + 2] := $F;  { set WR line to inactive HIGH      1   1   1   1  }
PORT[Lptx + 2] := $7;  { set CS line to inactive HIGH      0   1   1   1  }
END; { send data }

BEGIN { main }
ClrScr; Num := 2;
Lptx := Find_Lpt(Num); { in MY_Tpu }
   { Initilize the control lines }
Port[Lptx + 2] := $04; { 0000 0100 }
Data_Word := $7FFF;       { set initial frequency a about the middle of range }
  REPEAT
    REPEAT
      REPEAT UNTIL KEYPRESSED;
    Ch := ReadKey;
    UNTIL ORD(CH) IN [ 73, 81, 27 ];
    CASE ORD(CH) OF
      73 : IF Data_Word < $E000 THEN Data_Word := Data_Word + $0FFF;
      81 : IF Data_Word > $100F THEN Data_Word := Data_Word - $0FFF;
      27 : EXIT;        { pressing ESC key exits program }
      END;  { case }
  WRITELN(' DATA WORD = ',Data_Word);
  Send_Control_Word;
  Send_Data(Lo(Data_Word));
  Send_Data(Hi(Data_Word));
  UNTIL ORD(Ch) = 27; { pressing ESC key exits program }
END. { main }
```

C Source Code Listing

```
/*                     PROGRAM OSC_825
              Code conversion by Eugene Klein
           Produce a square wave on Intel's 8253
*/


#include <dos.h>
#include <stdio.h>
#include <conio.h>
#include <stdlib.h>
#include <string.h>
#include <bios.h>
#include "My_TPU.h"

const int A0 = 1; // D0, Bit 1, = Strobe at Base-Address + 2
const int A1 = 2; // D1, Bit 2, = Auto-Feed at Base-Address + 2
const int WR = 4; // D2, Bit 3, = Initialize at Base-Address + 2
const int CS = 8; // D3, Bit 4, = Select-Input at Base-Address + 2
unsigned char Control_Word, Data, Control_Lines;
unsigned int LPTx, Lpt_Num, Data_Word;
int Num, E;
char Ch;
```

```c
void Send_Control_Word(void)
{
    // set up Counter 0 to Mode 3, Square Wave Generator
    //                               D7   D6   D5   D4      D3   D2   D1   D0
    //                               Sc1  Sc0  RL1  RL0     M2   M1   M0   BCD
    //          select counter        0    0
    //     Load LSB then MSB                     1    1
    //          Select Mode 3                                0    1    1
    // No Binary Coded Decimal                                             0
    //                                                   _____
    Control_Word = 0x36; //                       0    0    1    1    0    1    1    0      }
    outport(LPTx,Control_Word); //place control word on printer port's data lines

                //                  INTEL 8253 PINS:  CS    WR    A1    A0
                //                                    __          __    __
                //                  PRINTER PORT PINS: D3    D2    D1    D0
    outport(LPTx + 2,0x4); // Set ALL  control lines HIGH;    0    1    0    0    }
    outport(LPTx + 2,0xC); // set CS line to active LOW       1    1    0    0    }
    outport(LPTx + 2,0x8); // set WR line to active LOW       1    0    0    0    }
    outport(LPTx + 2,0xC); // set WR line to inactive HIGH    1    1    0    0    }
    outport(LPTx + 2,0x4); // set CS line to inactive HIGH    0    1    0    0    }
}

void Send_Data(int Data)
{
 outport(LPTx,Data);
                //                  INTEL 8253 PINS:  CS    WR    A1    A0
                //                                    __          __    __
                //                  PRINTER PORT PINS: D3    D2    D1    D0
    outport(LPTx + 2,0x4); // turn ALL lines to inactive HIGHs  0    1    0    0
    outport(LPTx + 2,0x7); // Set A0 and A1 to LOW              0    1    1    1
    outport(LPTx + 2,0xF); // set CS line to active LOW         1    1    1    1
    outport(LPTx + 2,0xB); // set WR line to active LOW         1    0    1    1
    outport(LPTx + 2,0xF); // set WR line to inactive HIGH      1    1    1    1
    outport(LPTx + 2,0x7); // set CS line to inactive HIGH      0    1    1    1
}

void main()
{
 int x;
 clrscr(); Num = 2;
 Lpt_Num = Select_Printer_Port();
 LPTx = Init_Printer_Port(Lpt_Num);
 clrscr();
   // Initialize the control lines
 outport(LPTx + 2,0x04); // 0000 0100
 Data_Word = 0x7FFF;       // set initial frequency a about the middle of range
 do
 {
  do
  {
   Ch = getch();
   if(Ch==0)
    Ch=getch();
  }while(Ch!=73 & Ch!=81 & Ch!=27 & Ch!=57 & Ch!=51);
  switch(Ch)
  {
```

```c
    case 73:
     if(Data_Word < 0xE000)
      Data_Word = Data_Word + 0x0FFF;
     break;

    case 57:
     if(Data_Word < 0xE000)
      Data_Word = Data_Word + 0x0FFF;
     break;
    case 51:
     if(Data_Word > 0x100F)
      Data_Word = Data_Word - 0x0FFF;
     break;
    case 81:
     if(Data_Word > 0x100F)
      Data_Word = Data_Word - 0x0FFF;
     break;
    case 27:
     exit(0);          //pressing ESC key exits program
   }
   printf(" DATA WORD = %u\n",Data_Word);
   Send_Control_Word();
   Send_Data(Data_Word & 0xff);
   Send_Data(Data_Word>>8);
  }while(Ch !='\'');     //pressing ESC key exits program
}
```

Pulse Width Modulation Using the Printer Port

Circuit Theory

Intel's 8253, described in Application 18, can also be used in pulse width modulation (PWM) applications. As detailed in the previous circuit, the 8253 contains three independent 16-bit counters. Each counter has five modes of operation. You tell each counter which mode to use by sending it a control word. (The Intel handbook referenced in Application 18 describes the control words in detail.) Once the control word is sent, the counter will operate without further attention. The software accompanying Application 18 sent out a control word to have counter 1 output square waves. The software in this application uses two of the chip's three counters to generate a variable pulse width signal.

In the circuit shown in Figure 19, counter 1 is set for mode 2, "rate generator" operation. In mode 2, the counter generates a continuous stream of pulses, each one clock pulse wide. For example, if counter 1 is set to 1000, the output at pin 13 will be high for 999 clock ticks and then go low for 1 clock tick. The process continues until a new control word is received.

Next, counter 2 is set to mode 5, "hardware triggered strobe" operation. Every time counter 2's input gate, at pin 16, receives a low going pulse, counter 2 will count to a previously programed control word value and then output a one clock tick pulse. For instance, suppose counter 2 is loaded with the number 10. After the input gate at pin 16 receives a low going pulse, the counter's output gate_2, at pin 17, will remain high for 10 clock pulses and then go low for one clock pulse.

The output of counter 1, Out_1, is fed to counter 2's input at gate_2. The software changes the number stored in counter_2 based on keyboard number key-

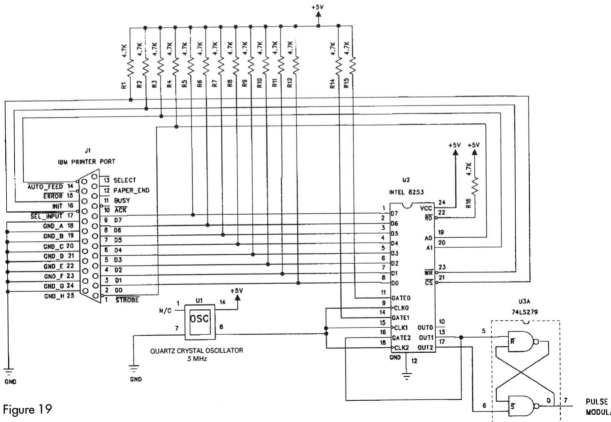

Figure 19

pad input. As the number stored in counter 2 is changed, the time between counter_1's output pulse and counter 2's output pulse will change. Out_1 and Out_2 are fed to opposite sides of the 74LS279, a RS latch device. Counter 1's pulse SETs the latch. Counter 2's pulse resets the latch. The latch's output is a pulse width modulation signal.

For this scheme to work, the number stored in counter 2 must be a minimum of two units smaller than the number stored in counter 1. For example, if counter 1 is programmed with the number 1000, counter 2's value can vary from 1 to 998. This insures that the set and reset signals sent to the 74LS279 do not overlap, which is a no-no for proper 74LS279 operation. Note that a 5 MHz quartz crystal oscillator is used with this circuit and that the circuit also produces a square wave output as a by-product.

Software

Programs PWM_8253.PAS, and PWM_8253.C set up counter 0 for mode 3 (square wave generator) operation. The square wave has no bearing on the variable pulse width generation which is the main purpose of the circuit in Figure 19.

Pascal Source Code Listing

```
PROGRAM PWM_8253;
{ Generate Pulse Width Modulation from Intel's 8253 Interval Timer IC }
USES CRT, PRINTER, My_Tpu;
TYPE  Ctrl_Wd_Type = ARRAY[0..2] OF BYTE;

CONST   A0 = 1; { D0, Bit 1, = Strbe at Base-Address + 2         }
        A1 = 2; { D1, Bit 2, = Auto-Feed at Base-Address + 2     }
        WR = 4; { D2, Bit 3, = Initialize at Base-Address + 2    }
        CS = 8; { D3, Bit 4, = Select-Input at Base-Address + 2 }

VAR Data, Counter_Number, Control_Lines : BYTE;
                   Lptx, Data_Word : WORD;
              Initial_Word, Num, E : INTEGER;
                                Ch : CHAR;
                      Control_Word : Ctrl_Wd_Type;

PROCEDURE Set_Control_Words( VAR Control_Word : Ctrl_Wd_Type );
{ computer Control Word Values to set Counter 0  for square wave output,
  Counter 1 for pulse generator, and Counter 2 as a software triggered
  one-shot pulse generator.
}
BEGIN
{ -=[ COUNTER 0 Control Word  ]=- }
     { Set Control-Word for Counter 0 to Mode 3, "Square Wave Rate Gen."
          Mode 3 allows the counter to output a continuous square wave.
       For example if the counter is programmed with a 10, the
       output will be low for five clock counts, and high for five clock
       counts.  The gate is used to start ( logic 1 ) and stop ( logic 0 )
       the count.                                                        }
     {                                                                   }
     { Base + 2 pin labels =       D7  D6  D5  D4     D3  D2  D1  D0      }
     { 8253's pin labels   =       Sc1 Sc0 RL1 RL0    M2  M1  M0  BCD     }
     {        select counter       0   0                                 }
     {        Load LSB then MSB             1   1                         }
     {             Select Mode 3                      0   1   1          }
     { No Binary Coded Decimal                                     0      }
     {                             _____               }
```

```
Control_Word[0] := $36;              {    0   0   1   1   0   1   1   0      }

{ -=[ COUNTER 1 Control Word ]=- }
    { Set Control Word for counter 1, to Mode 2, "Rate Generator"
       Mode 2 allows the counter to generate a series of continuous
    pulses that are one clock pulse in width.  The separation between
    pulses is determined by the count.  For example,  if the count is a
    10, the output will be a logic 1 for nine clock pulses and low
    ( logic 0 ) for one.  This cycle is repeated until the counter is
    reprogrammed with a new count.  The gate input is used to start
    ( logic 1 ) and stop ( Logic 0 ) the count.                          }
    {                                                                     }
    { Base + 2 pin labels =        D7  D6  D5  D4    D3  D2  D1  D0       }
    {                                                                     }
    { 8253's pin lables   =        Sc1 Sc0 RL1 RL0   M2  M1  M0  BCD      }
    {          select counter       0   1                                }
    {       Load LSB then MSB               1   1                         }
    {            Select Mode 2                       0   1   0            }
    { No Binary Coded Decimal                                     0       }
    {                             _____   }
Control_Word[1] := $74;      {    0   1   1   1   0   1   0   0      }

{ -=[ COUNTER 2 Control Word ]=- }
    { Set Counter 2 to Mode 5, "Hardware Triggered Strobe"
       Mode 5 allows the counter to generate a single pulse after it is
    triggered by a gate input.   For example, if a count of 5 is
    programmed, the output will remain high until five clock  counts
    after the gate trigger pulse ( logic 1 ) and then go low for an
    additional clock count.  The output is a, one shot, pulse.
    {                                                                     }
    { Base + 2 pin labels =        D7  D6  D5  D4    D3  D2  D1  D0       }
    { 8253's pin labels   =        Sc1 Sc0 RL1 RL0   M2  M1  M0  BCD      }
    {          select counter       1   0                                }
    {       Load LSB then MSB               1   1                         }
    {            Select Mode 5                       1   0   1            }
    { No Binary Coded Decimal                                     0       }
    {                             _____   }
Control_Word[2] := $BA; {    1   0   1   1   1   0   1   0      }
END; { set control words }


PROCEDURE Send_Control(Counter_Num : BYTE);
  BEGIN
  PORT[Lptx] := Control_Word[Counter_Num];
                                   {    INTEL 8253 PINS:  CS    WR    A1    A0   }
                                   {                      __    __    __    __   }
                                   { PRINTER PORT PINS:   D3    D2    D1    D0   }
  PORT[Lptx + 2] := $4; { Set ALL  control lines HIGH;    0     1     0     0   }
  PORT[Lptx + 2] := $C; { set CS line to active LOW       1     1     0     0   }
  PORT[Lptx + 2] := $8; { set WR line to active LOW       1     0     0     0   }
  PORT[Lptx + 2] := $C; { set WR line to inactive HIGH    1     1     0     0   }
  PORT[Lptx + 2] := $4; { set CS line to inactive HIGH    0     1     0     0   }
  END; { send control word }


PROCEDURE Send_Data(Counter_Num, Data : BYTE);
    { The procedure demonstrates how to send data to an 8253 counter.        }
    { YES, I know this code can be compressed, BUT then it would loose        }
```

```pascal
    { it's clarity.                                                                          }
BEGIN   { send data }
PORT[Lptx] := Data;           { load the data onto the data lines                            }
CASE Counter_Num OF
  0 :
    BEGIN                      {                       INTEL 8253 PINS:  CS   WR   A1   A0   }
                              {                                          __        __   __   }
                              {                    PRINTER PORT PINS:   D3   D2   D1   D0   }
    PORT[Lptx + 2] := $4; { turn ALL lines to inactive HIGHs  0    1    0    0   }
    PORT[Lptx + 2] := $7; { Set A0 and A1 to binary zero       0    1    1    1   }
    PORT[Lptx + 2] := $F; { set CS line to active LOW          1    1    1    1   }
    PORT[Lptx + 2] := $B; { set WR line to active LOW          1    0    1    1   }
    PORT[Lptx + 2] := $F; { set WR line to inactive HIGH       1    1    1    1   }
    PORT[Lptx + 2] := $7; { set CS line to inactive HIGH       0    1    1    1   }
    writeln('case = ', Counter_num);
    END; { counter # 0 }

  1 :
    BEGIN                      {                       INTEL 8253 PINS:  CS   WR   A1   A0   }
                              {                                          __        __   __   }
                              {                    PRINTER PORT PINS:   D3   D2   D1   D0   }
    PORT[Lptx + 2] := $4; { turn ALL lines to inactive HIGHs  0    1    0    0   }
    PORT[Lptx + 2] := $7; { Set A0 and A1 to binary one        0    1    1    0   }
    PORT[Lptx + 2] := $F; { set CS line to active LOW          1    1    1    0   }
    PORT[Lptx + 2] := $B; { set WR line to active LOW          1    0    1    0   }
    PORT[Lptx + 2] := $F; { set WR line to inactive HIGH       1    1    1    0   }
    PORT[Lptx + 2] := $7; { set CS line to inactive HIGH       0    1    1    0   }
    writeln('case = ', Counter_num);
    END; { counter # 1 }

  2 :
    BEGIN                      {                       INTEL 8253 PINS:  CS   WR   A1   A0   }
                              {                                          __        __   __   }
                              {                    PRINTER PORT PINS:   D3   D2   D1   D0   }
    PORT[Lptx + 2] := $4; { turn ALL lines to inactive HIGHs  0    1    0    0   }
    PORT[Lptx + 2] := $7; { Set A0 and A1 to binary two        0    1    0    1   }
    PORT[Lptx + 2] := $F; { set CS line to active LOW          1    1    0    1   }
    PORT[Lptx + 2] := $B; { set WR line to active LOW          1    0    0    1   }
    PORT[Lptx + 2] := $F; { set WR line to inactive HIGH       1    1    0    1   }
    PORT[Lptx + 2] := $7; { set CS line to inactive HIGH       0    1    0    1   }
    writeln('case = ', Counter_num);
    END; { counter # 2}
  END { case }
END; { send data }



PROCEDURE Adjust_Frequency(Counter_Number : BYTE; Initial_Word : WORD);
BEGIN { adj freq }
IF Counter_Number IN [0,1] THEN CASE Counter_Number OF
0 : BEGIN { case # 1 }  { set up counter 1 as a square wave generator }
    WRITELN('Setting up COUNTER 1 as a square wave generator ');
    REPEAT
      REPEAT
        REPEAT UNTIL KEYPRESSED;
      Ch := ReadKey;
```

```pascal
       UNTIL ORD(CH) IN [ 73, 81, 27 ];
      CASE ORD(CH) OF
        73 : IF Data_Word < $E000 THEN Data_Word := Data_Word + $0FFF;
        81 : IF Data_Word > $100F THEN Data_Word := Data_Word - $0FFF;
        27 : EXIT;        { pressing ESC key exits program }
        END;   { case, ord(ch) }
       WRITELN(' DATA WORD = ',Data_Word);
       Counter_Number := 0;
       Send_Control(Counter_Number);
       Send_Data(Counter_Number, Lo(Data_Word));
       Send_Data(Counter_Number, Hi(Data_Word));
       UNTIL ORD(Ch) = 27; { pressing ESC key exits program }
      END; { case # 0}

1 : BEGIN { case # 1 }
    WRITELN('Set up counters 1 and 2 for Pulse Width Modulation ');
{ set Counter 1 as a software triggered, pulse generator                       }
     Counter_Number := 1;
     Send_Control(Counter_Number);
     Data_Word := $FFFF;               { set to longest time period possible     }
     Send_Data(Counter_Number, Lo(Data_Word));
     Send_Data(Counter_Number, Hi(Data_Word));
     REPEAT
       REPEAT
         REPEAT UNTIL KEYPRESSED;
       Ch := ReadKey;
       UNTIL ORD(CH) IN [ 73, 81, 27 ];
       IF ORD(CH) IN [ 73, 81, 27 ] THEN CASE ORD(CH) OF
          73 : IF Data_Word < $E000 THEN Data_Word := Data_Word + $0FFF;
          81 : IF Data_Word > $100F THEN Data_Word := Data_Word - $0FFF;
          27 : EXIT;        { pressing ESC key exits program }
          END;   { case, ord(ch) }
{ set counter 2 as a hardware triggered, one shot, pulse generator             }
       Counter_Number := 2;
       Send_Control(Counter_Number);
       Send_Data(Counter_Number, Lo(Data_Word));
       Send_Data(Counter_Number, Hi(Data_Word));
       UNTIL ORD(Ch) = 27; { pressing ESC key exits program }
      END; { case # 1}
   END; { case }
END;  { adjust frequency }

BEGIN { main }
ClrScr; Num := 2;         { use 1 to find LPT1, and 3 to find LPT3              }
Lptx := Find_Lpt(Num); { in My_Tpu }
Set_Control_Words(Control_Word);
Port[Lptx + 2] := $04;  { = 0000 0100 Binary,   Initialize the control lines  }
  { start counter 0, as a square wave generator }
Initial_Word := $7FFF; { set initial frequency a about the middle of range     }
{          -=[ SET UP COUNTER 0 AS A SQUARE WAVE GENERATOR ]=-                  }
Counter_Number := 0;
Send_Control(Counter_Number);
Send_Data(Counter_Number, Lo(Initial_Word));
Send_Data(Counter_Number, Hi(Initial_Word));
Adjust_Frequency(Counter_Number, Initial_Word);
{          -=[ SET UP COUNTERS 1 and 2 AS A PULSE WIDTH GENERATOR              }
```

```
Counter_Number := 1;
Send_Control(Counter_Number);
Send_Data(Counter_Number, Lo(Initial_Word));
Send_Data(Counter_Number, Hi(Initial_Word));
Adjust_Frequency(Counter_Number, Initial_Word);

END. { main }
```

C Source Code Listing

```c
/*
                          PROGRAM PWM_8253
              Code conversion by Eugene Klein
     Generate Pulse Width Modulation from Intel's 8253 Interval Timer IC
*/


#include <dos.h>
#include <stdio.h>
#include <conio.h>
#include <stdlib.h>
#include <string.h>
#include <bios.h>
#include "My_TPU.h"

const int ESC = 0x1B;

const int A0 = 1;    // D0, Bit 1, = Strobe at Base-Address + 2
const int A1 = 2;    // D1, Bit 2, = Auto-Feed at Base-Address + 2
const int WR = 4;    // D2, Bit 3, = Initialize at Base-Address + 2
const int CS = 8;    // D3, Bit 4, = Select-Input at Base-Address + 2

unsigned char  Data, Counter_Number, Control_Lines,Control_Word[2],Lpt_Num;
unsigned int LPTx, Data_Word;
int Initial_Word, Num, E;
char Ch;

void Set_Control_Words(void)
{
/* Computer Control Word Values to set Counter 0  for squarewave output.
   Counter 1 for pulse generator, and Counter 2 as a software triggered
    one-shot pulse generator.

   -=[ COUNTER 0 Control Word  ]=- }
   Set Control-Word for Counter 0 to Mode 3, "Square Wave Rate Gen."
   Mode 3 allows the counter to output a continuous square wave.
   For example if the counter is programmed with a 10, the
   output will be low for five clock counts, and high for five clock
   counts.  The gate is used to start ( logic 1 ) and stop ( logic 0 )
   the count.

      Base + 2 pin labels =         D7  D6  D5  D4    D3  D2  D1  D0
      8253's pin labels   =         Sc1 Sc0 RL1 RL0   M2  M1  M0 BCD
           select counter        0   0
              Load LSB then MSB                1   1
```

```c
                Select Mode 3                        0   1   1
          No Binary Coded Decimal                                    0
                    _____     */
Control_Word[0] = 0x36;          //    0   0   1   1     0   1   1   0


/*-=[ COUNTER 1 Control Word ]=- }
     Set Control Word for counter 1, to Mode 2, "Rate Generator"
     Mode 2 allows the counter to generate a series of continuous
     pulses that are one clock pulse in width.  The separation between
     pulses is determined by the count.  For example,  if the count is a
     10, the output will be a logic 1 for nine clock pulses and low
     ( logic 0 ) for one.  This cycle is repeated until the counter is
     reprogrammed with a new count.  The gate input is used to start
     ( logic 1 ) and stop ( Logic 0 ) the count.

     // Base + 2 pin labels =        D7  D6  D5  D4     D3  D2  D1  D0
     //
     // 8253's pin labels    =       Sc1 Sc0 RL1 RL0    M2  M1  M0  BCD
     //         select counter        0   1
     //      Load LSB then MSB               1   1
     //          Select Mode 2                          0   1   0
     // No Binary Coded Decimal                                     0
     //                   _____     */
Control_Word[1] = 0x74;     //     0   1   1   1     0   1   0   0


/*   =[ COUNTER 2 Control Word ]=- }
     Set Counter 2 to Mode 5, "Hardware Triggered Strobe"
     Mode 5 allows the counter to generate a single pulse after it is
     triggered by a gate input.  For example, if a count of 5 is
     programmed, the output will remain high until five clock  counts
     after the gate trigger pulse ( logic 1 ) and then go low for an
     additional clock count.  The output is a, one shot, pulse.

     Base + 2 pin labels =          D7  D6  D5  D4     D3  D2  D1  D0
     8253's pin labels    =         Sc1 Sc0 RL1 RL0    M2  M1  M0  BCD
        select counter       1   0
        Load LSB then MSB                1   1
        Select Mode 5                            1   0   1
     No Binary Coded Decimal                                        0
                    _____     */
Control_Word[2] = 0xBA; //         1   0   1   1     1   0   1   0
}

void Send_Control(unsigned char Counter_Num)
{
 outport(LPTx,Control_Word[Counter_Num]);
                     //   INTEL 8253 PINS:  CS   WR   A1   A0   }
                     //                     __   __   __   __   }
                     //   PRINTER PORT PINS: D3   D2   D1   D0   }
 outport(LPTx + 2,0x4); // Set ALL  control lines HIGH;    0    1    0    0   }
 outport(LPTx + 2,0xC); // set CS line to active LOW       1    1    0    0   }
 outport(LPTx + 2,0x8); // set WR line to active LOW       1    0    0    0   }
 outport(LPTx + 2,0xC); // set WR line to inactive HIGH    1    1    0    0   }
 outport(LPTx + 2,0x4); // set CS line to inactive HIGH    0    1    0    0   }
}
```

}

```c
void Send_Data(unsigned char Counter_Num, unsigned char Data)
// The procedure demonstrates how to send data to an 8253 counter.        }
// YES, I know this code can be compressed, BUT then it would loose        }
// it's clarity.                                                           }
{
 outport(LPTx,Data);          // load the data onto the data lines         }
 switch(Counter_Num)
 {
  case 0 :
                    //                    INTEL 8253 PINS:  CS   WR   A1   A0   }
                    //                                      __        __   __   }
                    //            PRINTER PORT PINS:  D3   D2   D1   D0   }
   outport(LPTx + 2,0x4); // turn ALL lines to inactive HIGHs 0    1    0    0   }
   outport(LPTx + 2,0x7); // Set A0 and A1 to binary zero      0    1    1    1   }
   outport(LPTx + 2,0xF); // set CS line to active LOW         1    1    1    1   }
   outport(LPTx + 2,0xB); // set WR line to active LOW         1    0    1    1   }
   outport(LPTx + 2,0xF); // set WR line to inactive HIGH      1    1    1    1   }
   outport(LPTx + 2,0x7); // set CS line to inactive HIGH      0    1    1    1   }
   printf("case = %i\n", Counter_Num);
   break;

  case 1 :
                    //                    INTEL 8253 PINS:  CS   WR   A1   A0   }
                    //                                      __        __   __   }
                    //            PRINTER PORT PINS:  D3   D2   D1   D0   }
   outport(LPTx +2,0x4); // turn ALL lines to inactive HIGHs   0    1    0    0   }
   outport(LPTx +2,0x7); // Set A0 and A1 to binary one        0    1    1    0   }
   outport(LPTx +2,0xF); // set CS line to active LOW          1    1    1    0   }
   outport(LPTx +2,0xB); // set WR line to active LOW          1    0    1    0   }
   outport(LPTx +2,0xF); // set WR line to inactive HIGH       1    1    1    0   }
   outport(LPTx +2,0x7); // set CS line to inactive HIGH       0    1    1    0   }
   printf("case = %i\n", Counter_Num);
   break;

  case 2 :
                    //                    INTEL 8253 PINS:  CS   WR   A1   A0   }
                    //                                      __        __   __   }
                    //            PRINTER PORT PINS:  D3   D2   D1   D0   }
   outport(LPTx +2,0x4); // turn ALL lines to inactive HIGHs   0    1    0    0   }
   outport(LPTx +2,0x7); // Set A0 and A1 to binary two        0    1    0    1   }
   outport(LPTx +2,0xF); // set CS line to active LOW          1    1    0    1   }
   outport(LPTx +2,0xB); // set WR line to active LOW          1    0    0    1   }
   outport(LPTx +2,0xF); // set WR line to inactive HIGH       1    1    0    1   }
   outport(LPTx +2,0x7); // set CS line to inactive HIGH       0    1    0    1   }
   printf("case = %i\n", Counter_Num);
 }
}

void Adjust_Frequency(unsigned char Counter_Number)
{
 if(Counter_Number==0 | Counter_Number==1)
 {
  switch(Counter_Number)
  {
   case 0 :  // set up counter 1 as a square wave generator }
    printf("Setting up COUNTER 1 as a square wave generator \n");
```

```
     do
     {
      do
      {
       Ch  = getch();
      }while(Ch != 73 & Ch != 81 & Ch != 27);
       switch(Ch)
       {
       case 73 :
         if(Data_Word < 0xE000)
Data_Word  = Data_Word + 0x0FFF;
break;
       case 81 :
         if(Data_Word > 0x100F)
Data_Word  = Data_Word - 0x0FFF;
break;
       //case 27 :
         //exit(0);         // pressing ESC key exits program }
       }
      printf(" DATA WORD = %u\n\n",Data_Word);
      Counter_Number  = 0;
      Send_Control(Counter_Number);
      Send_Data(Counter_Number, (Data_Word & 0xff));
      Send_Data(Counter_Number, Data_Word >>8);
      // pressing ESC key exits program }
     }while(Ch != ESC);
    break;

    case 1 :
     printf("Set up counters 1 and 2 for Pulse Width Modulation \n");
// set Counter 1 as a software triggered, pulse generator                          }
     Counter_Number  = 1;
     Send_Control(Counter_Number);
     Data_Word  = 0xFFFF;                   // set to longest time period possible     }
     Send_Data(Counter_Number, Data_Word & 0xff);
     Send_Data(Counter_Number, Data_Word >> 8);
     do
     {
       do
       {
        Ch  = getch();
       }while(Ch != 73 & Ch != 81 & Ch != 27);
       switch(Ch)
       {
        case 73 :
     if(Data_Word < 0xE000)
       Data_Word  = Data_Word + 0x0FFF;
       break;
        case  81 :
     if(Data_Word > 0x100F)
      Data_Word  = Data_Word - 0x0FFF;
      break;
       //case 27:
     //exit(0);         // pressing ESC key exits program }
       }
      printf(" DATA WORD = %u\n\n",Data_Word);
```

```
           // set counter 2 as a hardware triggered, one shot, pulse generator              }
         Counter_Number  = 2;
         Send_Control(Counter_Number);
         Send_Data(Counter_Number, Data_Word & 0xff);
         Send_Data(Counter_Number, Data_Word >> 8);
       }while(Ch != ESC);
   } // pressing ESC key exits program }
  }
}


void main()
{
 Lpt_Num = Select_Printer_Port();
 LPTx = Init_Printer_Port(Lpt_Num);
 clrscr();
 Set_Control_Words();
 outport(LPTx + 2,0x04);   // = 0000 0100 Binary,    Initialize the control lines  }
 // start counter 0, as a square wave generator }
 Initial_Word  = 0x7FFF; // set initial frequency a about the middle of range   }
 //          -=[ SET UP COUNTER 0 AS A SQUARE WAVE GENERATOR ]=-                  }
 Counter_Number  = 0;
 Send_Control(Counter_Number);
 Send_Data(Counter_Number, Initial_Word & 0xff);
 Send_Data(Counter_Number, Initial_Word >> 8);
 Adjust_Frequency(Counter_Number);
 //          -=[ SET UP COUNTERS 1 and 2 AS A PULSE WIDTH GENERATOR               }
 Counter_Number  = 1;
 Send_Control(Counter_Number);
 Send_Data(Counter_Number, Initial_Word & 0xff);
 Send_Data(Counter_Number, Initial_Word >> 8);
 Adjust_Frequency(Counter_Number);

}
```

Controlling a 5-Wire Stepping Motor

Circuit Theory

If you're not familiar with stepping motor theory and operation, read Appendix A before experimenting with this or the next few applications.

The simplest wiring configuration for a stepping motor is one with five leads. One side of each coil is factory hard wired together. Figure 20 demonstrates how to control a 5-wire stepping motor from a parallel printer port. WARNING: The following discussion is presented only to permote a better understanding of stepping motor operation. The actual use of this circuit is highly discouraged. You can obtain far greater motor efficiencies using bipolar stepping motor drivers.

The ULN2803 is designed to accept TTL inputs and amplifies the signals to control inductive loads up to 50 volts at 500 mA. The ULN2803 contains built in back-EMF protection for inductive loads like relays and stepping motors. Resistor R helps reduce back-EMF and permits higher operating speeds. It is common to use a value down to $1/_7$ of the coil's resistance. For example, if you find a stepping motor rated at 3.5 volts, it was probably designed to operate from 12 to 24 volts with an appropriate low resistance, high wattage resistor in series with the coil. This wiring scheme works, but is very inefficient.

Using the configuration in Figure 20, only one field winding at a time may be energized. Each winding is controlled by a bit on the parallel printer port. D0 controls coil A, D1 controls coil B, D2 controls coil C, and D3 controls coil D4. Resistors R1 and R2 are pull-up resistors for the ACK and ERROR lines. By tying the ACK and ERROR lines to logic high, while securing the BUSY and PAPER-END lines to logic low, the computer is fooled into thinking it is connected to an on line printer ready to receive data. Thus, BASIC's LPRINT and Pascal's WRITE statements can easily output data.

Software

A coil winding is energized when the printer port's corresponding data bit is high. By setting printer port data bits, D0, D1, D2, and D3, to logic low, and then sequentially setting bits D0, D1, D2, and D3, high (one bit at a time), the motor shaft will turn clockwise. By setting printer port data bits, D0, D1, D2, and D3, to logic low, and then sequentially setting bits D3, D2, D1, and D0, high (one bit at a time), the motor shaft will turn counterclockwise.

Figure 20 requires four control lines to control a 5-wire stepping motor. A maximum of two stepping motors can be simultaneously controlled from one printer port. Since data remains latched in the printer port's data buffer until new data is received, the stepping motor will maintain its position even if your software "goes away" to do something else.

Sending the numbers 1, 2, 4, and 8, will energize windings A, B, C, and D in sequence. Listings MOT_3.BAS, MOT_3.PAS, and MOT_3.C, demonstrate the process. Using this method, you can operate up to two stepping motors form a single parallel printer port.

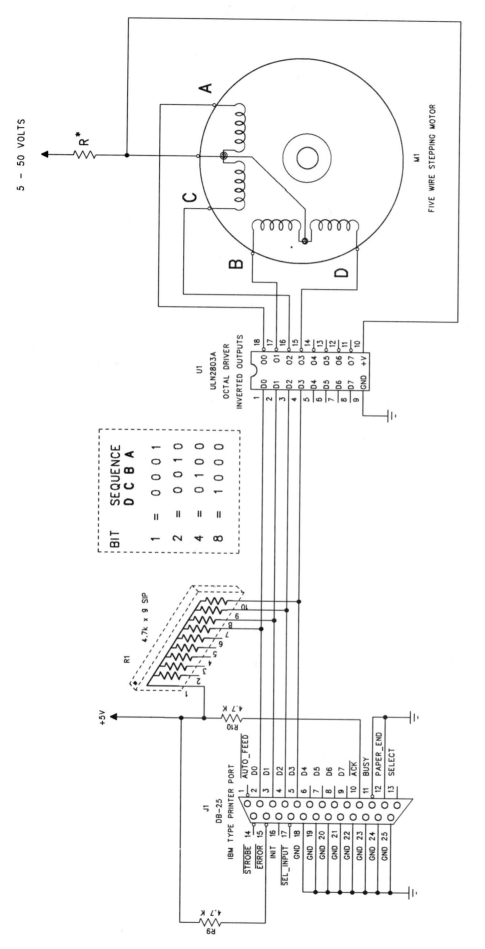

5-WIRE STEPPING MOTOR CONTROL

* R HELPS COUNTERACT BACK EMF FROM COIL DURING STEPS
R VALUES DOWN TO 1/7 OF COIL RESISTANCE ARE COMMON
COIL IS ENERGIZED WHEN ULN2803'S INPUT LOGIC IS HIGH

BASIC Source Code Listing

```
1    REM   FILE: MOT_3.BAS,   WRITTEN IN QBASIC
2    REM
3    REM  Printer port control of 5-wire stepping motor via LPRINT command.
4    REM  Efficient code, but stepping motor must be conntcted to LPT1.
7    REM
100  D0 = 1
110  D1 = 2
120  D2 = 4
130  D3 = 8
135  T = 300
137  REM
138  REM   %%%%%%%%%%%%%%%%%% -=[ METHOD ONE ]=- %%%%%%%%%%%%%%%%%%%%%%%%
140  REM
142  REM  Semicolens at end of LPRINT statement tells BASIC to not add
145  REM  carrage return and line feed to transmitted data.
147  REM
150  FOR e = 1 TO 10: REM  step motor 40 steps in clockwise direction
160  LPRINT CHR$(D0); : GOSUB 500
170  LPRINT CHR$(D1); : GOSUB 500
180  LPRINT CHR$(D2); : GOSUB 500
190  LPRINT CHR$(D3); : GOSUB 500
200  NEXT e
210  FOR e = 1 TO 10: REM step motor 40 steps in counter-clockwise direction
220  LPRINT CHR$(D3); : GOSUB 500
230  LPRINT CHR$(D2); : GOSUB 500
240  LPRINT CHR$(D1); : GOSUB 500
250  LPRINT CHR$(D0); : GOSUB 500
260  NEXT e
270  REM
280  REM   %%%%%%%%%%%%%%%%%%%%%%%%%  -=[ METHOD TWO ]=- %%%%%%%%%%%%%%%%%%%%%
282  REM
283  REM   This method permits sending control signals to LPT1, LPT2, and LPT3
290  REM
300  GOSUB 600: REM   get port's base address
310  FOR e = 1 TO 10: REM  step motor clockwise through 40 steps
320  OUT LptPortAddress, D0: GOSUB 500
340  OUT LptPortAddress, D1: GOSUB 500
350  OUT LptPortAddress, D2: GOSUB 500
360  OUT LptPortAddress, D3: GOSUB 500
370  NEXT e
380  FOR e = 1 TO 10: REM step motor counterclockwise through 40 steps
390  OUT LptPortAddress, D3: GOSUB 500
400  OUT LptPortAddress, D2: GOSUB 500
410  OUT LptPortAddress, D1: GOSUB 500
420  OUT LptPortAddress, D0: GOSUB 500
430  NEXT e
499  END
500  REM   -=[ delay ]=-
510  FOR V = 1 TO T: NEXT V
520  RETURN
600  REM
605  PRINT
610  PRINT " Which printer port do you want to use? "
620  PRINT "              1) LPT1"
```

```
630 PRINT "                   2) LPT1"
640 PRINT "                   3) LPT3"
650 n = VAL(INPUT$(1))
670 IF (n < 1) OR (n > 3) THEN GOTO 605
675 DEF SEG = 0
680 OffSet = (n * 2) + 6: Address = 1024 + OffSet
690 LptPortAddress = PEEK(Address) + (PEEK(Address + 1) * 256)
700 RETURN
```

Pascal Source Code Listing

```
PROGRAM MOT_3;

USES CRT, PRINTER, My_Tpu;
CONST D0 = 1;
      D1 = 2;
      D2 = 4;
      D3 = 8;
       t = 100;
VAR                           E : INTEGER;
    Lpt_Num, Lpt_Port_Address : WORD;

BEGIN
   (* %%%%%%%%%%%%%%%%%%%%%%%%  -=[ METHOD ONE ]=-  %%%%%%%%%%%%%%%%%% *)
  {
   Basic 5-wire stepping motor control.  Uses Pascal's WRITE command to
   transmit data through computer's LPT1 printer port.  The WRITE commands
   sends data WITHOUT generating printer Line Feed, or Carriage Return
   instructions.
  }
FOR E := 1 TO 10 DO  { step motor clockwise through 40 steps }
    BEGIN
    WRITE(LST, CHAR(D0)); DELAY(t);
    WRITE(LST, CHAR(D1)); DELAY(t);
    WRITE(LST, CHAR(D2)); DELAY(t);
    WRITE(LST, CHAR(D3)); DELAY(t);
    END;
  FOR E := 1 TO 10 DO  { step motor counter-clockwise through 40 steps }
    BEGIN
    WRITE(LST, CHAR(D3)); DELAY(t);
    WRITE(LST, CHAR(D2)); DELAY(t);
    WRITE(LST, CHAR(D1)); DELAY(t);
    WRITE(LST, CHAR(D0)); DELAY(t);
    END;

   (* %%%%%%%%%%%%%%%%%%%%%%%%%  -=[ METHOD TWO ]=-  %%%%%%%%%%%%%%%%% *)
  {
   Alternitive 5-wire stepping motor control.  Data is sent to printer port
   LPT1, LPT2, or LPT3.  From users keyboard input of the number 1, 2, or 3,
   port's address is computed, and used to route data.

   Since the printer port latches data sent to it, data sent to a printer
   port will remain on the output pins until new data replaces it.  That
   means stepping motors, directly driven by printer port logic, will hold
   there position between transmitted instructions.
```

```
    }
  Select_Printer_Port(Lpt_Num, Lpt_Port_Address);
  FOR E := 1 TO 10 DO     { step motor clockwise through 40 steps }
      BEGIN
      PORT[Lpt_Port_Address] := D0; DELAY(t);
      PORT[Lpt_Port_Address] := D1; DELAY(t);
      PORT[Lpt_Port_Address] := D2; DELAY(t);
      PORT[Lpt_Port_Address] := D3; DELAY(t);
      END;
    FOR E := 1 TO 10 DO   { step motor counter-clockwise through 40 steps }
      BEGIN
      PORT[Lpt_Port_Address] := D3; DELAY(t);
      PORT[Lpt_Port_Address] := D2; DELAY(t);
      PORT[Lpt_Port_Address] := D1; DELAY(t);
      PORT[Lpt_Port_Address] := D0; DELAY(t);
      END;
  END.
```

C Source Code Listing

```
/*                        PROGRAM MOT_3
   5-wire stepping motor single phase control. Only one motor winding
   is energized at a time.

   Code conversion by Eugene Klein
*/
#include <dos.h>
#include <stdio.h>
#include <conio.h>
#include <stdlib.h>
#include <string.h>
#include <bios.h>
#include "My_TPU.h"

const int       D0 = 1;
const int       D1 = 2;
const int       D2 = 4;
const int       D3 = 8;
const int       t = 100;
int E;
unsigned int Lpt_Num, Lpt_Port_Address;

void main()
{
  /* %%%%%%%%%%%%%%%%%%%%%%%%%  -=[ METHOD ONE ]=-  %%%%%%%%%%%%%%%%%% *

   Basic 5-wire stepping motor control.  Uses Pascal's WRITE command to
   transmit data through computer's LPT1 printer port.  The WRITE commands
   sends data WITHOUT generating printer Line Feed, or Carriage Return
   instructions.
  */
  for(E=1;E<=10;E++)          // step motor clockwise through 40 steps
  {
   putc(D0,stdprn);
   delay(t);
   putc(D1,stdprn);
```

```
  delay(t);
  putc(D2,stdprn);
  delay(t);
  putc(D3,stdprn);
  delay(t);
 }
  for(E=1;E<=10;E++)           // step motor counter-clockwise through 40 steps
  {
  putc(D3,stdprn);
  delay(t);
  putc(D2,stdprn);
  delay(t);
  putc(D1,stdprn);
  delay(t);
  putc(D0,stdprn);
  delay(t);
 }


  /* * %%%%%%%%%%%%%%%%%%%%%%%%%%  -=[ METHOD TWO ]=-  %%%%%%%%%%%%%%%%%% *

  Alternitive 5-wire stepping motor control.  Data is sent to printer port
  LPT1, LPT2, or LPT3.  From users keyboard input of the number 1, 2, or 3,
  port's address is computed, and used to route data.

  Since the printer port latches data sent to it, data sent to a printer
  port will remain on the output pins until new data replaces it.  That
  means stepping motors, directly driven by printer port logic, will hold
  there position between transmitted instructions.
*/
Lpt_Num = Select_Printer_Port();
Lpt_Port_Address = Init_Printer_Port(Lpt_Num);
clrscr();

for(E=1;E<=10;E++)      // step motor clockwise through 40 steps
{
 outport(Lpt_Port_Address,D0);
 delay(t);
 outport(Lpt_Port_Address,D1);
 delay(t);
 outport(Lpt_Port_Address,D2);
 delay(t);
 outport(Lpt_Port_Address,D3);
 delay(t);
}
for(E=1;E<=10;E++)      // step motor counter-clockwise through 40 steps
{
 outport(Lpt_Port_Address,D3);
 delay(t);
 outport(Lpt_Port_Address,D2);
 delay(t);
 outport(Lpt_Port_Address,D1);
 delay(t);
 outport(Lpt_Port_Address,D0);
 delay(t);
 }
}
```

Controlling a 6-Wire Stepping Motor

Circuit Theory

Six-wire stepping motors provide more flexibility in control logic than 5-wire steppers. They can be controlled by single phase, dual phase, half step, or bipolar drivers. Six-wire steppers allow you to simultaneously drive multiple coil windings, thus generating more torque than 5-wire stepping motors. You can even hard-wire a 6-wire stepper to behave like a 5-wire stepper, although it is usually not practical.

There are four driver-logic methods of controlling a 6-wire stepping motor: single phase, dual phase, half step, and bipolar. Bipolar operation is the most efficient, and is covered separately in a future circuit. This time, we'll discuss the first three.

* *Single phase.* A 6-wire motor can use control logic that energizes only one coil at a time. The sequence would be A, B, C, D. Use the software developed for Circuit 20, MOT_3.PAS, .MOT_3.C, and MOT_3.BAS for single phase operation.

* *Dual phase.* Control logic that keeps two coil windings energized for each step is called dual phase logic. The sequence would be AB, BC, CD, DA. Two coils share a series resistor. This sequence energizes only one coil from each group at a time. Since two coils are always energized, this arrangement provides twice the torque of single phase operation.

* *Half step.* Half step logic will not turn your 200 steps per revolution stepping motor into a 400 steps per revolution device. Half step was designed to smooth out the shaft's movement as it "snaps" from one position to the next. The idea is to ease the shaft from one position to the next by energizing the closest coil that makes up a pair. The sequence is AB, B, BC, C, CD, D, DA. It takes eight half steps to move four full steps. You should never rest on the half steps. Your software should force the motor to only stop at positions where two coils are energized.

Figure 21 shows the simplest driver configuration. The motor is drawn for visual simplicity. In a real stepping motor, the coils are physically arranged A, B, C, D. The drawing clearly shows which coils are connected to which resistor.

The ULN2803 contains eight inverting drivers. The ULN2803 was designed to drive inductive loads, like motor coils and relays, containing back-EMF. Each section contains back-EMF logic protection.

Each stepping motor coil is controlled by a separate printer port data bit. The ULN2803 drivers take their inputs from the printer port's TTL logic and amplifies the signals. Each section of the ULN2803 is able to drive a load requiring 5 to 50 volts at up to 500 mA. Its big brother, the ULN2813, has the same pin configuration, and can drive 60 volt loads.

The resistor in series with two coils has two functions. First, it reduces the coils' back-EMF. Values down to $1/7$ of the coil's resistance are common. Since each set of two coils share one resistor, only one coil from each pair should be energized at once. If you find a stepping motor rated at a very low voltage, it was probably designed to run from a much higher supply voltage with a voltage dropping resistor in series. Resistors values down to $1/7$ of the stepping motor's coil resistance are common. Second, the series resistors dampen stepping motor oscillation. Their presence allows the steppers to operate at a higher speed.

I find I can use a longer ribbon cable when I include the 4.7K pull-up resistors. However, you must exercise caution in making sure the control logic is low when you apply power to the driver circuit. If control logic does not initialize the driver's inputs to low, the pull-up resistors will supply inactive high input logic. The ULN2803 will invert the input logic, driver outputs will all be low, and all four coil windings will be energized. That could put twice the rated load current on each coil, with possibly deleterious results.

Resistors R1 and R2 are pull-up resistors for the ACK and ERROR lines. By tying the ACK and ERROR lines to logic high while securing the BUSY and PAPER-END lines to logic low, the computer is fooled into thinking it is connected to an on line printer ready to receive data. Thus, BASIC's LPRINT and Pascal's WRITE statements can easily be used to output data.

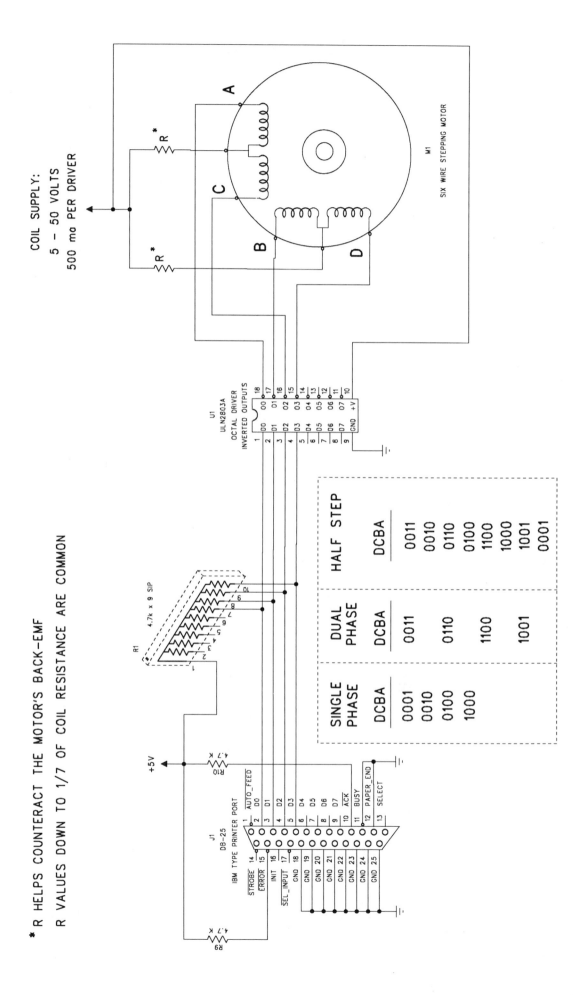

* R HELPS COUNTERACT THE MOTOR'S BACK-EMF

R VALUES DOWN TO 1/7 OF COIL RESISTANCE ARE COMMON

COIL SUPPLY:
5 - 50 VOLTS
500 ma PER DRIVER

M1
SIX WIRE STEPPING MOTOR

U1
ULN2803A
OCTAL DRIVER
INVERTED OUTPUTS

R1
4.7k x 9 SIP

J1
DB-25
IBM TYPE PRINTER PORT

R9
4.7 K

R10
4.7 K

+5V

SINGLE PHASE	DUAL PHASE	HALF STEP
DCBA	DCBA	DCBA
0001	0011	0011
0010		0010
0100	0110	0110
1000		0100
	1100	1100
		1000
	1001	1001
		0001

Software

The program listings DUALFAZE.PAS, DUALFAZE.C, and DUALFAZE.BAS demonstrate dual phase operation. Two methods are shown. The first uses BASIC's and Pascal's built-in procedures for sending characters to the LPT1 printer port. With this method, a strobe signal is automatically generated. The details are hidden from the programmer. This method requires the least amount of code. Pascal's WRITE command sends the data while telling the compiler NOT to send a carriage return or linefeed. BASIC's LPRINT command, with a trailing semicolon yealds the same results. Remember, this method only works with LPT1.

The second method requires a little more code, but allows you to send data to any of the three printer ports, LPT1, LPT2, and LPT3. Also, the program should run a little faster. Data is placed on the base address data lines using Pascal's PORT command and BASIC's OUT command. Since the circuit in Figure 21, does not require a strobe signal, none is generated.

The printer port will automatically latch the data onto the data output lines with either method. Data will remain on the printer ports output lines until new data arrives. Since the coils are directly driven by printer port data logic, they will remain energized between transmitted data.

Listings HALFSTEP.PAS, HALFSTEP.C, HALFSTEP.BAS demonstrate how to control a 6-wire stepping motor with half step logic. All comments above related to software construction apply to this listing as well.

BASIC Source Code Listing for Dual Phase Motors

```
1     REM   FILE: DUALFAZE.BAS,   WRITTEN IN QBASIC
2     REM
3     REM   Printer port control of 6-wire stepping motor via LPRINT command.
4     REM   Two of the four windings are always energized
7     REM
100   D0 = 1
110   D1 = 2
120   D2 = 4
130   D3 = 8
135   T = 300
137   REM
138   REM     %%%%%%%%%%%%%%%%%%%% -=[ METHOD ONE ]=- %%%%%%%%%%%%%%%%%%%%%%%%%
140   REM
142   REM   Semicolens at end of LPRINT statement tells BASIC to not add
145   REM   carriage return and line feed to transmitted data.
147   REM
150   FOR e = 1 TO 10: REM   step motor 40 steps in clockwise direction
160   LPRINT CHR$(D0 + D1); : GOSUB 500
170   LPRINT CHR$(D1 + D2); : GOSUB 500
180   LPRINT CHR$(D2 + D3); : GOSUB 500
190   LPRINT CHR$(D3 + D0); : GOSUB 500
200   NEXT e
210   FOR e = 1 TO 10: REM step motor 40 steps in counter-clockwise direction
220   LPRINT CHR$(D3 + D0); : GOSUB 500
230   LPRINT CHR$(D2 + D3); : GOSUB 500
240   LPRINT CHR$(D1 + D2); : GOSUB 500
250   LPRINT CHR$(D0 + D1); : GOSUB 500
260   NEXT e
270   REM
280   REM   %%%%%%%%%%%%%%%%%%%%%%%%%  -=[ METHOD TWO ]=- %%%%%%%%%%%%%%%%%%%%%%%%
282   REM
283   REM     This method permits sending control signals to LPT1, LPT2, and LPT3
290   REM
300   GOSUB 600: REM   get port's base address
310   FOR e = 1 TO 10: REM   step motor clockwise through 40 steps
```

```basic
320 OUT LptPortAddress, D0 + D1: GOSUB 500
340 OUT LptPortAddress, D1 + D2: GOSUB 500
350 OUT LptPortAddress, D2 + D3: GOSUB 500
360 OUT LptPortAddress, D3 + D0: GOSUB 500
370 NEXT e
380 FOR e = 1 TO 10: REM step motor counterclockwise through 40 steps
390 OUT LptPortAddress, D3 + D0: GOSUB 500
400 OUT LptPortAddress, D2 + D3: GOSUB 500
410 OUT LptPortAddress, D1 + D2: GOSUB 500
420 OUT LptPortAddress, D0 + D1: GOSUB 500
430 NEXT e
499 END
500 REM   -=[ delay ]=-
510 FOR V = 1 TO T: NEXT V
520 RETURN
600 REM
605 PRINT
610 PRINT " Which printer port do you want to use? "
620 PRINT "              1) LPT1"
630 PRINT "              2) LPT1"
640 PRINT "              3) LPT3"
650 n = VAL(INPUT$(1))
670 IF (n < 1) OR (n > 3) THEN GOTO 605
675 DEF SEG = 0
680 OffSet = (n * 2) + 6: Address = 1024 + OffSet
690 LptPortAddress = PEEK(Address) + (PEEK(Address + 1) * 256)
700 RETURN
```

Pascal Source Code Listing for Dual Phase Motors

```pascal
PROGRAM DualFaze
  {
    DUAL PHASE opteration of a six wire stepping motor.

    This method will also work with 8-wire stepping motors configured for
    6-wire operation.
  }
USES CRT, PRINTER, My_Tpu;
CONST T = 300;
      D0 = 1;
      D1 = 2;
      D2 = 4;
      D3 = 8;
VAR                         E : INTEGER;
    Lpt_Num, Lpt_Port_Address : WORD;

BEGIN
  (* %%%%%%%%%%%%%%%%%%%%%%%%  -=[ METHOD ONE ]=-  %%%%%%%%%%%%%%%%% *)
{
   Dual Phase operation of 6-wire stepping motor.  Uses Pascal's
   WRITE command to transmit data through computer's LPT1 printer port.
   The WRITE commands sends data WITHOUT generating printer Line Feed, or
   Carriage Return instructions.
}
FOR E := 1 TO 10 DO  { step motor clockwise through 40 steps }
    BEGIN
    WRITE(LST, CHAR(D0 + D1)); DELAY(t);
```

```
      WRITE(LST, CHAR(D1 + D2)); DELAY(t);
      WRITE(LST, CHAR(D2 + D3)); DELAY(t);
      WRITE(LST, CHAR(D3 + D0)); DELAY(t);
      END; { for e }
   FOR E := 1 TO 10 DO   { step motor counter-clockwise through 40 steps }
      BEGIN
      WRITE(LST, CHAR(D3 + D0)); DELAY(t);
      WRITE(LST, CHAR(D2 + D3)); DELAY(t);
      WRITE(LST, CHAR(D1 + D2)); DELAY(t);
      WRITE(LST, CHAR(D0 + D1)); DELAY(t);
      END; { for e }
        (* %%%%%%%%%%%%%%%%%%%%%%%%%  -=[ METHOD TWO ]=-  %%%%%%%%%%%%%%%%%% *)
   {
     Dual Phase 6-wire stepping motor.  Data is sent to printer port
     LPT1, LPT2, or LPT3.  From users keyboard input of the number 1, 2, or 3,
     port's address is computed, and used to route data.

     Since the printer port latches data sent to it, data sent to a printer
     port will remain on the output pins until new data replaces it.  That
     means stepping motors, directly driven by printer port logic, will hold
     there position between transmitted instructions.
   }
Select_Printer_Port(Lpt_Num, Lpt_Port_Address);
FOR E := 1 TO 10 DO    { step motor clockwise through 40 steps }
     BEGIN
     PORT[Lpt_Port_Address] := D0 + D1; DELAY(t);
     PORT[Lpt_Port_Address] := D1 + D2; DELAY(t);
     PORT[Lpt_Port_Address] := D2 + D3; DELAY(t);
     PORT[Lpt_Port_Address] := D3 + D0; DELAY(t);
     END; { for e }
   FOR E := 1 TO 10 DO  { step motor counter-clockwise through 40 steps }
     BEGIN
     PORT[Lpt_Port_Address] := D3 + D0; DELAY(t);
     PORT[Lpt_Port_Address] := D2 + D3; DELAY(t);
     PORT[Lpt_Port_Address] := D1 + D2; DELAY(t);
     PORT[Lpt_Port_Address] := D0 + D1; DELAY(t);
     END; { for e }
END. { dual phase }
```

C Source Code Listing for Dual Phase Motors

```
/*                        PROGRAM DualFaze
              Code convesion by Eugene Klein

    DUAL PHASE opteration of a six wire stepping motor.

    This method will also work with 8-wire stepping motors configured for
    6-wire operation.
*/

#include <dos.h>
#include <stdio.h>
#include <conio.h>
#include <stdlib.h>
#include <string.h>
#include <bios.h>
#include "My_TPU.h"
```

```
const int        t = 300;
const int        D0 = 1;
const int        D1 = 2;
const int        D2 = 4;
const int        D3 = 8;
int   E;
unsigned int   Lpt_Num, Lpt_Port_Address;

void main()
    /* %%%%%%%%%%%%%%%%%%%%%%%%%%   -=[ METHOD ONE ]=-   %%%%%%%%%%%%%%%%%%%

    Dual Phase operation of 6-wire stepping motor.  Uses Pascal's
    WRITE command to transmit data through computer's LPT1 printer port.
    The WRITE commands sends data WITHOUT generating printer Line Feed, or
    Carriage Return instructions.
*/

{
 for(E=1;E<=10;E++)                      // step motor clockwise through 40 steps
 {
  putc((D0 + D1),stdprn); delay(t);
  putc((D1 + D2),stdprn); delay(t);
  putc((D2 + D3),stdprn); delay(t);
  putc((D3 + D0),stdprn); delay(t);
 }
 for(E=1;E<=10;E++)                      // step motor counter-clockwise through 40 steps }
 {
  putc((D3 + D0),stdprn); delay(t);
  putc((D2 + D3),stdprn); delay(t);
  putc((D1 + D2),stdprn); delay(t);
  putc((D0 + D1),stdprn); delay(t);
 }


/*       %%%%%%%%%%%%%%%%%%%%%%%%%%%   -=[ METHOD TWO ]=-   %%%%%%%%%%%%%%%%%%%

    Dual Phase 6-wire stepping motor.  Data is sent to printer port
    LPT1, LPT2, or LPT3.  From users keyboard input of the number 1, 2, or 3,
    port's address is computed, and used to route data.

    Since the printer port latches data sent to it, data sent to a printer
    port will remain on the output pins until new data replaces it.  That
    means stepping motors, directly driven by printer port logic, will hold
    there position between transmitted instructions.
*/

Lpt_Num = Select_Printer_Port();
Lpt_Port_Address = Init_Printer_Port(Lpt_Num);

for(E=1;E<=10;E++)                       // step motor clockwise through 40 steps
{
 outport(Lpt_Port_Address,(D0 + D1)); delay(t);
 outport(Lpt_Port_Address,(D1 + D2)); delay(t);
 outport(Lpt_Port_Address,(D2 + D3)); delay(t);
 outport(Lpt_Port_Address,(D3 + D0)); delay(t);
}
for(E=1;E<=10;E++)                       // step motor counter-clockwise through 40 steps }
```

```
  {
  outport(Lpt_Port_Address,(D3 + D0)); delay(t);
  outport(Lpt_Port_Address,(D2 + D3)); delay(t);
  outport(Lpt_Port_Address,(D1 + D2)); delay(t);
  outport(Lpt_Port_Address,(D0 + D1)); delay(t);
  }
}
```

BASIC Source Code Listing for Half Step Motors

```
1    REM   FILE: HALFSTEP.BAS,   WRITTEN IN QBASIC
2    REM
3    REM   Printer port control stepping motor using HALF STEP code logic
7    REM
100  T = 500
102 Motor(1) = 3:   REM 00000011
104 Motor(2) = 2:   REM 00000010
106 Motor(3) = 6:   REM 00000110
108 Motor(4) = 4:   REM 00000100
110 Motor(5) = 12:  REM 00001100
112 Motor(6) = 8:   REM 00001000
114 Motor(7) = 9:   REM 00001001
116 Motor(8) = 1:   REM 00000001
137 REM
138 REM   %%%%%%%%%%%%%%%%%%% -=[ METHOD ONE ]=- %%%%%%%%%%%%%%%%%%%%%%%%%%%
140 REM
142 REM   Semicolens at end of LPRINT statement tells BASIC to not add
145 REM   carrage return and line feed to transmitted data.
147 REM
150 FOR E = 1 TO 10: REM  step 40 full steps in clockwise direction using
155 FOR D = 1 TO 8
160 LPRINT CHR$(Motor(D)); : GOSUB 500
170 NEXT D: NEXT E
210 FOR E = 1 TO 10: REM step motor 40 steps in counter-clockwise direction
220 FOR D = 8 TO 1 STEP -1
230 LPRINT CHR$(Motor(D)); : GOSUB 500
240 NEXT D: NEXT E
270 REM
280 REM   %%%%%%%%%%%%%%%%%%%%%%%%%  -=[ METHOD TWO ]=- %%%%%%%%%%%%%%%%%%%%%%%%
282 REM
283 REM    This method permits sending control signals to LPT1, LPT2, and LPT3
290 REM
300 GOSUB 600: REM   get port's base address
310 FOR E = 1 TO 10: REM  step motor clockwise through 40 steps
320 FOR D = 1 TO 8
340 OUT LptPortAddress, Motor(D): GOSUB 500
370 NEXT D: NEXT E
380 FOR E = 1 TO 10: REM step motor counterclockwise through 40 steps
390 FOR D = 8 TO 1 STEP -1
400 OUT LptPortAddress, Motor(D): GOSUB 500
410 NEXT D: NEXT E
499 END
500 REM  -=[ delay ]=-
510 FOR V = 1 TO T: NEXT V
520 RETURN
600 REM
605 PRINT
610 PRINT " Which printer port do you want to use? "
```

```
620 PRINT "                  1) LPT1"
630 PRINT "                  2) LPT1"
640 PRINT "                  3) LPT3"
650 n = VAL(INPUT$(1))
670 IF (n < 1) OR (n > 3) THEN GOTO 605
675 DEF SEG = 0
680 OffSet = (n * 2) + 6: Address = 1024 + OffSet
690 LptPortAddress = PEEK(Address) + (PEEK(Address + 1) * 256)
700 RETURN
```

Pascal Source Code Listing For Half Step Motors

```pascal
PROGRAM HalfStep;
 {
   HALF STEP opteration of a six wire stepping motor.

   This method will also work with 8-wire stepping motors configured for
   6-wire operation.
 }
USES CRT, PRINTER, My_Tpu;
CONST T = 300;
VAR                     A, E : INTEGER;
                   Motor_Step : ARRAY[1..8] OF BYTE;
    Lpt_Num, Lpt_Port_Address : WORD;
BEGIN
Motor_Step[1] := 3;  { 00000011 }
Motor_Step[2] := 2;  { 00000010 }
Motor_Step[3] := 6;  { 00000110 }
Motor_Step[4] := 4;  { 00000100 }
Motor_Step[5] := 12; { 00001100 }
Motor_Step[6] := 8;  { 00001000 }
Motor_Step[7] := 9;  { 00001001 }
Motor_Step[8] := 1;  { 00000001 }
       (* %%%%%%%%%%%%%%%%%%%%%%%%  -=[ METHOD ONE ]=-  %%%%%%%%%%%%%%%% *)
 {
   Dual Phase operation of 6-wire stepping motor.  Uses Pascal's
   WRITE command to transmit data through computer's LPT1 printer port.
   The WRITE commands sends data WITHOUT generating printer Line Feed, or
   Carriage Return instructions.

   Note that to move through 40 steps, the counter is set to 80. The
   purpose of Half Stepping is to smooth out the snap action of Dual Step.
   Normally, you only count the full-step positions as actual steps.
   In other words, using Half Step logic, will not turn your 200 step / rev.
   stepping motor into a 400 step / rev. stepping motor. ( unless your
   load is VERY, VERY LIGHT! )
 }
FOR A := 1 TO 10 DO    { step motor clockwise through 40 steps        }
  FOR E := 1 TO 8 DO BEGIN WRITE(LST, CHAR(Motor_Step[e])); DELAY(t); END;
FOR A := 1 TO 10 DO    { step motor counter-clockwise through 40 steps }
  FOR E := 8 DOWNTO 1 DO BEGIN WRITE(LST, CHAR(Motor_Step[e])); DELAY(t); END;

   (* %%%%%%%%%%%%%%%%%%%%%%%%  -=[ METHOD TWO ]=-  %%%%%%%%%%%%%%%% *)
 {
   Dual Phase 6-wire stepping motor. Uses Pascal's PORT command to "poke"
   port address with data.  Allows use of LPT1, LPT2, or LPT3.
```

From users keyboard input of the number 1, 2, or 3,
port's address is computed, and used to route data.

Since the printer port latches data sent to it, data sent to a printer
port will remain on the output pins until new data replaces it. That
means stepping motors, directly driven by printer port logic, will hold
there position between transmitted instructions.

```
}
Select_Printer_Port(Lpt_Num, Lpt_Port_Address);
FOR A := 1 TO 10 DO     { step motor clockwise through 40 steps }
  FOR E := 1 TO 8 DO
    BEGIN PORT[Lpt_Port_Address] := Motor_Step[e]; DELAY(t); END;
FOR A := 1 TO 10 DO  { step motor counter-clockwise through 40 steps }
  FOR E := 8 DOWNTO 1 DO
    BEGIN PORT[Lpt_Port_Address] := Motor_Step[e]; DELAY(t); END;
END. { half step }
```

C Source Code Listing For Half Step Motors

```
/*                    PROGRAM HalfStep2

    HALF STEP opteration of a six wire stepping motor.

    This method will also work with 8-wire stepping motors configured for
    6-wire operation.
 */


#include <dos.h>
#include <stdio.h>
#include <conio.h>
#include <stdlib.h>
#include <string.h>
#include <bios.h>
#include "My_TPU.h"

const t = 300;
int A, E;
unsigned char  Motor_Step[8];
unsigned int Lpt_Port_Address, Lpt_Num;
void main()
{
 Motor_Step[1] = 3;             // 00000011
 Motor_Step[2] = 2;             // 00000010
 Motor_Step[3] = 6;             // 00000110
 Motor_Step[4] = 4;             // 00000100
 Motor_Step[5] = 12;            // 00001100
 Motor_Step[6] = 8;             // 00001000
 Motor_Step[7] = 9;             // 00001001
 Motor_Step[8] = 1;             // 00000001

 /*    * %%%%%%%%%%%%%%%%%%%%%%%%  -=[ METHOD ONE ]=-  %%%%%%%%%%%%%%%%%% *

    Dual Phase operation of 6-wire stepping motor.  Uses Pascal's
    WRITE command to transmit data through computer's LPT1 printer port.
```

The WRITE commands sends data WITHOUT generating printer Line Feed, or Carriage Return instructions.

Note that to move through 40 steps, the counter is set to 80. The purpose of Half Stepping is to smooth out the snap action of Dual Step. Normally, you only count the full-step positions as actual steps. In other words, using Half Step logic, will not turn your 200 step / rev. stepping motor into a 400 step / rev. stepping motor. (unless your load is VERY, VERY LIGHT!)

```c
*/
for(A=1;A<=10;A++)          // step motor clockwise through 40 steps
{
  for(E=1;E<=8;E++)
  {
   putc(Motor_Step[E],stdprn);
   delay(t);
  }
  for(A=1;A<=10;A++)        // step motor counter-clockwise through 40 steps
  {
   for(E=8;E>=1;E--)
   {
    putc(Motor_Step[E],stdprn);
    delay(t);
   }
  }
}


/* * %%%%%%%%%%%%%%%%%%%%%%%%%  -=[ METHOD TWO ]=-  %%%%%%%%%%%%%%%%%% *
```

Dual Phase 6-wire stepping motor. Uses Pascal's PORT command to "poke" port address with data. Allows use of LPT1, LPT2, or LPT3.

From users keyboard input of the number 1, 2, or 3, port's address is computed, and used to route data.

Since the printer port latches data sent to it, data sent to a printer port will remain on the output pins until new data replaces it. That means stepping motors, directly driven by printer port logic, will hold there position between transmitted instructions.

```c
*/
Lpt_Num = Select_Printer_Port();
Lpt_Port_Address = Init_Printer_Port(Lpt_Num);

for(A=1;A<=10;A++)          // step motor clockwise through 40 steps } FOR E := 1 TO 8 DO
{
 outport(Lpt_Port_Address,Motor_Step[E]);
 delay(t);
}
for(A=1;A<=10;A++)          // step motor counter-clockwise through 40 steps
{
 for(E=8;E>=1;E--)
 {
  outport(Lpt_Port_Address,Motor_Step[E]);
  delay(t);
 }
}
}
```

An Alternate Method of Controlling a 6-Wire Stepping Motor

Circuit Theory

Application 21 allows you to operate only two stepping motors from a printer port. Figure 22 shows a more efficient method of controlling a 6-wire stepping motor. This circuit requires only two control bits for proper operation, meaning you can operate four stepping motors from a single parallel port. Series resistors are included to dampen stepping motor oscillation, which allows the steppers to operate at a higher speed.

The circuit in Figure 22 drives stepping motors with dual phase logic. The software sends out binary numbers 0 to 3. Hardware converts the binary logic to gray code, and then uses additional logic to insure that two coils are always energized. Since all these IC chips contain additional logic gates, you would need almost no additional IC logic to control four stepping motors from a single parallel printer port!

The ULN2803 drivers take their inputs from the output of the dual phase logic circuitry. Each section of the ULN2803 is able to drive a load requiring 5 to 50 volts at up to 500 mA. Its big brother, the ULN2813, has the same pin configuration and can drive 60 volt loads.

In addition to dampening stepper motor oscillations, the resistor in series with two coils also reduces the coils' back-EMF. Values down to $1/7$ of the coil's resistance are common. Since each set of two coils share one resistor, only one coil from each pair should be energized at once. If you find a stepping motor rated at a very low voltage, it was probably designed to run from a much higher supply voltage with a voltage dropping resistor in series. Resistors values down to $1/7$ of the stepping motor's coil resistance are common.

Software

The software listings MOT_BIN.PAS, MOT_BIN.C, and MOT_BIN.BAS demonstrate how to control a stepping motor with binary control logic.

Pascal's WRITE command sends the binary data while telling the compiler NOT to send a carriage return or linefeed. BASIC's LPRINT command with a trailing semicolon yields the same results. Remember, this method only works with LPT1.

The second method requires a little more code, but allows you to send data to any of the three printer ports: LPT1, LPT2, and LPT3. Binary data is placed on the base address data lines using Pascal's PORT command, and BASIC's OUT command. Since the circuit in Figure 22 does not require a strobe signal, none is generated.

Using either method, the printer port will automatically latch the data onto the data output lines. Data will remain on the printer port's output lines until new data arrives. Since the coils are directly driven by printer port data logic, they will remain energized between data transmissions.

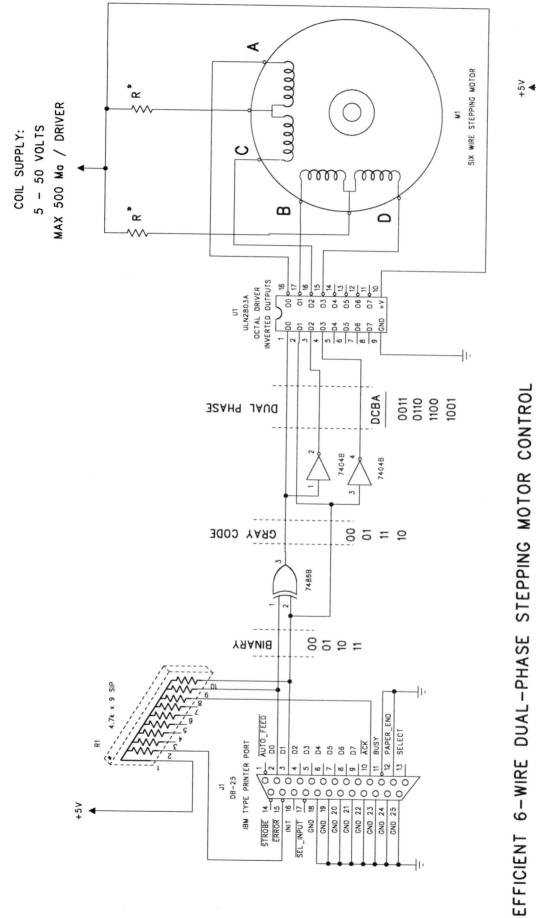

EFFICIENT 6-WIRE DUAL-PHASE STEPPING MOTOR CONTROL

* R HELPS COUNTERACT COIL'S BACK-EMF

R VALUES DOWN TO 1/7 OF COIL RESISTANCE ARE COMMON

BASIC Source Code Listing

```
1    REM   FILE: MOT_BIN,   WRITTEN IN QBASIC
2    REM
3    REM   Printer port control of stepping motor using binary codes
7    REM
100  T = 300
137  REM
138  REM    %%%%%%%%%%%%%%%%%%% -=[ METHOD ONE ]=- %%%%%%%%%%%%%%%%%%%%%%%%%%
139  REM   Send control signals to LPT1
140  REM
142  REM   Semicolens at end of LPRINT statement tells BASIC to not add
145  REM   carriage return and line feed to transmitted data.
147  REM
150  FOR e = 1 TO 10: REM   step motor 40 steps in clockwise direction
155  FOR D = 0 TO 3
160  LPRINT CHR$(D); : GOSUB 500
170  NEXT D: NEXT e
210  FOR e = 1 TO 10: REM step motor 40 steps in counter-clockwise direction
220  FOR D = 3 TO 0 STEP -1
230  LPRINT CHR$(D); : GOSUB 500
240  NEXT D: NEXT e
270  REM
280  REM    %%%%%%%%%%%%%%%%%%%%%%%%%  -=[ METHOD TWO ]=- %%%%%%%%%%%%%%%%%%%%%%
282  REM
283  REM    This method permits sending control signals to LPT1, LPT2, or LPT3
290  REM
300  GOSUB 600: REM    get port's base address
310  FOR e = 1 TO 10: REM   step motor clockwise through 40 steps
320  FOR D = 0 TO 3
340  OUT LptPortAddress, D: GOSUB 500
370  NEXT D: NEXT e
380  FOR e = 1 TO 10: REM step motor counterclockwise through 40 steps
390  FOR D = 3 TO 0 STEP -1
400  OUT LptPortAddress, D: GOSUB 500
410  NEXT D: NEXT e
490  END
492  REM
494  REM      -=[ subroutine for delay ]=-
296  REM
500  REM  -=[ delay ]=-
510  FOR V = 1 TO T: NEXT V
520  RETURN
600  REM
601  REM      -=[ subroutine to input character ]=-
602  REM
605  PRINT
610  PRINT " Which printer port do you want to use? "
620  PRINT "            1) LPT1"
630  PRINT "            2) LPT1"
640  PRINT "            3) LPT3"
650  n = VAL(INPUT$(1))
670  IF (n < 1) OR (n > 3) THEN GOTO 605
675  DEF SEG = 0
680  OffSet = (n * 2) + 6: Address = 1024 + OffSet
690  LptPortAddress = PEEK(Address) + (PEEK(Address + 1) * 256)
700  RETURN
```

Pascal Source Code Listing

```pascal
PROGRAM MOT_BIN;
{
   Stepping motor control via BINARY code. Written in Turbo Pascal 6.0

   Since the printer port latches data sent to it, data sent to a printer
   port will remain on the output pins until  new data replaces it.  That
   means stepping motors, directly driven by printer port logic, will hold
   there position between transmitted instructions.
}
USES CRT, PRINTER, My_Tpu;
CONST t = 300;
VAR                        D, E : INTEGER;
     Lpt_Num, Lpt_Port_Address : WORD;

BEGIN
   (* %%%%%%%%%%%%%%%%%%%%%%%%%  -=[ METHOD ONE ]=-  %%%%%%%%%%%%%%%%%% *)
   {
   Uses Pascal's WRITE command to transmit data through computer's LPT1
   printer port.  The WRITE command sends data WITHOUT generating printer
   Line Feed, or Carriage Return, instructions.
   }
FOR E := 1 TO 10 DO  { step motor clockwise through 40 steps }
  FOR D := 0 TO 3 DO
    BEGIN
    WRITE(LST, CHAR(D));  { transmit binary value }
    DELAY(t);
    END;

FOR E := 1 TO 10 DO  { step motor counter-clockwise through 40 steps }
  FOR D := 3 DOWNTO 0 DO
    BEGIN
    WRITE(LST, CHAR(D));  { transmit binary value }
    DELAY(t);
    END;


   (* %%%%%%%%%%%%%%%%%%%%%%%%%%  -=[ METHOD TWO ]=-  %%%%%%%%%%%%%%%%%% *)
   {
   Stepping Motor control via binary logic is sent to printer port LPT1, LPT2,
   or LPT3.  From users keyboard input of the number 1, 2, or 3, port's
   address is computed, and used to route control code.
   }
Select_Printer_Port(Lpt_Num, Lpt_Port_Address);
FOR E := 1 TO 10 DO     { step motor clockwise through 40 steps }
  FOR D := 0 TO 3 DO
    BEGIN
    PORT[Lpt_Port_Address] := D;  { transmit binary value }
    DELAY(t);
    END;

FOR E := 1 TO 10 DO  { step motor counter-clockwise through 40 steps }
  FOR D := 3 DOWNTO 0 DO
    BEGIN
    PORT[Lpt_Port_Address] := D;  { transmit binary value }
    DELAY(t);
    END;
END.
```

C Source Code Listing

```
/*                            PROGRAM MOT_BIN
                    Code conversion by Eugene Klein

    Stepping motor control via BINARY code. Written in Turbo Pascal 6.0

    Since the printer port latches data sent to it, data sent to a printer
    port will remain on the output pins until  new data replaces it.  That
    means stepping motors, directly driven by printer port logic, will hold
    there position between transmitted instructions.
*/


#include <dos.h>
#include <stdio.h>
#include <conio.h>
#include <stdlib.h>
#include <string.h>
#include <bios.h>
#include "My_TPU.h"

const int t = 300;
int D, E;
unsigned int Lpt_Num, Lpt_Port_Address;

void main()
{
/*    * %%%%%%%%%%%%%%%%%%%%%%%%  -=[ METHOD ONE ]=-  %%%%%%%%%%%%%%%%%% *

    Uses Pascal's WRITE command to transmit data through computer's LPT1
    printer port.  The WRITE command sends data WITHOUT generating printer
    Line Feed, or Carriage Return, instructions.
 */
for(E=1;E<=40;E++)          // Step motor clockwise through 40 steps
  for(D=0;D<=3;D++)
  {
   putc(D,stdprn);          // Transmit binary value
   delay(t);
  }
 for(E=1;E<=40;E++)
 {      // Step motor counter-clockwise through 40 steps
  for(D=3;D>=0;D—)
  {
   putc(D,stdprn);          // Transmit binary value
   delay(t);
  }
 }


/*    (* %%%%%%%%%%%%%%%%%%%%%%%%%  -=[ METHOD TWO ]=-  %%%%%%%%%%%%%%%%% *)

    Stepping Motor control via binary logic is sent to printer port LPT1, LPT2,
    or LPT3.  From users keyboard input of the number 1, 2, or 3, port's
    address is computed, and used to route control code.
 */

Lpt_Num = Select_Printer_Port();
Lpt_Port_Address = Init_Printer_Port(Lpt_Num);
```

```c
 clrscr();

 for(E=1;E<=40;E++)        // Step motor clockwise through 40 steps
  for(D=1;D<=3;D++)
  {
   outport(Lpt_Port_Address,D);    // Transmit binary value
   delay(t);
  }
 for(E=1;E<=40;E++)
 {       // Step motor counter-clockwise through 40 steps
  for(D=3;D>=0;D--)
  {
   outport(Lpt_Port_Address,D);    // Transmit binary value
   delay(t);
  }
 }
}
```

Bipolar Operation of Stepping Motors Using Gray Code

Circuit Theory

Bipolar operation is the most efficient method of driving stepping motors. Since all four windings are always energized, bipolar operation provides four times the torque of single phase operation.

Bipolar stepping motors are designed to have all their coils continually energized. In order for this scheme to work, the coil current is reversed for some steps. You could design your own circuit to reverse the coil current. However, the IC logic needed to prevent short circuits is tricky. Using off-the-shelf ICs can save you time and grief.

There are four different control logic methods for operating bipolar stepping motors. Each requires only two data bits for proper operation, meaning you can operate four bipolar steppers from a single parallel port. In this circuit, we'll examine the "gray code" method of stepper control.

Here's a quick explanation of the gray code. Suppose you had a disk with binary numbers between 1 and 360 represented as punched holes. Phototransistors placed near one side of the disk are positioned to detect a light source from the opposite side. As the disk turns, binary numbers are sent to your computer. The disk stops turning right on the boundary between 7 and 8. What would the output be? The output could be any number between Ø and 15. What you need is a feedback system that would oscillate between 7 and 8. That's what gray code was designed for.

The gray code can, among other things, provide reliable position feedback of rotating and straight line movement. Like binary, gray code is made of ones and zeros. However, with gray code only one bit

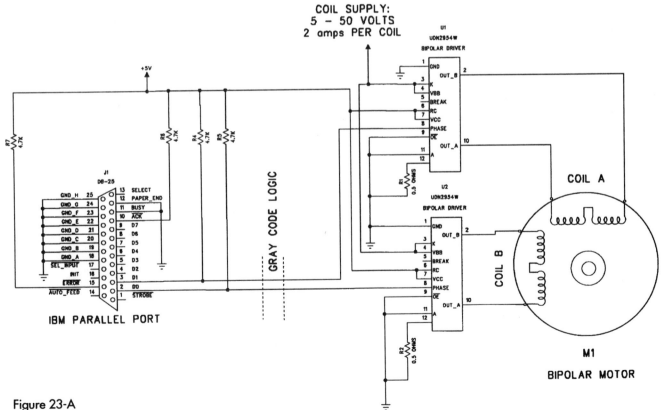

Figure 23-A

changes while in transition from one logic state to the next. Gray code can be generated with any number of bits.

Through observation and experimentation, I discovered that gray code matches the sequential logic used for dual phase and bipolar stepping motor movement. I have not seen this concept documented anywhere else. Armed with this knowledge, you can simplify you stepping motor control software by adding a little hardware glue logic.

Figure 23-A demonstrates how to directly control a bipolar stepping motor using Gray Code logic. Each winding is controlled by a UDN2954W bipolar driver. The UDN2954 come in two packages: the in-line SIP package used here and a conventional DIP IC. The in-line chip is packaged with a heat sink. The ULN2954 takes TTL signals for input through PHASE, pin 8. The chip has on-board logic to protect itself from shorting the power supply and protecting the input from coil back-EMF. It can supply up to 2 amps from a 5 to 50 volt supply. Figure 23-B shows a 6-wire stepping motor adapted for series-wired bipolar operation.

Resistors R6 and R7 are pull-up resistors for the ACK and ERROR lines. By tying the ACK and ERROR lines to logic high, while securing the BUSY and PAPER-END lines to logic low, the computer is fooled into thinking it is connected to an on line printer ready to receive data. Thus, BASIC's LPRINT and Pascal's WRITE statements can easily be used to output data.

Software

Listings GRAYCODE.BAS, GRAYCODE.C, and GRAYCODE.PAS demonstrate how gray code logic can be used to control the stepping motor shown in Figure 23. Two ways are used to transmit the gray code control logic. The first uses the the language's built-in procedures for sending characters to the LPT1 printer port. With this method, a strobe signal is automatically generated. The details are hidden from the programmer. This method is requires the least amount of code. Pascal's WRITE command sends the data while telling the compiler NOT to send a carriage return or linefeed. BASIC's LPRINT command, with a trailing semicolon yields the same results. Remember, this method only works with LPT1.

The second method requires a little more code, but allows you to send data to any of the three printer ports: LPT1, LPT2, and LPT3. Also, the program should also run a little faster. Data is placed on the base address data lines using Pascal's PORT command and BASIC's OUT command. Since the circuit in Figure 23 does not require a strobe signal, none is generated.

The printer port will automatically latch the data onto the data output lines with either method. Data will remain on the printer ports output lines until new data arrives. Since the coils are directly driven by printer port data logic, they will remain energized between transmitted data.

BASIC Source Code Listing

```
1    REM   FILE: GrayCode.BAS,  WRITTEN IN QBASIC
2    REM
3    REM   Bipolar stepping motor control from printer port using GRAYCODE
7    REM
100     T = 500
120  REM
130  REM    %%%%%%%%%%%%%%%%%%% -=[ METHOD ONE ]=- %%%%%%%%%%%%%%%%%%%%%%%%%%%
140  REM
142  REM   Semicolens at end of LPRINT statement tells BASIC to not add
145  REM   carriage return and line feed to transmitted data.
147  REM
150  FOR e = 1 TO 10: REM  step motor 40 steps in clockwise direction
160  LPRINT CHR$(0); : GOSUB 500
170  LPRINT CHR$(1); : GOSUB 500
180  LPRINT CHR$(3); : GOSUB 500
190  LPRINT CHR$(2); : GOSUB 500
200  NEXT e
210  FOR e = 1 TO 10: REM step motor 40 steps in counter-clockwise direction
220  LPRINT CHR$(2); : GOSUB 500
230  LPRINT CHR$(3); : GOSUB 500
```

```
240 LPRINT CHR$(1); : GOSUB 500
250 LPRINT CHR$(0); : GOSUB 500
260 NEXT e
270 REM
280 REM  %%%%%%%%%%%%%%%%%%%%%%  -=[ METHOD TWO ]=-  %%%%%%%%%%%%%%%%%%%%%%%
282 REM
283 REM    This method permits sending control signals to LPT1, LPT2, and LPT3
290 REM
300 GOSUB 600: REM   get port's base address
310 FOR e = 1 TO 10: REM  step motor clockwise through 40 steps
320 OUT LptPortAddress, 0: GOSUB 500
340 OUT LptPortAddress, 1: GOSUB 500
350 OUT LptPortAddress, 3: GOSUB 500
360 OUT LptPortAddress, 2: GOSUB 500
370 NEXT e
380 FOR e = 1 TO 10: REM step motor counterclockwise through 40 steps
390 OUT LptPortAddress, 2: GOSUB 500
400 OUT LptPortAddress, 3: GOSUB 500
410 OUT LptPortAddress, 1: GOSUB 500
420 OUT LptPortAddress, 0: GOSUB 500
430 NEXT e
499 END
500 REM  -=[ delay ]=-
510 FOR V = 1 TO T: NEXT V
520 RETURN
600 REM
605 PRINT
610 PRINT " Which printer port do you want to use? "
620 PRINT "              1) LPT1"
630 PRINT "              2) LPT1"
640 PRINT "              3) LPT3"
650 n = VAL(INPUT$(1))
670 IF (n < 1) OR (n > 3) THEN GOTO 605
675 DEF SEG = 0
680 OffSet = (n * 2) + 6: Address = 1024 + OffSet
690 LptPortAddress = PEEK(Address) + (PEEK(Address + 1) * 256)
700 RETURN
```

Pascal Source Code Listing

```
PROGRAM GrayCode;
{
  control a bipolar stepping motor via GRAY CODE logic
}
USES CRT, PRINTER, My_Tpu;
CONST T = 300;
VAR                            E : INTEGER;
    Lpt_Num, Lpt_Port_Address : WORD;

BEGIN
   (* %%%%%%%%%%%%%%%%%%%%%%%%  -=[ METHOD ONE ]=-  %%%%%%%%%%%%%%%%% *)
 {
   Basic 4-wire, bipolar, stepping motor control.  Uses Pascal's WRITE
   command to transmit data through computer's LPT1 printer port.  The
   WRITE commands sends data WITHOUT generating printer Line Feed, or
```

Carriage Return instructions.

```
    NOTE the sequence of the transmitted numbers.  Bipolar stepping motors
    require Gray Code.
  }
FOR E := 1 TO 10 DO  { step motor clockwise through 40 steps }
    BEGIN
    WRITE(LST, CHAR(0)); DELAY(t);
    WRITE(LST, CHAR(1)); DELAY(t);
    WRITE(LST, CHAR(3)); DELAY(t);
    WRITE(LST, CHAR(2)); DELAY(t);
    END;
  FOR E := 1 TO 10 DO  { step motor counter-clockwise through 40 steps }
    BEGIN
    WRITE(LST, CHAR(2)); DELAY(t);
    WRITE(LST, CHAR(3)); DELAY(t);
    WRITE(LST, CHAR(1)); DELAY(t);
    WRITE(LST, CHAR(0)); DELAY(t);
    END;


    (* %%%%%%%%%%%%%%%%%%%%%%%%  -=[ METHOD TWO ]=-  %%%%%%%%%%%%%%%%%% *)
  {
    4-wire stepping motor control.  Data is sent to printer port
    LPT1, LPT2, or LPT3.  From users keyboard input of the number 1, 2, or 3,
    port's address is computed, and used to route data.

    Since the printer port latches data sent to it, data sent to a printer
    port will remain on the output pins until new data replaces it.  That
    means stepping motors, directly driven by printer port logic, will hold
    there position between transmitted instructions.

    NOTE the sequence of the transmitted numbers.  Bipolar stepping motors
    require Gray Code.
  }
Select_Printer_Port(Lpt_Num, Lpt_Port_Address);
FOR E := 1 TO 10 DO    { step motor clockwise through 40 steps }
    BEGIN
    PORT[Lpt_Port_Address] := 0; DELAY(t);
    PORT[Lpt_Port_Address] := 1; DELAY(t);
    PORT[Lpt_Port_Address] := 3; DELAY(t);
    PORT[Lpt_Port_Address] := 2; DELAY(t);
    END;
  FOR E := 1 TO 10 DO  { step motor counter-clockwise through 40 steps }
    BEGIN
    PORT[Lpt_Port_Address] := 2; DELAY(t);
    PORT[Lpt_Port_Address] := 3; DELAY(t);
    PORT[Lpt_Port_Address] := 1; DELAY(t);
    PORT[Lpt_Port_Address] := 0; DELAY(t);
    END;
END.
```

C Source Code Listing

```
/*                        PROGRAM GrayCode
                     Code conversion by Eugene Klein
            control a bipolar stepping motor via GRAY CODE logic
*/


#include <dos.h>
#include <stdio.h>
#include <conio.h>
#include <stdlib.h>
#include <string.h>
#include <bios.h>
#include "My_TPU.h"

const int t = 300;
int    E;
unsigned int Lpt_Port_Address, Lpt_Num;
void main()
{
 /*    * %%%%%%%%%%%%%%%%%%%%%%%  -=[ METHOD ONE ]=-  %%%%%%%%%%%%%%%%% *

   Basic 4-wire, bipolar, stepping motor control.  Uses Pascal's WRITE
   command to transmit data through computer's LPT1 printer port.  The
   WRITE commands sends data WITHOUT generating printer Line Feed, or
   Carriage Return instructions.

   NOTE the sequence of the transmitted numbers.  Bipolar stepping motors
   require Gray Code.
 */
 for(E=1;E<=10;E++)               // step motor clockwise through 40 steps
 {
  putc(0,stdprn); delay(t);
  putc(1,stdprn); delay(t);
  putc(3,stdprn); delay(t);
  putc(2,stdprn); delay(t);
 }
 for(E=1;E<=10;E++)               // step motor counter-clockwise through 40 steps }
 {
  putc(2,stdprn); delay(t);
  putc(3,stdprn); delay(t);
  putc(1,stdprn); delay(t);
  putc(0,stdprn); delay(t);
 }

 /*    * %%%%%%%%%%%%%%%%%%%%%%%%%  -=[ METHOD TWO ]=-  %%%%%%%%%%%%%%%%% *

   4-wire stepping motor control.  Data is sent to printer port
   LPT1, LPT2, or LPT3.  From users keyboard input of the number 1, 2, or 3,
   port's address is computed, and used to route data.

   Since the printer port latches data sent to it, data sent to a printer
   port will remain on the output pins until new data replaces it.  That
   means stepping motors, directly driven by printer port logic, will hold
   there position between transmitted instructions.
```

```
  NOTE the sequence of the transmitted numbers.  Bipolar stepping motors
  require Gray Code.
*/

Lpt_Num = Select_Printer_Port();
Lpt_Port_Address = Init_Printer_Port(Lpt_Num);

for(E=1;E<=10;E++)                  // step motor clockwise through 40 steps
{
 outport(Lpt_Port_Address,0); delay(t);
 outport(Lpt_Port_Address,1); delay(t);
 outport(Lpt_Port_Address,3); delay(t);
 outport(Lpt_Port_Address,2); delay(t);
}
for(E=1;E<=10;E++)                  // step motor counter-clockwise through 40 steps }
{
 outport(Lpt_Port_Address,2); delay(t);
 outport(Lpt_Port_Address,3); delay(t);
 outport(Lpt_Port_Address,1); delay(t);
 outport(Lpt_Port_Address,0); delay(t);
}
}
```

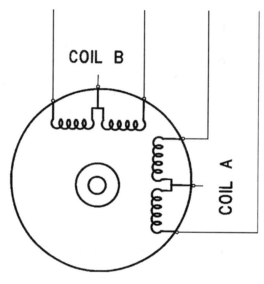

Figure 23-B: 6-Wire Stepping Motor Adapted for Series-Wired Bipolar Operation

Bipolar Operation of Stepping Motors Using Binary Code

Circuit Theory

Figure 24 demonstrates how to directly control a bipolar stepping motor using binary logic. It is identical to Figure 23 in Application 23, but with the addition of a 7486 logic gate. The 7486 converts its binary logic input to gray code logic (gray code logic is discussed in detail in Application 23). The gray code logic is input to the UDN2954 through pin 8, PHASE.

Each coil is controlled by a UDN2954 bipolar driver. The UDN2954 comes in two packages: the in-line SIP package used here and a conventional DIP IC. The in-line chip configuration contains a heat sink. The ULN2954W takes TTL signals for input through PHASE, pin 8. The chip has on-board logic to protect itself from shorting the power supply, and protecting the input from the coil's back-EMF. It can supply up to 2 amps from a 5 to 50 volt supply.

Resistors R6 and R7 are pull-up resistors for the ACK and ERROR lines. By tying the ACK and ERROR lines to logic high, while securing the BUSY and PAPER-END lines to logic low, the computer is fooled into thinking it is connected to an on-line printer ready to receive data. This lets BASIC's LPRINT and Pascal's WRITE statements easily output data.

The wattage ratings of resistors R1 and R2 must be high enough for your chosen power supply. If the coil current is 2 amps, the power rating of R1 and R2 should be at least 5 watts.

Software

The bipolar stepping motor in Figure 24 is controlled by binary logic. Program listings MOT_BIN.PAS, MOT_BIN.C, and MOT_BIN.BAS, given in Application 22, are also used here to demonstrate how binary logic can control a bipolar stepping motor.

Two ways are used to transmit the binary control logic. The first uses the the language's built-in procedures for sending characters to the LPT1 printer port. With this method, a strobe signal is automatically generated. The details are hidden from the programmer. This method requires the least amount of code. Pascal's WRITE command sends the data while telling the compiler NOT to send a carriage return or linefeed. BASIC's LPRINT command, with a trailing semicolon, yealds the same results. Remember, this method only works with LPT1.

The second method requires a little more code, but allows you to send data to any of the three printer ports: LPT1, LPT2, and LPT3. Also, the program should run a little faster. Data is placed on the base address data lines using Pascal's PORT command and BASIC's OUT command. Since the circuit in Figure 24 does not require a strobe signal, none is generated.

The printer port will automatically latch the data onto the data output lines with either method. Data will remain on the printer ports output lines until new data arrives. Since the coils are directly driven by printer port data logic, they will remain energized between transmitted data.

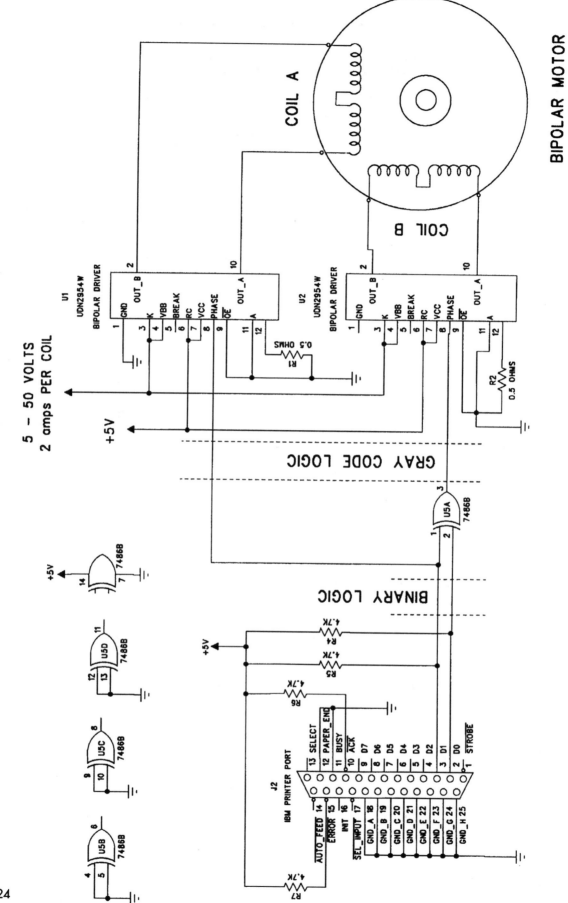

Figure 24

Bipolar Operation of Stepping Motors Using Clock/Direction Logic

Figure 25 demonstrates how to directly control a bipolar stepping motor using clock/direction Logic. The SSA1042 has on-board logic and driver circuitry to power both coils of a bipolar stepping motor. The chip can supply up to 500 mA to each coil from a 6 to 12 volt supply. Its pin-compatible little brother, the MC3479, will supply up to 350 mA to each coil form a 7.2 to 16.6 volt supply.

Each CLOCK pulse on sent to the SAA1042's pin 7 will advance the stepper's shaft to the next position. Pin 10, CCW/CW, determines the motors DIRECTION. If you want the shaft to turn clockwise, then pin 10 should be held low. If you want the shaft to turn counter clockwise, then pin 10 should be held high.

The SAA1042 can generate half step and full step drive currents. Pin 8, H/F, determines which logic the chip will use. Half step logic will not turn your 200

steps per revolution stepping motor into a 400 steps per revolution device. Half step logic was designed to smooth out the shaft's movement as it "snaps" from one position to the next. The idea is to ease the shaft from one full position to the next. Bipolar half step operation involves energizing only one of the two coils used in the next full step. This helps smooth the shaft's "snap" movement from step to step. You should never rest on the half steps. Your software should force the motor to only stop at positions where two coils are energized for maximum holding torque.

Resistors R3 and R4 are pull-up resistors for the ACK and ERROR lines. By tying the ACK and ERROR lines to logic high while securing the BUSY and PAPER-END lines to logic low, the computer is fooled into thinking it is connected to an on-line printer ready to receive data. Thus, BASIC's LPRINT and Pascal's WRITE statements can easily be used to output data.

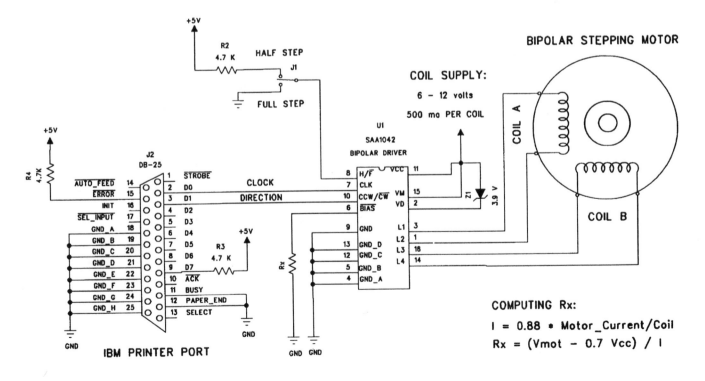

Figure 25

Software

Listings MOT_1042.BAS, MOT_1042.C, and MOT_1042.PAS demonstrate how clock/direction logic can be used to control the stepping motor shown in Figure 25. Two ways are used to transmit the CLK/DIR control logic. The first uses each language's built in procedures for sending characters to the LPT1 printer port. With this method, a strobe signal is automatically generated. The details are hidden from the programmer. This method is requires the least amount of code.

Pascal's WRITE command sends the data while telling the compiler NOT to send a carriage return or linefeed. BASIC's LPRINT command, with a trailing semicolon, yields the same results. Remember, this method only works with LPT1.

The second method requires a little more code, but allows you to send data to any of the three printer ports: LPT1, LPT2, and LPT3. Also, the program should also run a little faster. Data is placed on the base address data lines using Pascal's PORT command, and BASIC's OUT command. Since the circuit in Figure 25 does not require a strobe signal, none is generated.

The printer port will automatically latch the data onto the data output lines with either method. Data will remain on the printer ports output lines until new data arrives. Since the coils are directly driven by printer port data logic, they will remain energized between transmitted data.

BASIC Source Code Listing

```
1 REM FILE: MOT_1042.BAS,   WRITTEN IN QBASIC
2 REM
3 REM Printer port control  of stepping motor using CLOCK/DIRECTION code logic
7 REM
100   T = 300: REM  time delay, dependent on your computer's clock speed
110 Clk = 1: REM   clock pulse data bit, D0
120 Dir = 2: REM   direction data bit, D1
137 REM
138 REM    %%%%%%%%%%%%%%%%%%% -=[ METHOD ONE ]=- %%%%%%%%%%%%%%%%%%%%%%%%%%
140 REM
142 REM   Semicolens at end of LPRINT statement tells BASIC to not add
145 REM   carrage return and line feed to transmitted data.
147 REM
150 FOR E = 1 TO 40: REM  step 40 full steps in clockwise direction using
160 LPRINT CHR$(Clk); : GOSUB 500
170 LPRINT CHR$(0); : GOSUB 500
180 NEXT E
210 FOR E = 40 TO 1 STEP -1: REM step motor 40 steps in CCW direction
230 LPRINT CHR$(Clk + Dir); : GOSUB 500
240 LPRINT CHR$(Dir); : GOSUB 500
250 NEXT E
270 REM
280 REM   %%%%%%%%%%%%%%%%%%%%%%%%  -=[ METHOD TWO ]=- %%%%%%%%%%%%%%%%%%%%%%%
282 REM
283 REM   This method permits sending control signals to LPT1, LPT2, and LPT3
290 REM
300 GOSUB 600: REM   get port's base address
310 FOR E = 1 TO 40: REM  step motor clockwise through 40 steps
340 OUT LptPortAddress, Clk: GOSUB 500
350 OUT LptPortAddress, 0: GOSUB 500
370 NEXT E
380 FOR E = 40 TO 1 STEP -1: REM step motor counterclockwise through 40 steps
400 OUT LptPortAddress, Clk + Dir: GOSUB 500
410 OUT LptPortAddress, Dir: GOSUB 500
420 NEXT E
```

```
499 END
500 REM  -=[ delay ]=-
510 FOR V = 1 TO T: NEXT V
520 RETURN
600 REM
605 PRINT
610 PRINT " Which printer port do you want to use? "
620 PRINT "              1) LPT1"
630 PRINT "              2) LPT1"
640 PRINT "              3) LPT3"
650 n = VAL(INPUT$(1))
670 IF (n < 1) OR (n > 3) THEN GOTO 605
675 DEF SEG = 0
680 OffSet = (n * 2) + 6: Address = 1024 + OffSet
690 LptPortAddress = PEEK(Address) + (PEEK(Address + 1) * 256)
700 RETURN
```

Pascal Source Code Listing

```pascal
PROGRAM Mot_1042;
{
  Bidirectional stepping motor control from parallel printer port using
  CLOCK & DIRECTION control logic.
}
USES CRT, My_Tpu, PRINTER;
CONST Clk = 1;    { clock data bit, D0     }
      Dir = 2;    { direction data bit, D1 }
        t = 100;  { time delay dependent on your computer's clock speed }
VAR                        E : INTEGER;
     Lpt_Num, Lpt_Port_Address : WORD;

BEGIN
    (* %%%%%%%%%%%%%%%%%%%%%%% -=[ METHOD ONE ]=- %%%%%%%%%%%%%%%%%%%% *)

{
   Advance stepper motor shaft 40 steps in clockwise direction.
   With Dir, bit D1, held low, strobe the clock line, D0, 40 times.
   This method only works with LPT1.
}
WRITE(LST, CHAR(0)); { intitilize to clockwise direction, data = 0 }
FOR E := 1 TO 40 DO
  BEGIN
  WRITE(LST, CHR(CLK)); { 00000001 } DELAY(t);
  WRITE(LST, CHR(0));   { 00000000 } DELAY(t);
  END; { for e }
{
   Advance stepper motor shaft 40 steps in counter-clockwise direction.
   With Dir, bit D1, held high, strobe the clock line, D0, 40 times.
}
FOR E := 1 TO 40 DO
  BEGIN
  WRITE(LST, CHR(CLK + DIR));   { 00000011 }  DELAY(t);
  WRITE(LST, CHR(DIR));         { 00000010 }  DELAY(t);
  END; { for e }
```

```
        (* %%%%%%%%%%%%%%%%%%% -=[ METHOD TWO ]=- %%%%%%%%%%%%%%%%%%%% *)
  Select_Printer_Port(Lpt_Num, Lpt_Port_Address);
  {

      Advance stepper motor shaft 40 steps in clockwise direction.
      With Dir, bit D1, held low, strobe the clock line, D0, 40 times.
      This method permits selection of LPT1, LPT2 or LPT3.
  }

  FOR E := 1 TO 40 DO
    BEGIN
    PORT[Lpt_Port_Address] :=  CLK;  { 00000001 } DELAY(t);
    PORT[Lpt_Port_Address] :=  0;    { 00000000 } DELAY(t);
    END; { for e }
  {
      Advance stepper motor shaft 40 steps in counter-clockwise direction.
      With Dir, bit D1, held high, strobe the clock line, D0, 40 times.
  }
  FOR E := 1 TO 40 DO
    BEGIN
    PORT[Lpt_Port_Address] :=  CLK + DIR; { 00000011 } DELAY(t);
    PORT[Lpt_Port_Address] :=  DIR;       { 00000010 } DELAY(t);
    END; { for e }
  END.
```

C Source Code Listing

```
/*
                         PROGRAM Mot_1042
            Code   conversion by Eugene Klein
   Bidirectional stepping motor control from parallel printer port using
    CLOCK & DIRECTION control logic.
*/

#include <dos.h>
#include <stdio.h>
#include <conio.h>
#include <stdlib.h>
#include <string.h>
#include <bios.h>
#include "My_TPU.h"

const int   CLK = 1;                        // clock data bit, D0
const int   DIR = 2;                        // direction data bit, D1
const int   t   = 100; // time delay dependent on your computer's clock speed
int E;
unsigned int  Lpt_Num, Lpt_Port_Address;

void main()
{
    /* %%%%%%%%%%%%%%%%%%%%% -=[ METHOD ONE ]=- %%%%%%%%%%%%%%%%%%%% *


      Advance stepper motor shaft 40 steps in clockwise direction.
      With Dir, bit D1, held low, strobe the clock line, D0, 40 times.
      This method only works with LPT1.
*/
```

```
 putc(0,stdprn);                     // intitilize to clockwise direction, data = 0
 for(E=1;E<=40;E++)
 {
  putc(CLK,stdprn);                  //00000001
  delay(t);
  putc(0,stdprn);                    // 00000000
  delay(t);
 }
/*
    Advance stepper motor shaft 40 steps in counter-clockwise direction.
    With Dir, bit D1, held high, strobe the clock line, D0, 40 times.
*/
 for(E=1;E<=40;E++)
 {
  putc((CLK + DIR),stdprn);     // 00000011
  delay(t);
  putc(DIR,stdprn);             // 00000010
  delay(t);
 }
   // (* %%%%%%%%%%%%%%%%%%%%%%%% -=[ METHOD TWO ]=- %%%%%%%%%%%%%%%%%%%%%%% *)

 Lpt_Num = Select_Printer_Port();
 Lpt_Port_Address = Init_Printer_Port(Lpt_Num);
 clrscr();

/*
    Advance stepper motor shaft 40 steps in clockwise direction.
    With Dir, bit D1, held low, strobe the clock line, D0, 40 times.
    This method permits selection of LPT1, LPT2 or LPT3.
*/

 for(E=1;E<=40;E++)
 {
  outport(Lpt_Port_Address,CLK);   // 00000001
  delay(t);
  outport(Lpt_Port_Address,0);     // 00000000
  delay(t);
 }
/*
    Advance stepper motor shaft 40 steps in counter-clockwise direction.
    With Dir, bit D1, held high, strobe the clock line, D0, 40 times.
*/
 for(E=1;E<=40;E++)
 {
 outport(Lpt_Port_Address,CLK+DIR);   // 00000011
  delay(t);
  outport(Lpt_Port_Address,DIR);      // 00000010
  delay(t);
 }
}
```

Bipolar Operation of Stepping Motors Using Clock Pulses

Circuit Theory

Some circuits require you to use only a series of pulses to control a stepping motor's rotation. One clock pulse turns the motor in a clockwise direction, while a separate clock pulse turns the stepping motor in a counterclockwise direction.

Figure 26 demonstrates how to use only clock pulses to control a bipolar stepping motor. The printer port's clock pulses are fed to the input of the 74193 up/down counter. The counter sequentially generates binary numbers from 0 to 3. The binary logic is converted to gray code logic by a single 7486 gate. The gray code tells the UDN2954 which coil current polarity to use. Each CLOCK pulse on sent from the printer port's pin 2, D0, will advance the motor's shaft counterclockwise one full step. Each CLOCK pulse sent from the printer port's pin 3, D1, will advance the motor's shaft clockwise one full step.

Resistors R6 and R7 are pull-up resistors for the ACK and ERROR lines. By tying the ACK and ERROR lines to logic high, while securing the BUSY and PAPER-END lines to logic low, the computer is fooled into thinking it is connected to an on-line printer ready to receive data. This means BASIC's LPRINT and Pascal's WRITE statements can easily be used to output data.

Each coil winding is controlled by a UDN2954W bipolar driver. The UDN2954 comes in two packages: the in-line SIP package used here and a conventional DIP IC. The in-line chip is packaged with a heat sink. The ULN2954 takes TTL signals for input through PHASE, pin 8. The chip has on-board logic to protect itself from shorting the power supply, and protecting the input from coil back-EMF. It can supply up to 2 amps from a 5 to 50 volt supply.

Software

Program listings MOT_CLK.BAS, MOT_CLK.C, and MOT_CLK.PAS demonstrate how clock/clock logic can be used to control the stepping motor of Figure 26. Two ways are used to transmit the CLK/CLK control logic. The first uses each language's built-in procedures for sending characters to the LPT1 printer port. With this method, a strobe signal is automatically generated. The details are hidden from the programmer. This method requires the least amount of code.

Pascal's WRITE command sends the data while telling the compiler NOT to send a carriage return or linefeed. BASIC's LPRINT command, with a trailing semicolon, yields the same results. Remember, this method only works with LPT1.

The second method requires a little more code, but allows you to send data to any of the three printer ports: LPT1, LPT2, and LPT3. The program should also run a little faster than when using LPRINT and WRITE commands. Data is placed on the printer port's base address data lines using Pascal's PORT command, or BASIC's OUT command. Since the circuit in Figure 26 does not require a strobe signal, none is generated.

The printer port will automatically latch the data onto the data output lines with either method. Data will remain on the printer ports output lines until new data arrives. Since the coils are directly driven by printer port data logic, they will remain energized between transmitted data.

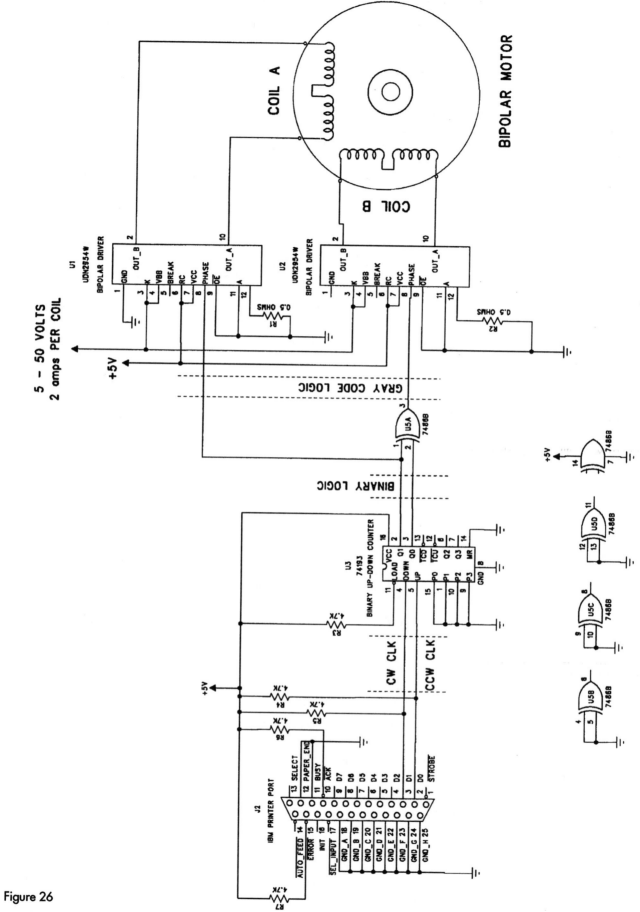

Figure 26

APPLICATION 26 Bipolar Operation of Stepping Motors Using Clock Pulses

```
1    REM   FILE: MOT_CLK.BAS,  WRITTEN IN QBASIC
2    REM
3    REM Bipolar stepping motor control from printer port using CLOCK pulses
7    REM
100  CW = 1: REM printer port D0, pin 2, provides clockwise rotation pulses
110  CCW = 2: REM printer port D1, pin 3, provides CounterClockWise pulses
135  T = 300
137  REM
138  REM    %%%%%%%%%%%%%%%%%%%% -=[ METHOD ONE ]=- %%%%%%%%%%%%%%%%%%%%%%%%%%
140  REM
142  REM   Semicolens at end of LPRINT statement tells BASIC to not add
145  REM   carrage return and line feed to transmitted data.
146  REM   This method only works with LPT1.
147  REM
150  FOR e = 1 TO 40: REM  step motor 40 steps in clockwise direction
160  LPRINT CHR$(CW); : GOSUB 500
170  LPRINT CHR$(0); : GOSUB 500
200  NEXT e
210  FOR e = 1 TO 40: REM step motor 40 steps in counter-clockwise direction
220  LPRINT CHR$(CCW); : GOSUB 500
230  LPRINT CHR$(0); : GOSUB 500
260  NEXT e
270  REM
280  REM    %%%%%%%%%%%%%%%%%%%%%%%%%  -=[ METHOD TWO ]=- %%%%%%%%%%%%%%%%%%%%%%%%
282  REM
283  REM   This method permits sending control signals to LPT1, LPT2, and LPT3
290  REM
300  GOSUB 600: REM   get port's base address
310  FOR e = 1 TO 40: REM  step motor clockwise through 40 steps
320  OUT LptPortAddress, CW: GOSUB 500
340  OUT LptPortAddress, 0: GOSUB 500
370  NEXT e
380  FOR e = 1 TO 40: REM step motor counterclockwise through 40 steps
390  OUT LptPortAddress, CCW: GOSUB 500
400  OUT LptPortAddress, 0: GOSUB 500
430  NEXT e
499  END
500  REM   -=[ delay ]=-
510  FOR V = 1 TO T: NEXT V
520  RETURN
600  REM
605  PRINT
610  PRINT " Which printer port do you want to use? "
620  PRINT "              1) LPT1"
630  PRINT "              2) LPT1"
640  PRINT "              3) LPT3"
650  n = VAL(INPUT$(1))
670  IF (n < 1) OR (n > 3) THEN GOTO 605
675  DEF SEG = 0
680  OffSet = (n * 2) + 6: Address = 1024 + OffSet
690  LptPortAddress = PEEK(Address) + (PEEK(Address + 1) * 256)
700  RETURN
```

Pascal Source Code Listing

```
PROGRAM Mot_Clk;
{
    Bidirectional stepping motor control from parallel printer port using
    CLOCK PULSES. ClockWise on D0, CounterClockWise on D1.
}
USES CRT, My_Tpu, PRINTER;
CONST  CW = 1;    {         clockwise data bit, D0      }
       CCW = 2;   { counterclockwise data bit, D1 }
         t = 100; { time delay dependent on your computer's clock speed }
VAR                          E : INTEGER;
     Lpt_Num, Lpt_Port_Address : WORD;

BEGIN
    (* %%%%%%%%%%%%%%%%%%%%%%% -=[ METHOD ONE ]=- %%%%%%%%%%%%%%%%%%%%% *)

{
    Advance stepper motor shaft 40 steps in clockwise direction.
    Strobe the ClockWise clock line, D0, 40 times.
    This method only works with LPT1.
}
WRITE(LST, CHAR(0)); { intitilize all control bits }
FOR E := 1 TO 40 DO
  BEGIN
  WRITE(LST, CHR(CW));    { 00000001 } DELAY(t);
  WRITE(LST, CHR(0));     { 00000000 } DELAY(t);
  END; { for e }
{
    Advance stepper motor shaft 40 steps in counter-clockwise direction.
    Strobe the counterclockwise clock line, D1, 40 times.
}
FOR E := 1 TO 40 DO
  BEGIN
  WRITE(LST, CHR(CCW));   { 00000010 }  DELAY(t);
  WRITE(LST, CHR(0));     { 00000000 }  DELAY(t);
  END; { for e }


    (* %%%%%%%%%%%%%%%%%%%%%%%% -=[ METHOD TWO ]=- %%%%%%%%%%%%%%%%%%%%% *)


Select_Printer_Port(Lpt_Num, Lpt_Port_Address);
{
    Advance stepper motor shaft 40 steps in clockwise direction.
    Strobe the Clockwise clock line, D0, 40 times.
    This method permits selection of LPT1, LPT2 or LPT3.
}

FOR E := 1 TO 40 DO
  BEGIN
  PORT[Lpt_Port_Address] :=  CC;      { 00000001 } DELAY(t);
  PORT[Lpt_Port_Address] :=  0;       { 00000000 } DELAY(t);
  END; { for e }
{
    Advance stepper motor shaft 40 steps in counter-clockwise direction.
    Strobe the counterclockwise clock line, D1, 40 times.
}
```

```
FOR E := 1 TO 40 DO
  BEGIN
  PORT[Lpt_Port_Address] :=  CCW;        { 00000010 } DELAY(t);
  PORT[Lpt_Port_Address] :=  0;          { 00000000 } DELAY(t);
  END; { for e }
END.
```

C Source Code Listing

```
/*                        PROGRAM Mot_Clk
              Code conversion by Eugene Klein

   Bidirectional stepping motor control from parallel printer port using
   CLOCK PULSES. ClockWise on D0, CounterClockWise on D1.
*/

#include <dos.h>
#include <stdio.h>
#include <conio.h>
#include <stdlib.h>
#include <string.h>
#include <bios.h>
#include "My_TPU.h"

const int  CW = 1;    //          clockwise data bit, D0
const int  CCW = 2;   //          counterclockwise data bit, D1
const int  t = 100;   // time delay dependent on your computer's clock speed
int E;
unsigned int Lpt_Num, Lpt_Port_Address;

void main()
{
/*    * %%%%%%%%%%%%%%%%%%%%%%%%% -=[ METHOD ONE ]=- %%%%%%%%%%%%%%%%%%%%% *


   Advance stepper motor shaft 40 steps in clockwise direction.
   Strobe the ClockWise clock line, D0, 40 times.
   This method only works with LPT1.
*/

 putc(0,stdprn);                   // intitilize all control bits
 for(E=1;E<=40;E++)
 {
  putc(CW,stdprn);                 //00000001
  delay(t);
  putc(0,stdprn);                  // 00000000
  delay(t);
 }

/*
   Advance stepper motor shaft 40 steps in counter-clockwise direction.
   Strobe the counterclockwise clock line, D1, 40 times.
*/
  for(E=1;E<=40;E++)
  {
  putc(CCW,stdprn);                    //00000010
```

```
   delay(t);
   putc(0,stdprn);                    // 00000000
   delay(t);
  }


//     (* %%%%%%%%%%%%%%%%%%%%%%%% -=[ METHOD TWO ]=- %%%%%%%%%%%%%%%%%%%%%% *)

  Lpt_Num = Select_Printer_Port();
  Lpt_Port_Address = Init_Printer_Port(Lpt_Num);
  clrscr();

 /*
    Advance stepper motor shaft 40 steps in clockwise direction.
    Strobe the Clockwise clock line, D0, 40 times.
    This method permits selection of LPT1, LPT2 or LPT3.
 */

 for(E=1;E<=40;E++)
 {
  outport(Lpt_Port_Address,CW);    // 00000001
  delay(t);
  outport(Lpt_Port_Address,0);     // 00000000
  delay(t);
 }

 /*
    Advance stepper motor shaft 40 steps in counter-clockwise direction.
    Strobe the counterclockwise clock line, D1, 40 times.
 */
 for(E=1;E<=40;E++)
 {
  outport(Lpt_Port_Address,CCW);   // 00000010
  delay(t);
  outport(Lpt_Port_Address,0);     // 00000000
  delay(t);
 }
}
```

Controlling DC Servo Motors

Circuit Theory

Servo motors, such as those sold in hobby shops, are a special breed of DC motor. They are designed to move the output shaft through an arc of 180 degrees. Any position within that arc is selected, and held, based on input control signals. Servo motors allow your computer to control a straight line movement.

Cramped within a small DC servo motor package lies the DC servo motor itself, a lot of reduction gearing, and an IC chip. That's a lot of hardware, but because these servo motors are so widely used in remote control airplanes, boats, and cars they are relatively inexpensive.

The control logic generates positive going pulse width control. With power applied and no pulses, the output shaft is free turning. The length of the pulse tells the on-board electronics what angular position to move to and then stay at. Pulse widths between 0.5 milliseconds, and 2.5 milliseconds will result in the output shaft moving 0 to 180 degrees. For example, a pulse width of 1.5 milliseconds would position the output shaft at 90 degrees, while a pulse width of 1 millisecond would position the shaft at a 45 degree position. The output shaft will maintain its position as long as pulse width signals are repeated.

The on-board electronics does all the work. It reads the servo's feedback loop, keeps track of the shaft's position, and maintains the motor's position. Other circuitry protects the chip and input logic from back-EMF spikes. Figure 27 shows how to interface a miniature servo motor to a parallel printer port. Since the motor requires only one control line, eight servos can easily be controlled from one printer port.

Software

In order to send pulse width modulation information with durations of 0.5 to 2.5 milliseconds, a very fast timer routine is needed. No high level language can provide such an accurate time base. Many BIOS interrupts take precedence over a running program, routinely interrupting executing programs to take care of computer related overhead tasks. Therefore, your high level program can not provide an accurate timer function.

Assembly language can. Both Turbo Pascal and Turbo C++, permit you to include assembly language source code within your program listings. Assembly language can halt interrupt operations long enough to complete a dedicated task (in this case, timing an interval between 0.5 and 2.5 milliseconds. Listings SERVO.PAS and SERVO.C demonstrate this technique.

Inside your IBM/IBM clone computer is a timer chip, the 8253. The 8253 is actually three indepen-

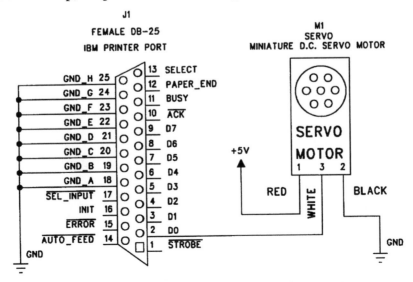

Figure 27

dent timers in one plastic package. Two sections of the 8253 are dedicated to computer related operations. The third is used to generate an audible frequency for your computer's speaker (hardly a priority!). Through software, you can set and read this timer's values.

The crystal oscillator input frequency to the 8253 is the same on every IBM/IBM clone computer. That means that regardless of your computer model the 8253 is always running from a uniform time base. Using assembly language, your program can initialize one of the 8253 timer sections with a particular count, monitor the timer's progress, and return the results.

The program takes numeric keypad input for de-sired servo motor position. The keyboard input is converted to a number between 0 and 255. This number, in variable "r", represents an output shaft angular position of 0 to 180 degrees.

A square wave is output through the printer port's D0, at pin 2. The PROCEDURE PULSE sets the printer port's output bit 1 to high, initializes the 8253's third timer section, waits for the requested count to be reached, and then sets the printer port's data bit 1 low again. Assembly language is used to initialize the 8253 timer and monitor the elapsed time.

Many thanks to my good friend Mike Mensch for contributing this material, including the software listings that follow.

Pascal Source Code Listing

```
PROGRAM SERVO;
{
 - Control R/C Model Servo Motors from a parallel printer port.
 - A Servo Motor is a DC motor with feedback.
 - All IBM / clone 8253 timer generates frequencies up to 1,193,180 Hertz
 - For R/C model servos, pulse width should be 0.5ms to 2.5ms.
 - Motors may oscillate due to delay increase cause by timer and other
   internal interrupt calls.  The effect is more noticeable on slower machines.
 - Many thanks to my good friend, Mike Mensch, who developed this program
}
USES DOS, CRT, My_Tpu;
CONST   PIA_8255B    =  $0061;     { 8255 port B address               }
        TIM_8253C    =  $0043;     { 8253 timer control register       }
        TIM_8253T2   =  $0042;     { 8253 timer 2 register             }

        Time_10_ms   =  $2e9a;     { 10 milli-seconds                  }
        time_2_ms    =  $0952;     { computed time for 2 millisecond delay  }
        time_1_ms    =  $04a9;     { computed time for 1 millisecond delay  }
        time_half_ms =  $0255;     { computed time for half a millisecond delay  }
        Survo      :   BYTE = 0;   { byte = unsigned char              }

VAR                                     Ch : CHAR;
                        PBbits, r,y ,motor : BYTE;
        Lpt_Num, Lpt_Port_Address, Delay_Value : WORD;

PROCEDURE Do_Pulse( Delay_Value : WORD); ASSEMBLER;
{
 Send three copies of bit at three-phase zero crossings
 Waits for next zero crossing and restarts timer
 Gets bit value from global bitval
 Mashes BL and DX
}
LABEL  ReGet, L1, L2, L3, L4;     { must pre declare subroutine names in TP }
{
 NOTE: Jumps to lables L1, L2, L3, and L4 are not needed on XT machines
       XT machines do not have a pre-fetch.
}
ASM
```

```
        PUSH    bx
        MOV     bx,Delay_Value   { load the contents of Delay_Value into Bx }
        PUSH    bp
        MOV     bp,sp
        CLI
        IN      AL,PIA_8255B        {   get current port B bit         }
        OR      AL,$01              {   turn on timer gate             }
        JMP     L1                  {   flush CPU's internal buffer    }
L1:     OUT     PIA_8255B,AL        {   update timer gate bits         }
        STI                         {   get 16 bit timer count         }
ReGet:
        MOV     AL,10000000B        {   latch Timer 2                  }
        JMP     L2                  {   flush CPU's internal buffer    }
L2:     CLI
        OUT     TIM_8253C,AL        {   load 8255 control register w/AL }
        JMP     L3                  {   flush CPU's internal buffer    }
L3:     IN      AL,TIM_8253T2       {   get LSB from timer             }
        MOV     AH,AL
        JMP     L4                  {   flush CPU's internal buffer    }
L4:     IN      AL,TIM_8253T2       {   get MSB from timer             }
        STI (* shift this one down to after jump, JB *)
        XCHG    AH,AL               {   swap bits around,              }
        NOT     AX                  {   and flip bits to count upward  }
        CMP     AX,bx  { compare until count ( in AX ) >=  Delay_Value }
        JB      reget
        (* try sti here instead of above *)
        POP     bp
        POP     bx
END; { do pulse }



PROCEDURE Init_Time; ASSEMBLER;
{
  Delay times measured in Timer-2 ticks These are found by computing
     (time/54.9ms)*64*1024 Delay required on AT after each I/O operation
  Sets up Timer2 Halts timer counting,
  sets FFFF reload value
  Sets Mode 2
  Clears "speaker enable" bit
  Does not start timer, leaves "gate speaker" bit low
}
LABEL   L1, L2, L3;          { must pre declare subroutine names in Turbo Pascal }
{
 NOTE: Jumps to lables L1, L2, and L3 are not needed on XT machines
       XT machines do not have a pre-fetch.
}
ASM     CLI                         {   clear control bits             }
        IN      AL,PIA_8255B        {   get current port B bits        }
        AND     AL,$FC              {   turn off timer gate and speaker }
        JMP     L1                  {   flush CPU's internal buffer    }
L1:     OUT     PIA_8255B,AL        {   load Port B bits               }
        STI
        CLI                         {   set Timer 2 to LSB/MSB mode 2  }
        MOV     AL,$B4              {   10110100B                      }
        OUT     TIM_8253C,AL        {   send control byte to 8253      }
        MOV     AL,$FF              {   set reload value to FFFF       }
```

```
          JMP     L2                      { flush CPU's internal buffer      }
L2:       OUT     TIM_8253T2,AL
          JMP     L3                      { flush CPU's internal buffer      }
L3:       OUT     TIM_8253T2,AL
          STI
          END; { asm }

PROCEDURE Delay_Between;
{
 set up for a ten millisecond delay between pulses sent to servo motor.
 may be eliminated if you are controlling only one motor
}
BEGIN
Init_Time;
Do_Pulse(time_10_ms);
END;


PROCEDURE Pulse(VAR r, MOTOR : BYTE; VAR Delay_Value : WORD);
{
 converts r value, (0 to 255), to appropriate pulse width, (0.5 to 2.5 ms)
}
BEGIN
Delay_Value := time_1_ms + ( 10 * r ) + 75;
Init_Time;
Do_Pulse(time_half_ms);
PORT[Lpt_Port_Address ] :=  motor;       { set printer port active bits HIGH }
Do_Pulse(Delay_Value);
PORT[Lpt_Port_Address] := $00;           { set printer port bits LOW         }
END; { pulse }


BEGIN { main }
Select_Printer_Port(Lpt_Num, Lpt_Port_Address); { in My_Tpu }
Ch := CHAR(32);
r := 128;
WHILE ORD(ch) <> 27 DO
  BEGIN { while }
  IF KeyPressed THEN
    BEGIN { if }
    Ch := ReadKey;
      CASE Ch OF
        '6', 'M' : if ( r < 255 ) THEN INC(R);
        '4', 'K' : if ( r > 0 ) THEN  DEC(r);
        '8', 'H' : if ( r > 250 ) THEN r := 255 ELSE R := R + 5;
        '2', 'P' : if ( r > 4 ) THEN r := R -5 else r := 0;
        '+' : r := 255;
        '-' : r := 1;
      END;  { case }
    WRITE('Ch = ',Ch); WRITELN(':   r value = ',r);writeln;
    END; { if }
  FOR y := 0 to 2 do
    BEGIN { for y }
    motor := $ff;
    Pulse(r,motor, Delay_Value);
    Delay_Between;
    END; { for y }
  END; { while }
END. { main }
```

C Source Code Listing

```c
/*
                        PROGRAM SERVO
              Code conversion by Eugene Klein

   Control R/C Model Servo Motors from a parallel printer port.
   A Servo Motor is a DC motor with feedback.
   All IBM / clone 8253 timer generates frequencies up to 1,193,180 Hertz
   For R/C model servos, pulse width should be 0.5ms to 2.5ms.
   Motors may oscillate due to delay increase cause by timer and other
    internal interrupt calls.  The effect is more noticeable on slower machines.
   Many thanks to my good friend, Mike Mench, who developed this program
*/


#include <dos.h>
#include <stdio.h>
#include <conio.h>
#include <stdlib.h>
#include <string.h>
#include <bios.h>
#include "My_TPU.h"

#define PIA_8255B      0x61;      // 8255 port B address
#define TIM_8253C      0x43;      // 8253 timer control register
#define TIM_8253T2     0x42;      // 8253 timer 2 register

const int ESC = 0x1B;
const unsigned int   Time_10_ms   = 0x2e9a;    // 10 milliseconds
const unsigned int   time_2_ms    = 0x0952;  // computed time for 2 millisecond delay
const unsigned int   time_1_ms    = 0x04a9;  // computed time for 1 millisecond delay
const unsigned int   time_half_ms = 0x0255;  // computed time for half a millisecond
delay

char Servo =0; // byte = unsigned char
char Ch;
unsigned char PBbits, r,y ,motor, Lpt_Num;
unsigned int LPTx, Delay_Value;

void Do_Pulse( unsigned int Delay_Value)
{
 /*
 Send three copies of bit at three-phase zero crossings
 Waits for next zero crossing and restarts timer
 Gets bit value from global bitval
 Mashes BL and DX

NOTE: Jumps to labels L1, L2, L3, and L4 are not needed on XT machines
      XT machines do not have a pre-fetch.
 */
 asm     {
      PUSH    bx
      MOV     bx,Delay_Value          // load the contents of Delay_Value into Bx
      PUSH    bp
      MOV     bp,sp
      CLI
      IN      AL,0x61                 //   get current port B bit
```

```
            OR       AL,0x01              //   turn on timer gate
            JMP      L1                   //   flush CPU's internal buffer
            }
    L1:
    asm      {
            OUT      0x61,AL              //   update timer gate bits
            STI                           //   get 16 bit timer count
            }
    Reget:
    asm      {
            MOV      AL,0x80              //   latch Timer 2
            JMP      L2                   //   flush CPU's internal buffer
            }
    L2:
    asm      {
            CLI
            OUT      0x43,AL              //   load 8255 control register w/AL
            JMP      L3                   //   flush CPU's internal buffer
            }
    L3:
    asm      {
            IN       AL,0x42              //   get LSB from timer
            MOV      AH,AL
            JMP      L4                   //   flush CPU's internal buffer
            }
    L4:
    asm      {
            IN       AL,0x42              //   get MSB from timer
            STI
            XCHG     AH,AL                //   swap bits around,
            NOT      AX                   //    and flip bits to count upward
            CMP      AX,BX               // compare until count ( in AX ) >=  Delay_Value
            JB       Reget
            POP      BP
            POP      BX
            }
}


void Init_Time(void)
{
/*
 Delay times measured in Timer-2 ticks These are found by computing
    (time/54.9ms)*64*1024 Delay required on AT after each I/O operation
 Sets up Timer2 Halts timer counting,
 sets FFFF reload value
 Sets Mode 2
 Clears "speaker enable" bit
 Does not start timer, leaves "gate speaker" bit low
*/

// NOTE: Jumps to labels L1, L2, and L3 are not needed on XT machines
//        XT machines do not have a pre-fetch.

    asm      {
            CLI                           //   clear control bits
            IN       AL,0x61              //   get current port B bits
            AND      AL, 0xFC             //   turn off timer gate and speaker
```

```
            JMP     L1                          //  flush CPU's internal buffer
        }
    L1:
    asm     {
            OUT     0x61,AL                     //  load Port B bits
            STI
            CLI                                 //  set Timer 2 to LSB/MSB mode 2
            MOV     AL,0xB4                      //  10110100B
            OUT     0x43,AL                      //  send control byte to 8253
            MOV     AL,0xFF                      //  set reload value to FFFF
            JMP     L2                          //  flush CPU's internal buffer
        }
    L2:
    asm     {
            OUT     0x42,AL
            JMP     L3                          //  flush CPU's internal buffer
        }
    L3:
    asm     {
            OUT     0x42,AL
            STI
        }
}


void Delay_Between(void)
/*
 set up for a ten millisecond delay between pulses sent to servo motor.
 may be eliminated if you are controlling only one motor
*/
{
 Init_Time();
 Do_Pulse(Time_10_ms);
}

void Pulse(unsigned char r, unsigned char motor,unsigned int Delay_Value)

 //converts r value, (0 to 255), to appropriate pulse width, (0.5 to 2.5 ms)

{
 Delay_Value = time_1_ms + ( 10 * r ) + 75;
 Init_Time();
 Do_Pulse(time_half_ms);
 outport(LPTx, motor);          // set printer port active bits HIGH
 Do_Pulse(Delay_Value);
 outport(LPTx,0x00);            // set printer port bits LOW
}

void main()
{
 char cmd[10] = " ";

 Lpt_Num = Select_Printer_Port();
 LPTx = Init_Printer_Port(Lpt_Num);
 clrscr();
 Ch = 0x32;
 r = 128;
```

```
      gotoxy(10,10);
      printf("Ch = %s  :    r value = %i",cmd,r);
      while(Ch != ESC)
      {
       if(kbhit())
       {
        Ch = getch();
        if(Ch==0)
         Ch=getch();
        if(Ch=='6'|| Ch=='M')
        {
         r++;
         strcpy(cmd,"right arrow");
        }
        if(Ch=='4' || Ch=='K')
        {
         r-;
         strcpy(cmd,"left arrow");
        }
        if(Ch=='8'|| Ch=='H')
        {
         if ( r > 250 )
          r = 255;
         else
          r += 5;
         strcpy(cmd,"Up arrow");
        }
        if(Ch=='2'|| Ch=='P')
        {
         if ( r > 4 )
          r -= 5;
         else
          r = 0;
         strcpy(cmd,"Down arrow");
        }
        if(Ch=='+')
        {
         r = 255;
         strcpy(cmd,"Plus");
        }
        if(Ch=='-')
        {
         r = 1;
         strcpy(cmd,"Minus");
        }
        clrscr();
        gotoxy(10,10);
        printf("Ch = %s  :    r value = %i",cmd,r);
       }
       for(y = 0;y<=2;y++)
       {
        motor = 0xff;
        Pulse(r,motor, Delay_Value);
        Delay_Between();
       }
      }
    }
```

8-Bit Data Input from a Parallel Printer Port

Circuit Theory

In order to input digital logic, we need a standardized method for dealing with input data. An IBM compatible printer port has nine control lines capable of inputting real world data. Each printer port has three address locations. The base address is used to transmit data. The next address can input five data bits, using D3 through D7, and the third port address can input or output a nibble of information via bits D0 through D3. A complete chart is shown in Appendix G.

The simplest method of inputting eight data bits is to read the high nibble from the base + 1 address and the low nibble from the base + 2 address. These two nibbles can be logically ORed together to form a data byte. Some of the bits are hard-wired on the printer card for inactive high operation. You could have your software reinvert the logic, but I find it more practical to do the job with hardware. I find this approach makes my software simpler, and more logical to follow. Like Steve Ciarcia, founder and editorial director of Circuit Cellar Inc., I believe the best software language is solder.

Figure 28 demonstrates how to input eight data bits from an IBM type parallel printer port. Each switch and related pull-up resistor can generate logic high and low signals. When a switch is open, the supply voltage is present at both ends of the pull-up resistor. The corresponding printer port data bit will see an active high logic bit. When a switch is closed, the switch will sink the current flowing through the pull-up resistor. The associated printer port data bit will see a logic low signal.

Since the printer port contains hard-wired gates to invert the ERROR, ACKNOWLEDGE, AUTO-FEED, AND SELECT-INPUT data lines, I use four sections of a 7404 to re-invert the inverted data lines.

The ninth input data bit, at pin 15, is not used. Decoding this bit, along with the other eight, would

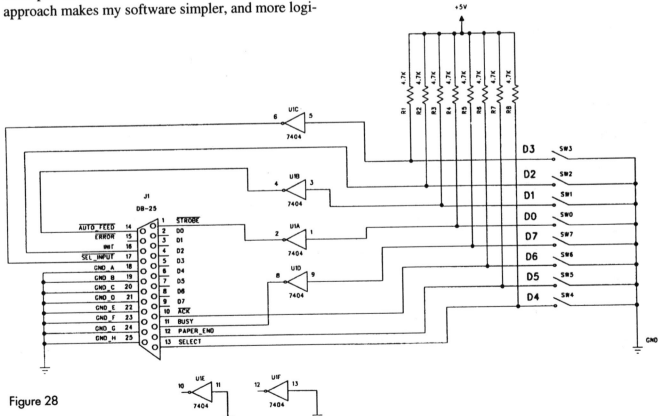

Figure 28

require only slightly more programming code. However, the code is awkward, using XOR statements, and less logical to follow. I only use the ERROR line if I must input all nine data bits or I want to use the ACK line for a hardware driven TSR interrupt. Check the TSR chapter for details.

This circuit comes in handy for testing software during prototyping. Most languages have a single step command for tracing software execution. Using a single step command with this circuit can greatly reduce debugging time.

Software

Program listings SW_IN.BAS, SW_IN.C, and SW_IN.PAS demonstrate how to input digital data bits through a parallel printer port. First the program reads data from address base + 1, and then base + 2. Next, the program isolates the high nibble information from base + 1, and the low nibble information form base + 2. Finally, the two nibbles are combined and displayed. The process is repeated until a key is pressed.

BASIC Source Code Listing

```
1    REM
2    REM    FILE: SW_IN.BAS
3    REM
100  REM    basic 8-bit switch input   from parallel printer port
105  REM
110  REM    input BUSY, ACK, PAPER END, INPUT, STROBE, AUTO FEED, ERROR,
120  REM    and SELECT INPUT signals from IBM type parallel printer port.
130  REM
140  REM    written in QBASIC
150  LPT = 0: BaseAddress = 0
160  DataByte = 0: HighNibble = 0:  LowNibble = 0: OffSet = 0
170  REM
200  REM    -=[ begin program ]=-
210  CLS 0
220  REM    find base address of LPT1, use 10 for LPT2, and 12 for LPT3
230  BaseAddress = &H400 + 8
240  DEF SEG = 0
245  LPT = PEEK(BaseAddress) + (PEEK(BaseAddress + 1) * 256)
250  REM
260  GOSUB 700: REM   read switches
270  GOSUB 860: REM   display data
280  IF INKEY$ = "" THEN GOTO 250
290  END: REM   -=[ program end ]=-
300  REM
310  REM
699  REM
700  REM    -=[ Subroutine,  Read Switches ]=-
710  REM
720  HighNibble = 0: LowNibble = 0
730  REM    first set all open collector output pins HIGH to read from base + 2
735  REM
740  OUT (LPT + 2), (INP(LPT + 2) OR 15)
750  FOR E = 1 TO 50: NEXT E:           REM delay dependent on your machine
760  LowNibble = INP(LPT + 2)
770  HighNibble = INP(LPT + 1)
780  LowNibble = (LowNibble AND &HF)
790  HighNibble = (HighNibble AND &HF0)
800  DataByte = (HighNibble OR LowNibble):   REM   combine nibbles into byte
810  RETURN: REM    end of subroutine, read switches
850  REM
860  REM       -=[ subroutine, display data ]=-
```

```
870 REM
880 LOCATE 1, 3
890 PRINT "Base Address = "; LPT; ";      Data Byte = "; DataByte; "    "
895 PRINT
900 PRINT "D0 = ";
902 IF (DataByte AND 1) = 1 THEN PRINT "HIGH" ELSE PRINT "LOW "
904 PRINT "D1 = ";
906 IF (DataByte AND 2) = 2 THEN PRINT "HIGH" ELSE PRINT "LOW "
908 PRINT "D2 = ";
910 IF (DataByte AND 4) = 4 THEN PRINT "HIGH" ELSE PRINT "LOW "
912 PRINT "D3 = ";
914 IF (DataByte AND 8) = 8 THEN PRINT "HIGH" ELSE PRINT "LOW "
916 PRINT "D4 = ";
918 IF (DataByte AND 16) = 16 THEN PRINT "HIGH" ELSE PRINT "LOW "
920 PRINT "D5 = ";
922 IF (DataByte AND 32) = 32 THEN PRINT "HIGH" ELSE PRINT "LOW "
924 PRINT "D6 = ";
926 IF (DataByte AND 64) = 64 THEN PRINT "HIGH" ELSE PRINT "LOW "
928 PRINT "D7 = ";
930 IF (DataByte AND 128) = 128 THEN PRINT "HIGH" ELSE PRINT "LOW "
932 RETURN: REM   end of subroutine, display data
934 SYSTEM
```

Pascal Source Code Listing

```
PROGRAM Sw_In;   { basic switch input }
{
   input BUSY, ACK, PAPER END, INPUT, STROBE, AUTO FEED, ERROR,
   and SELECT INPUT signals from IBM type parallel printer port.

   written in Turbo Pascal 6.0
}
USES CRT;

VAR   Base, Base_Address                    : INTEGER;
      Data_Byte, High_Nibble, Low_Nibble, OffSet : BYTE;

PROCEDURE Read_Switches(VAR Data_Byte : BYTE);

VAR High_Nibble, Low_Nibble : BYTE;

BEGIN { read switches }
{ first set all open collector output pins HIGH to read from base + 2        }
Port[Base + 2] := Port[Base_Address + 2] OR 15;
delay(50);
Low_Nibble :=  Port[Base + 2];
High_Nibble := Port[Base + 1];
Low_Nibble := Low_Nibble AND $0F;         { $0F = 00001111                   }
High_Nibble := High_Nibble AND $F0;       { $F0 = 11110000                   }
Data_Byte := High_Nibble OR Low_Nibble;
END;  { read switches  }

PROCEDURE Display_Data(Data_Byte : BYTE);
{
   display the bytes value and condition of each bit, HIGH or LOW
}
```

```
BEGIN
GoToXY(1,3); WRITELN('Base Address = ',Base, ';    Data Byte = ',Data_Byte:4);
WRITELN;
WRITE('D0 = '); IF (Data_Byte AND      1) =   1 THEN   { 00000001 }
  WRITELN('HIGH') ELSE WRITELN('LOW ');
WRITE('D1 = '); IF (Data_Byte AND      2) =   2 THEN   { 00000010 }
  WRITELN('HIGH') ELSE WRITELN('LOW ');
WRITE('D2 = '); IF (Data_Byte AND      4) =   4 THEN   { 00000100 }
  WRITELN('HIGH') ELSE WRITELN('LOW ');
WRITE('D3 = '); IF (Data_Byte AND      8) =   8 THEN   { 00001000 }
  WRITELN('HIGH') ELSE WRITELN('LOW ');
WRITE('D4 = '); IF (Data_Byte AND     16) =  16 THEN   { 00010000 }
  WRITELN('HIGH') ELSE WRITELN('LOW ');
WRITE('D5 = '); IF (Data_Byte AND     32) =  32 THEN   { 00100000 }
  WRITELN('HIGH') ELSE WRITELN('LOW ');
WRITE('D6 = '); IF (Data_Byte AND     64) =  64 THEN   { 01000000 }
  WRITELN('HIGH') ELSE WRITELN('LOW ');
WRITE('D7 = '); IF (Data_Byte AND    128) = 128 THEN   { 10000000 }
  WRITELN('HIGH') ELSE WRITELN('LOW ');
END;


BEGIN { basic switch input }
ClrScr;
{ find base address of LPT1, use 10 for LPT2, and 12 for LPT3 }
Base_Address := 1024; OffSet := 8;
Base := MemW[0: Base_Address + OffSet]; { Get base address }
  REPEAT
  Read_Switches(Data_Byte);
  Display_Data(Data_Byte);
  UNTIL KeyPressed;
END. { basic switch input }
```

C Source Code Listing

```c
/*                        PROGRAM Sw_In   { basic switch input }
        Code conversion by Eugene Klein
 input BUSY, ACK, PAPER END, INPUT, STROBE, AUTO FEED, ERROR,
 and SELECT INPUT signals.
*/.

#include <dos.h>
#include <stdio.h>
#include <conio.h>
#include <stdlib.h>
#include <string.h>
#include <bios.h>
#include "My_TPU.h"

int LPT1, Base_Address;
unsigned char Data_Byte, High_Nibble, Low_Nibble;

unsigned char Read_Switches(void)
{
 unsigned char High_Nibble, Low_Nibble;
// set all open collector output pins HIGH so you can read from base + 2
 outport(Base_Address + 2,inport(Base_Address + 2) ||15);
```

```c
  delay(50);
  Low_Nibble =  inport(Base_Address + 2);
  High_Nibble = inport(Base_Address + 1);
  Low_Nibble = Low_Nibble & 0x0F;          // 0x0F = 00001111
  High_Nibble = High_Nibble & 0xF0;        // 0xF0 = 11110000
  Data_Byte = High_Nibble | Low_Nibble;
  return(Data_Byte);
}

void Display_Data(unsigned char Data_Byte)
{
  gotoxy(1,3); printf("LPT1 = %i     Data Byte = %i \n",LPT1,Data_Byte);
}

void main()
{
  clrscr();
  Base_Address = 1024; LPT1 = peek(0, Base_Address + 8); // find base address
  do
  {
   Data_Byte=Read_Switches();
   Display_Data(Data_Byte);
  }while(!kbhit());
}
```

A Hardware-Activated TSR

Circuit Theory

Borland's popular "SideKick" software package and the Print-Screen key on your PC are examples of *terminate and stay resident* (TSR) interrupt driven software. When you press a key, the computer stops whatever it was doing to run the new program. When you exit the TSR program, the original software continues from where it left off.

Here's how a TSR works. Your computer can only do one task at a time. Well, sort of. Inside your computer is a microprocessor that directs all computer-related operations. The microprocessor can not do all the work. Other dedicated computers complete individual tasks. The hard disk, floppy disk, video, and internal timing are all handled by separate single-chip computers. One of these dedicated computers is the 8259 interrupt handler. It continually polls all the computer's hardware. The 8259 tells the main microprocessor when a hardware interrupt line on some piece of hardware has been triggered. The computer then determines which piece of hardware was triggered and executes special software—already buried in memory—designed to go into action after the interrupt request.

Your computer's SHIFT/Print-Screen key combination is an interrupt driven program. No matter what your computer is doing, when you press the SHIFT/Print-Screen key combination, the computer stops whatever it is doing and runs a program that prints a screen dump. After the screen dump is completed, control is returned to the orginal program.

Borland's SideKick was one of the earliest commerical programs developed around a keyboard interrupt. When you press a "hot key," your program stops running the current program and puts the SideKick main menu in the middle of your display screen. From that menu, you can select a text editor, appointment calender, phone book, or ASCII look-up table. When you exit from SideKick, the interrupted software continues.

Hardware devices can also trigger a TSR interrupt. Borland's Turbo Pascal and Turbo C++ separate the programmer from most of the overhead. The ACK line, pin 10, on a parallel printer card, can be used to create a processor interrupt. Your software enables and disables interrupt operation.

A hardware controlled TSR can be very useful. I have a computer dedicated to operating 24 hours a day as a voice mail answering machine. However,

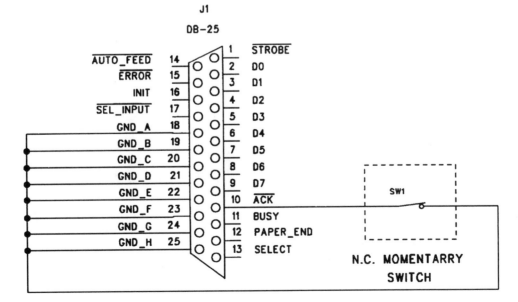

Figure 29

when anyone picks up a phone to call out, a simple circuit triggers a TSR. The TSR logs the phone number dialed along with the time and date.

A second hardware controlled TSR is connected to the same computer. It is triggered by the burglar alarm. When triggered, the commercial alarm calls the police and contacts the security service. In addition, it triggers a TSR on my computer. (Application 33 gives details on this alarm.)

Figure 29 illistrates the hardware interface. A switch is used to ground the ACK line, pin 10. After software has initilized the interrupt function, opening the normally closed switch will trigger the interrupt.

Note that the circuit uses a bounceless switch. If you are using a mechanical switch you must take steps to eliminate the bounce. For testing this software for publication, I simply shunted my microswitch with a 0.2 micofarad capacitor.

Software

Listing TSR_DEMO.PAS was written in Turbo Pascal. It is well documented and should be easy to read.

Grounding the printer port's ACK line will activate the interrupt. When activated, the interrupt driven TSR saves the current screen and replaces it with its own. When the ground is removed for the ACK line, the TSR restores the orginal screen and returns control to the orginal software. You can replace my screen display with your code.

The software lists several magizine articles and books which describe how to write a TSR. I have not found any definitive source. However, if you must choose one, look at "Mastering Turbo Pascal." I particularly enjoy Tom Swan's writings.

Pascal Source Code Listing

```
{$M 8000, 0, 10000}
{$N-,S-}
PROGRAM TSR_INTR;
{   This program will create a DEMO TSR HARDWARE INTERRUPT.            }
{   The Parallel Printer Port's ACK line, pin 10, can be set for       }
{      hardware interrupt operation.                                   }
{   Ref:1 "MICRO CORNUCOPIA,#38,Nov-Dec 1987"                          }
{      :2 "BYTE;Vol 10,Num 11, 'Inside the IBM PC's'"                  }
{      :3 "Mastering Turbo Pascal 4.0,second edition, Tom Swan"        }
{      :4 "Programmer's Guide to the IBM PC, Peter Norton"             }
{   The first working copy was finished at 2 pm, on Sept. 3, 1988.    }
USES DOS, CRT;
Const
  MaxWin = 5;
  Base = 888; {   BASE ADDRESS = 3BC HEX, 956 DECIMAL, Mono Card      }
              {   BASE ADDRESS = 378 HEX, 888 DECIMAL, CGA Card       }
              {   BASE ADDRESS = 278 HEX, 632 DECIMAL, 3ed Printer Port }
Type
  MaxStr = String[255];
  ScreenPtr = ^ScreenType;
  ScreenType = Record
     Pos : Array [1..80,1..25] of Record
       Ch :Char;
       At : Byte;
       End;
     CursX, CursY : Integer;
     End;
VAR
  Screen_2, Screen_1 : screenptr;
  Ch : Char;
  k, i, j, B, Int_Mask :INTEGER;
```

```pascal
PROCEDURE TSR_Code;
INTERRUPT;
 Var X, Y :integer;

Function Vidseg : Word;
{
  Is current video adapter a monochrome or color graphics adapter?  Video
  memory starts at a different address on the monochrome graphics adapter
}
  Begin { vidseg }
  IF Mem[$0000:$0449] = 7 THEN VidSeg := $B000 ELSE VidSeg := $B800;
  End; { VidSeg }

Begin  { TSR code, this section stays resident in memory }
X := WhereX; Y := WhereY;
Screen_2^.CursX := WhereX; Screen_2^.CursY := WhereY;
Screen_2 := Ptr(Vidseg,$0000);
screen_1^ := screen_2^;
clrscr;
gotoxy(1,3);
writeln('       Éffffffffffffffffffffffffffffffffffffffffffffffffffffffffffffffffffffffff»');
writeln('       º       TSR ON       TSR ON       TSR ON       TSR ON       º');
writeln('       º                                                           º');
writeln('       º  TSR ON       TSR ON       TSR ON       TSR ON            º');
writeln('       º                                                           º');
writeln('       º       TSR ON       TSR ON       TSR ON       TSR ON       º');
writeln('       º                                                           º');
writeln('       º  TSR ON       TSR ON       TSR ON       TSR ON            º');
writeln('       º                                                           º');
writeln('       º       TSR ON       TSR ON       TSR ON       TSR ON       º');
writeln('       º                                                           º');
writeln('       º  TSR ON       TSR ON       TSR ON       TSR ON            º');
writeln('       º                                                           º');
writeln('       º       TSR ON       TSR ON       TSR ON       TSR ON       º');
writeln('       º                                                           º');
writeln('       º  TSR ON       TSR ON       TSR ON       TSR ON            º');
writeln('       º                                                           º');
writeln('       º       TSR ON       TSR ON       TSR ON       TSR ON       º');
writeln('       º                                                           º');
writeln('       º  TSR ON       TSR ON       TSR ON       TSR ON            º');
writeln('       º                                                           º');
writeln('       Èffffffffffffffffffffffffffffffffffffffffffffffffffffffffffffffffffffffff_');

   REPEAT                        {       ___                                     }
   k := PORT[base + 1];          { Repeat until ACK is high again                }
   UNTIL (k and 64) <> 0;
screen_2^ := screen_1^;
gotoxy(X,Y);
B := PORT[base + 2];
B := (B OR 16);
PORT[base + 2] := B;
Port[$0020] := $20;             { Nonspecific End Of Interrupt to                }
END; { TSR code }

BEGIN { main, TSR intr }
SetIntVec( $0F, @TSR_CODE);    { set interrupt vector 15 to TSR_Code             }
```

```
B := PORT[base + 2];          { set printer card to accept Interrupts      }
B := (B OR 16);
PORT[base + 2] := B;          { To enable the interrupt on the printer card   }
Int_Mask    := PORT[33] AND 127;
PORT[33] := Int_Mask;         { To enable the interrupt in the  8259 PIC    }
writeln(' -=[ INTERRUPT INSTALLED ]=- , Paul Bergsman, and Mike Mensch');
New(Screen_1);  New(Screen_2);
KEEP( 0 );                    { install TSR                               }
END. { main, TSR intr }
```

Reflective Object Sensor

Circuit Theory

The OPB708 is a reflective photo-microsensor device known as an *optocoupler* or *optoisolator*. It consists of an LED and phototransistor in a single package, and will produce an output voltage when it detects a reflection of some of its light output. This makes it ideal for detecting the presence of nearby reflective objects. Figure 30-A shows a simple circuit using the OPB708. The 50K potentiometer, R3, is adjusted for the desired level of sensitivity to reflective surfaces. However, there may be situations where you need to boost the output level of the OPB708. Figure 30-B shows a circuit that will allow you to do that. Potentiometer R7, a 500K device, is used to set the level of hysteresis in the stage built around the LM311 voltage comparator.

Software

The circuits in Figures 30-A and 30-B can be used with the program listings SW_IN.BAS, SW_IN.PAS, and SW_IN.C which are given with Application 28.

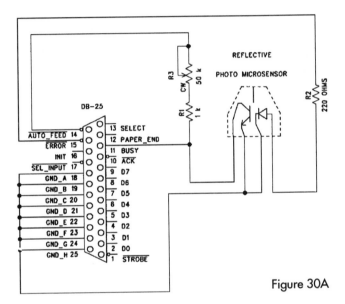

Figure 30A

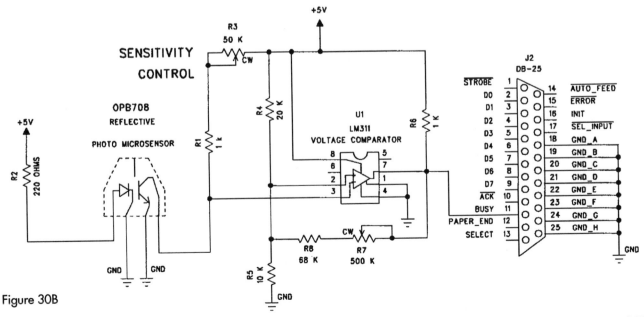

Figure 30B

Controlling Large Loads
with a Reflective Sensor

Circuit Theory

The OPB708 reflective microsensor device introduced in Application 30 can be part of a more elaborate circuit to control large loads through the printer parallel port. Figure 31 shows such an application. Data from the OPB708 is input to the computer through a parallel printer port, and, based on that information, some output device is manipulated.

The blender in Figure 31 represents any large power hungry load. It could be a conveyor belt, garage door opener, robotic arm, toaster oven, etc. The solid state relay permits a large electrical load to be safely controlled by your computer's relatively frail TTL logic.

The reflective microsensor could be replaced by other real-world sensing devices. In this application, it could be used for counting objects passing an observation point, responding to a person's arm movement, etc. Resistor R4, the 50K potentiometer, is used to set the sensitivity level of the OPB708 reflective microsensor.

Software

Listings IO_BASIC.BAS, IO_BASIC.PAS, and IO_BASIC.C can be used to control the circuit in Figure 31.

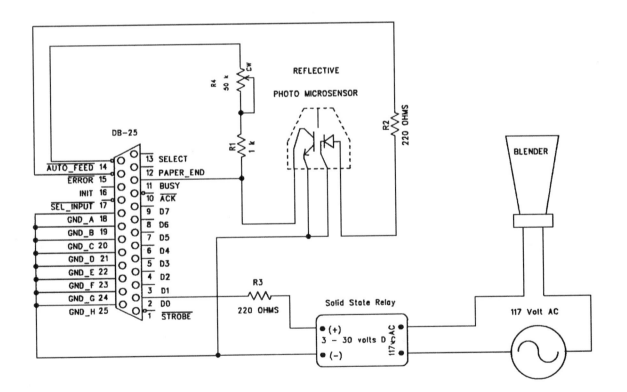

Figure 31

BASIC Source Code Listing

```
100 REM   FILE: IO_BASIC.BAS,  WRITTEN IN QBASIC
110 REM
120 REM   Demonstrate basic concept of computer I/O
130 REM
140 REM   When sensor data bit, D6, is high, turn blender on,  when
150 REM   sensor data bit, D6, is low, turn blender off.
160 D7 = 128
170 PortAddress = &H378: REM = CGA printer port base address,
180 REM                      use 956 for MGA, and 632 for 3rd printer port.
190 REM
200 OUT PortAddress, 1
210 IF INKEY$ <> "" THEN STOP
220 IF (INP(PortAddress + 1) AND D7) = D7 THEN OUT PortAddress, 0 ELSE GOTO 210
240 IF INKEY$ <> "" THEN STOP
250 IF (INP(PortAddress + 1) AND D7) = 0 THEN OUT PortAddress, 1 ELSE GOTO 240
260 GOTO 210
270 END
```

Pascal Source Code Listing

```
PROGRAM Io_Basic; {  FILE: IO_BASIC.PAS,  WRITTEN IN Turbo Pascal 6.0 }
USES CRT;
{
        Demonstrate basic concept of computer I/O

        When sensor data bit, D6, is high, turn blender on,  when
        sensor data bit, D6, is low, turn blender off.
}
CONST              D7 = 128;
      LptPortAddress = 888; { = CGA printer port base address,
                        { use 956 for MGA, and 632 for 3rd printer port.}
BEGIN

PORT[LptPortAddress] := 1;
REPEAT
 REPEAT
 IF KEYPRESSED THEN EXIT;
 IF PORT[LptPortAddress + 1] AND D7 = D7 THEN PORT[LptPortAddress] := 0
 UNTIL PORT[LptPortAddress + 1] AND D7 = D7;
 REPEAT
 IF KEYPRESSED THEN EXIT;
 IF PORT[LptPortAddress + 1] AND D7 = 0 THEN PORT[LptPortAddress] := 1
 UNTIL PORT[LptPortAddress + 1] AND D7 = 0;
UNTIL KEYPRESSED;
END.
```

C Source Code Listing

```
/*                          PROGRAM IO_Basic
                   Code converted by Eugene Klein


        Demonstrate basic concept of computer I/O

        When sensor data bit, D6, is high, turn blender on,  when
        sensor data bit, D6, is low, turn blender off.
*/

#include <dos.h>
#include <stdio.h>
#include <conio.h>
#include <stdlib.h>
#include <string.h>
#include <bios.h>
#include "My_TPU.h"

const int D7 = 128;
int LptPortAddress,Lpt_Num;

void main()
{
 Lpt_Num = Select_Printer_Port();
 LptPortAddress = Init_Printer_Port(Lpt_Num);
 clrscr();
 outport(LptPortAddress,1);
 do
 {
  if(kbhit())
    exit(0);
  if(inport(LptPortAddress + 1) && D7 == D7);
    outport(LptPortAddress,0);
 }while(LptPortAddress + 1 && D7 == D7);
 do
 {
  if(kbhit())
     exit(0);
  if(inport(LptPortAddress + 1) && D7 == 0);
    outport(LptPortAddress,1);
 }while(inport(LptPortAddress + 1) && D7 == 0);
 }
```

Input from Optoelectronics Devices

Circuit Theory

Optoelectronics devices, such as photodiodes and phototransistors, can be used as sensors to provide data to your PC. A *photodiode* is a solid state device in which light is allowed to strike an exposed PN junction, resulting in the generation of electron-hole pairs. The greater the intensity of light hitting the photodiode's PN junction, the greater the diode current. A *phototransistor* operates in a similar fashion, but can amplify the current generated by the light.

Figure 32-A shows an application of a MF0D71 photodiode. The 20K potentiometer, R5, sets the sensitivity of the photodiode. Figure 32-B shows an application of a MF0D72 phototransistor. Both of these circuits have TTL-level outputs. Figure 32-C shows how to use the OPB-816 slotted optical switch.

Software

The circuits in Figures 32-A and 32-C can be used with the program listings SW_IN.BAS, SW_IN.PAS, and SW_IN.C which are given with Application 28.

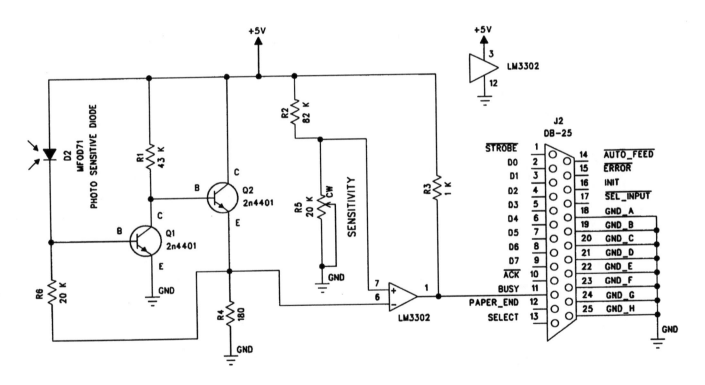

Figure 32-A

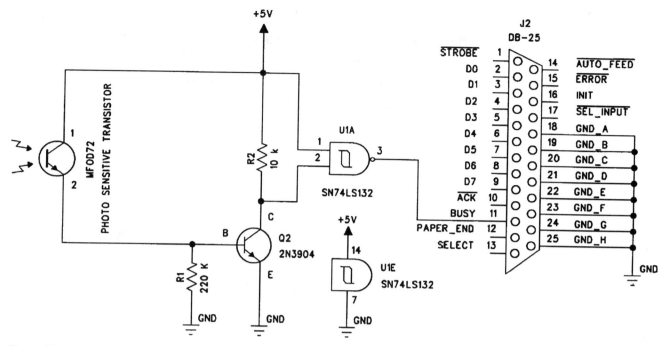

Figure 32-B

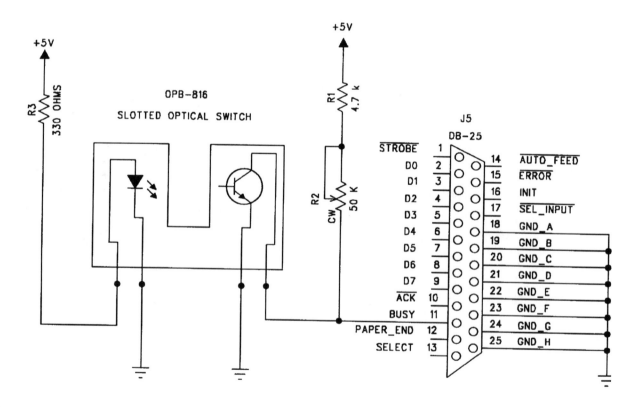

Figure 32-C

Using an Eddy Current Proximity Switch for Input

Circuit Theory

Every conductor that carries alternating current or any varying magnetic field will produce *eddy currents* in adjacent conductors. These eddy currents will circulate in the conductor and are a source of power loss in transformers and high frequency circuits. However, eddy currents also allow us to detect the presence of nearby metallic conductors (copper, iron, aluminum, etc.). Figure 33 shows a metal proximity detector based on a PE16 eddy current proximity switch from Gordon Products. The PE16 will detect the presence of eddy currents set up in nearby conductors; all necessary sensing, filtering, and output driver circuits are contained in the PE16 module housing.

Software

The circuit in Figure 33 can be used with the program listings SW_IN.BAS, SW_IN.PAS, and SW_IN.C which are given with Application 28.

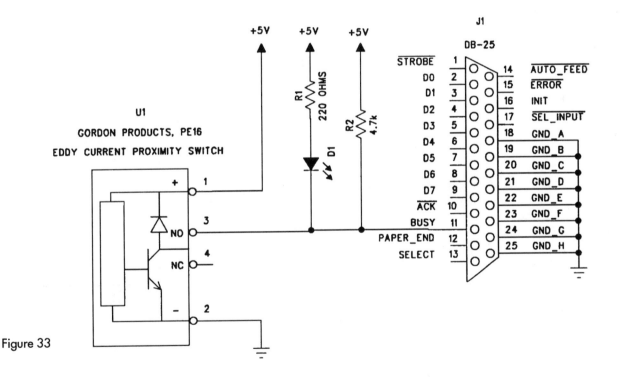

Figure 33

Using Hall Effect Devices

Circuit Theory

A Hall effect sensor is one that will respond to the presence of a magnetic field. The ULN3113 Hall effect switch shown in Figure 34-A will have a low logic output in the presence of a magnetic field. When the magnetic field is removed, the ULN3113's output will return to high. The UGN3175 latching Hall effect switch shown in Figure 34-B will "trip" to a low logic output will in the presence of the field of a north magnetic pole. The output will remain low until it detects the presence of a south pole magnetic field, at which point the output will reset to high and remain so until a north magnetic pole field is detected.

Software

The circuits 34-A and 34-B can be used with the program listings SW_IN.BAS, SW_IN.PAS, and SW_IN.C which are given with Application 28.

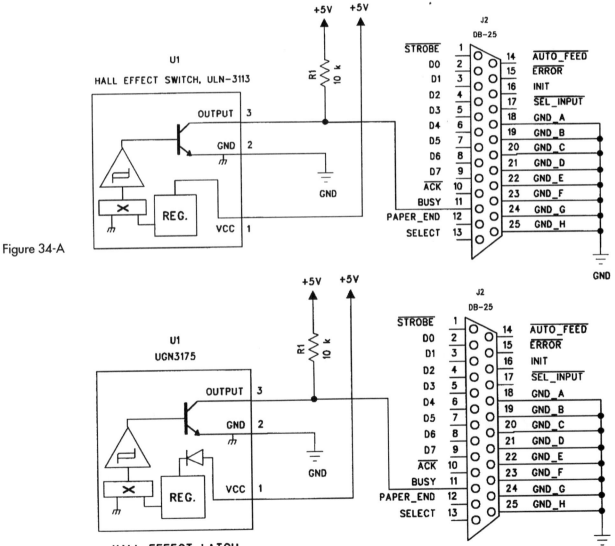

Figure 34-A

Figure 34-B   HALL EFFECT LATCH

Detecting Fluids and Moisture

Circuit Theory

The ULN-2429A device was originally designed to monitor a car radiator's coolant level. It contains all necessary oscillator, current detection, and filtering circuitry in a single package. When a complete AC current path is detected between pins 6 and 9, the output of the ULN-2429A is turned on. The chip can detect many liquids, including soap, as well as high levels of moisture. The IL74 optocoupler is used to interface the ULN-2429's 12 volt supply with the printer port's TTL logic.

Software

The circuit in Figure 35 can be used with the program listings SW_IN.BAS, SW_IN.PAS, and SW_IN.C which are given with Application 28.

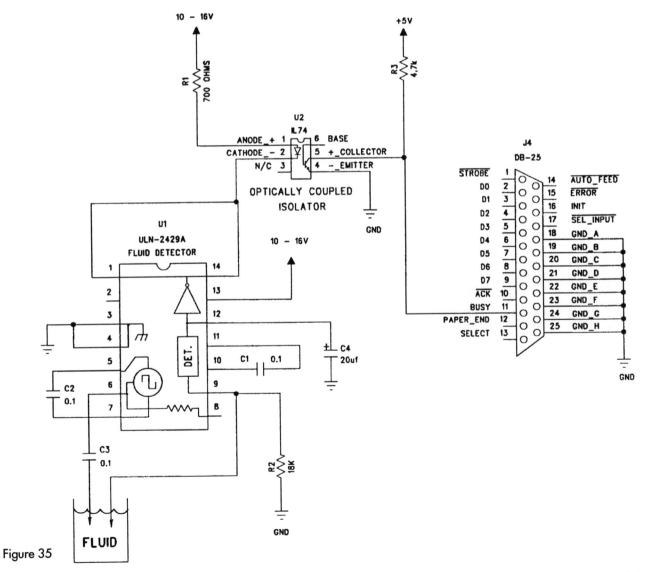

Figure 35

"Bounceless" Mechanical Key Input

Circuit Theory

Suppose you are constructing a science fair, trade show, or museum exhibit that requires user input to a computer. You include a keyboard as part of the display. However, the keyboard will be under constant assault. Users will drop things, spill drinks, or even "borrow" the keyboard. You could encase the keyboard in wood, place a clear plastic lid on the top, and drill access holes over the required keys, but this is costly, unsightly, and will still leave the keyboard susceptible to the same abuses cited above.

A better solution is to eliminate the computer keyboard and replace it with switches designed to accept constant abuse. They could be interfaced to your computer through the parallel printer port. However, all mechanical switches have "bounce." This is the tendency for a switch to send multiple signals to the keyboard decoder due to vibration and flexing of the switch when contact is made or broken. Even though the switch is activated only once, the decoder will interpret multiple signals. If you are inputting data from only one or two mechanical switches, you can hard-wire a separate debounce circuit for each switch. However, if you need to input data from a dozen switches, the circuitry can become an albatross.

The MM74C922 can monitor up to 16 normally open momentary switches (32 with the addition of a transistor and two resistors). If any switch is closed, the chip places binary data on its output lines Da, Db, Dc and Dd and then toggles the DATA AVAILABLE strobe line, pin 12. The DATA AVAILABLE line will remain at active high until the mechanical switch is released. Internal circuitry of the MM74C922 filters out mechanical bounce from all the switches.

The MM74C922 is a CMOS IC chip. However, all outputs are designed to directly drive up to two standard TTL loads. That means that no extra IC chips must be added to interface the MM74C922 CMOS logic with the printer port's TTL logic input lines.

In the circuit shown in Figure 36, 16 mechanical switches, arranged in a 4x4 matrix, are wired to the MM74C922's input lines. Each time a switch is closed, the MM74C922 outputs a binary number from 0 to 15 on its data lines Da, Db, Dc, and Dd. C1 and C2 provide a time delay for the chip's internal debounce circuitry. You can play with C1 and C2 values to fine tune the response time. However, data manual specs insist that C1's value must always be ten times that of C2.

The DATA AVAILABLE line provides a strobe signal to tell the computer that data is ready for reading. Transistor Q1 inverts the DATA AVAILABLE's active high logic to an active low. The inverted strobe signal is fed to the MM74C922's Output Enable line, OE. When the OE line goes LOW, data will appear at the Da, Db, Dc, and Dd Data Output pins.

The inverted OE control signal is also wired to the printer port's ACK line as an inactive high. The ACK line is brought to an active low while any switch is closed.

Software

Listings MM74C922.BAS, MM74C922.PAS, and MM74C922.C illustrate how to input debounced switch data using the MM74C922 IC chip. The software does the following:

- waits until the printer port's ACK line goes low.
- when ACK line is low, reads in and displays the data
- waits until the ACK line returns to an inactive high logic level
- erases the displayed value
- repeats the process until any keyboard key is pressed

The MM74C922 outputs a binary number between 0 and 15. Since the data is received by printer port data bit lines D7. D5, D4, and D3, software transfers the data to bits D3, D2, D1, and D0. Thus, the displayed byte is a restored number between 0 and 15.

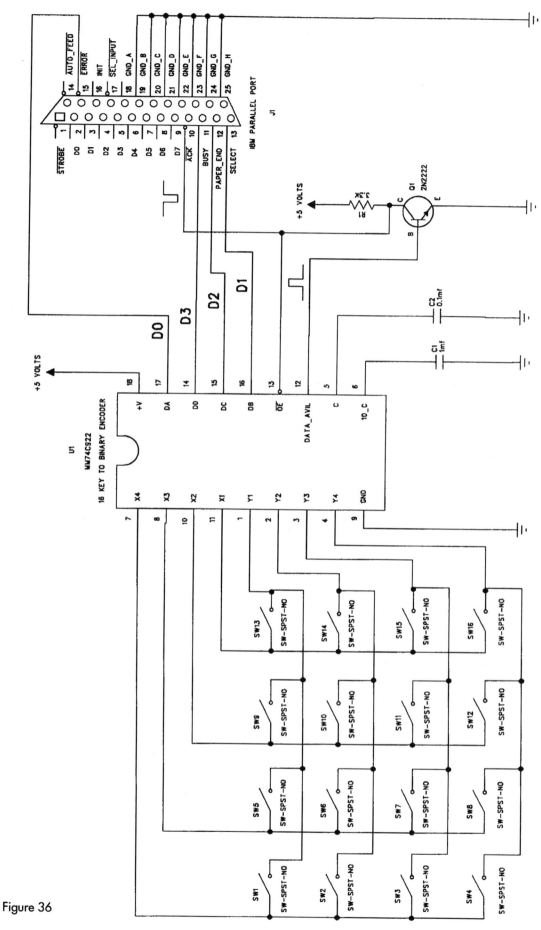

Figure 36

BASIC Source Code Listing

```
100 REM FILE: MM74C922.BAS,      WRITTEN IN QBASIC
102 REM
110 REM Inputs 4 bit data from National's MM74C922 matrix key pad encoder
120 REM via standard Centronics Parallel Printer Port. Output from the
130 REM '922 is read into the parallel port's ( Base Address + 1 ).  D6
140 REM of the (Base Address + 1), ACK, is used to input the '922 strobe
150 REM signal.  When D6 goes to an active LOW, the new byte value is
160 REM displayed on the screen.
162 REM
164 REM Since data is comming in on printer port data bits D3, D4, D5, and D7,
166 REM data is reformated to output numbers between 0 and 15
168
180 INPUTBITS = 0: LptPortAddress = 0
190 LptPortAddress = 888: REM  base address of Graphic Card's printer port
200 REM                              use 632 for 3ed printer port base address
210 REM                              and 956 for Monochrome Card's printer port
220 CLS
230 LOCATE 10, 1: PRINT "Inputs = ";
240 REM
245 D6 = 64
260    INPUTBITS = INP(LptPortAddress + 1)
270    IF (INPUTBITS AND D6) <> 0 THEN 330
290    LOCATE 10, 10
292    INPUTBITS = INPUTBITS XOR 128: REM 10000000 invert the inverted bit
294    IF (INPUTBITS AND 128) <> 128 THEN GOTO 297:  REM format for 0-15 out
296        INPUTBITS = ((INPUTBITS - 128) * 2) + 128: GOTO 298
297        INPUTBITS = INPUTBITS * 2
298    INPUTBITS = INPUTBITS \ 16
300    PRINT INPUTBITS; : PRINT "    ";
310    IF (INP(LptPortAddress + 1) AND D6) = 0 THEN GOTO 310
320    LOCATE 10, 10: PRINT "       ";
330    IF INKEY$ = "" THEN GOTO 260: REM   press any key to exit
340 END
```

Pascal Source Code Listing

```
Program MM74C922;
{
 Inputs 4 bit data from National's MM74C922 matrix key-pad encoder via
 standard Centronics Parallel Printer Port. Output from the '922 is read
 into the parallel port's ( Base Address + 1 ).  D6 of the (Base Address + 1),
 the ACK line, is used to input the '922's strobe signal.  When D6 goes to an
 active LOW, the new value is displayed on the screen.

 Since data is comming in on printer port data lines D7, D5, D4, and D3,
 the data is reformated to ouput numbers between 0 and 15
}

USES CRT;
CONST D6 = 64;
VAR        Input_Bits : BYTE;
     Lpt_Port_Address : WORD;

BEGIN { main }
Lpt_Port_Address := 888; { 632 = IBM's 3ed parallel port address        }
                         { use 888 for Graphics Card's printer port,    }
```

```
                  { and 956 for Monochrome Card's printer port              }
ClrScr;
gotoxy(1,10); write('Inputs = ');
  REPEAT
   Input_Bits := PORT[Lpt_Port_Address + 1]; { read Base + 1 data bits      }
   IF Input_Bits AND D6 = 0 THEN              { is there new data to display? }
     BEGIN  { reformat data bits D7, D5, D4, and D3, to D7, D6, D5, and D4   }
     Input_Bits := Input_Bits XOR 128;        { invert inverted bit, D7       }
     If (Input_Bits AND 128) = 128            { format data in high nibble     }
       THEN Input_Bits := (Input_Bits SHL 1) + 128
         ELSE Input_Bits := Input_Bits SHL 1;
     Input_Bits := Input_Bits SHR 4; { shift data to low nibble, D3, D2, D1, D0 }
     GOTOXY(10,10);                           { display new data              }
     WRITE(Input_Bits:3);
     REPEAT UNTIL (PORT[Lpt_Port_Address + 1] AND D6) = D6;  { switch released? }
     GOTOXY(10,10); WRITE('    ');             { clear data display            }
     END; { if }
  UNTIL KEYPRESSED;                            { press any key to exit         }
END.  { main }
```

C Source Code Listing

```c
/*
                        Program MM74C922
            Code conversion by Eugene Klein
   Inputs 4 bit data from National's MM74C922 matrix key pad encoder via standard
   Centronics Parallel Printer Port. Output from the '922 is read into the
   parallel port's ( Base Address + 1 ).  D7 of the ( Base Address + 1 ) is
   used to input the '922 strobe signal, DATA_AVIL.  When D7 goes to an active
   LOW, the byte value is displayed on the screen.
*/


#include <dos.h>
#include <stdio.h>
#include <conio.h>
#include <stdlib.h>
#include <string.h>
#include <bios.h>
#include "My_TPU.h"

const int D7 = 127;
unsigned char Inputs;
unsigned int LPTx, Lpt_Num;

void main()
{
 Lpt_Num = Select_Printer_Port();
 LPTx = Init_Printer_Port(Lpt_Num);
 clrscr();
 gotoxy(10,10); printf("Inputs = ");
 do
 {
  Inputs = inport(LPTx + 1);    // read bit's status
  if(Inputs != D7)
  {
   gotoxy(20,10);
   printf("%3i",Inputs);
  }
 }while(!kbhit());
}
```

Converting DTMF Tones to Binary

Circuit Theory

Dual tone multifrequency (DTMF) tones are the tone signals used for telephone dialing and switching. DTMF is also used for myriads of other communication applications. You can access data from a remote location over a twisted pair or DTMF tone signals can be transmitted through an inexpensive FM transmitter and decoded at a remote location using a matching FM receiver. I have used this method to control a small robotic vehicle from my computer.

In the past, you had to construct a separate circuit to decode each tone, but no more. Several companies manufacture dedicated IC chips designed to decode, filter, and convert DTMF tone signals to a binary number. Basically, you plug audio containing the DTMF tones in one end and get a binary number out the other. The IC does all the work.

Figure 37 illustrates how a decoded DTMF signal interfaces to an IBM type parallel printer port. The M8870's inactive high SI line, at pin 15, will go to active low each time a DTMF signal has been de-coded. The SI line is wired to the printer port's ACK line at pin 10. The computer waits for the ACK line to go to an active high. When it does, the DTMF conversion is read at the parallel printer port's ERROR, SELECT, PAPER-END, and BUSY LINES as a binary number between Ø and 16.

The M8870 is a CMOS IC chip. Six sections of a 4049 inverter/buffer are used to interface the CMOS M8870's output signals to the printer port's TTL logic levels.

Software

Listings MM74C922.PAS, MM74C922.C, and MM74C922.BAS used in Application 36 to input matrix keyboard data will work equally well for this circuit. Both circuits transmit a binary number to the parallel printer port and use the same data bits for data transfer. For both circuits, running these listings will display a byte of data whenever the ACK line is at an active high logic level.

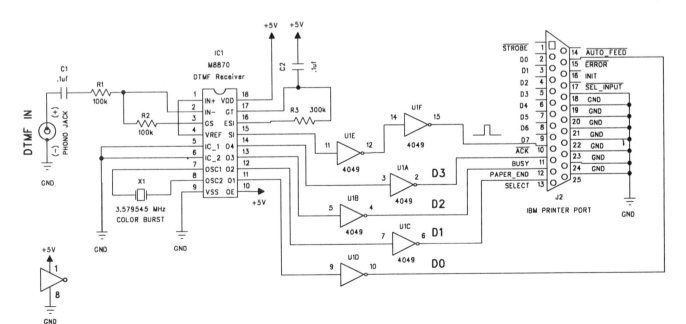

Figure 37

Controlling a Burglar Alarm System Through a Parallel Port

Circuit Theory

In my youth, I worked several years for two large central station burglar alarm companies. I quickly learned that there was more to installing a burglar alarm protective loop than simply running a series loop. Professionals follow strict guidelines.

Underwriters Laboratories (UL) sets the standards. Most people are familiar with the tests UL runs on household electrical equipment. If the equipment is electrically safe, will not electrocute you, or contribute to an electrical fire, then it gets a UL Listed "seal of approval." As their name implies, Underwriters Laboratories had its origins in the insurance industry, as insurance companies wanted to determine how safe various products were and minimize their risks. The insurance industry still depends on UL tests. If your home suffered fire damage and the cause could be traced back to non-UL listed electrical equipment, you might have real trouble collecting from your homeowner's policy.

However, Underwriters Laboratory also tests items related to other types of insurance and establishes standards. UL has also developed a list of guidelines on how a burglar alarm should be wired. Though the guidelines for burglar alarm system installation were developed for commercial buildings, the same techniques can be used when wiring you own home. In my youth, I spent over two years wiring UL-approved protective circuits. The actual equipment used in protective circuits may change, but the basic concepts do not. The following material describes how to wire a burglar alarm meeting UL's standards for a CLASS A supervised protective alarm circuit. You might want to check with the insurance company you have your homeowner's policy with to see whether you qualify for a discount or other special consideration in your coverage for having such an alarm installed.

What is the purpose of a burglar alarm? A burglar alarm is designed to sound an alarm if an intruder enters your home. If your home is being burglarized, then—by definition—you are not home. An alarm

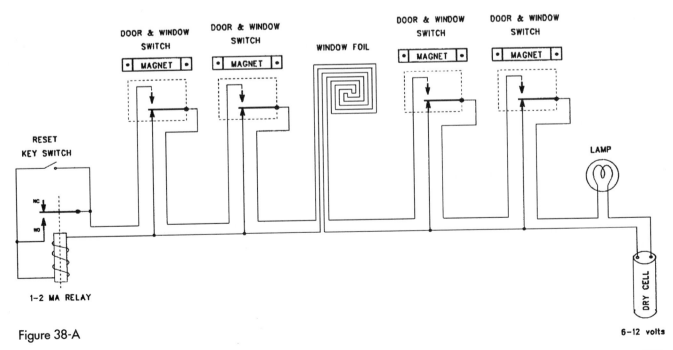

Figure 38-A

6–12 volts

device that is triggered while you are in your home is called a *hold-up* alarm. My home has a burglar alarm. It is a robotics security guard watching my home while I am away, not while I sleep. The following material explains how you can design a quality burglar alarm system for your home.

A burglar alarm's protective circuit should trigger an alarm if any part of the *protective loop* has been compromised. Figure 38-A shows the basic circuit. For now, let's assume the relay is energized. The circuit is not as trivial as it first appears. The battery at one end of the loop is in series with every sensor. A very sensitive mechanical relay is at the other end of the protective loop. If any wire in the protective loop is shorted or cut, the relay will default to an unenergized state. Reconnecting the wires or removing the short will not restore the relay to an energized state. A contact on the relay can trigger an alarm, and the only way to reset the system is to manually reset the relay.

Rather than draw a wiring diagram for each building, I always started wiring a room at the main entrance and then proceeded clockwise around the room. This procedure can save you a lot of time when you have to track down a fault in the protective loop.

The magnetic switches are used on doors and sliding windows. The magnetic switches have two parts. The switch has an internal spring holding it in one position. The magnet is installed to pull the switch away from the spring. When a door or window is opened, the magnet moves away from the switch and the spring pulls the switch to its normally closed (NC) position. As long as the magnet is close, the switch is part of the series loop. If the magnet moves away, the switch position flips, shorting the battery, and depriving the relay of current.

Any good motion detector, light beam, or infrared detector will come with a SPDT (single pole double throw) switch. You can easily integrate that switch into the protective circuit by using the same wiring methods used for a magnetic switch.

Sometimes you must use foil to protect a window or glass door panel. If the window pane breaks, the foil should tear, breaking the protective loop. I don't like foil. The cheap kind is relatively thick and has a sticky backing. I have seen broken windows held together by cheap foil WITHOUT BREAKING THE PROTECTIVE CIRCUIT! Good foil is very thin and has no sticky backing. With tailor's chalk, you lay a line on the glass. Using a very fine artist's brush, you paint the line with a very thin coat of varnish. Then, when the varnish gets tacky, lay the foil on top. Finally, with a wide artist brush coat the foil with clear high gloss varnish. The varnish forms an almost invisible protective coating for the foil. Regardless of how big the picture window is, the foil should be laid in one continuous piece. The hardest protective circuit fault to detect is patched foil.

I suggest that outside windows not be part of the protective loop. If you are away, and your neighbor's son hits a baseball through your picture window, the alarm will be triggered without anyone having ever gained access! In my township, you pay a fine for every false alarm. Window foil can end up costing you plenty. I want a protective circuit that will only be activated after an intruder has gained access to my home. One motion detector, properly placed, can cover an entire room. One light beam, deflected with mirrors, can blanket a whole floor with protection. Both work AFTER an intruder has gained access to your home.

The first thing a burglar does when he enters your home is look for an escape route. He will quickly walk through every room looking for avenues of quick exit. THEN he goes back and starts filling his backpack with your belongings. Knowing how a thief operates, my favorite defense is floor mats. Floor mats are often sold in rolls three feet wide and 50 feet long. A wire runs down each outside edge. You cut the mat to the desired length and place it under a carpet or area rug. Stepping on the mat shorts the wires. Alarm mats are like doorbells; they only work when they're supposed to. Your doorbell won't operate unless a human finger pushes on the face plate. A floor mat will not short its two edge wires unless the mat is walked on. Like other good alarm sensors, shorting or cutting a wire triggers the alarm. Mats placed in the second floor hallway and the first floor foyer might be all that is needed to protect your entire home!

The lamp in the protective loop serves two purposes. First, it acts as a current limiting device. If a short occurs in the protective loop, the lamp will brightly light while limiting the battery's current drain. Therefore, if the relay will not energize and the lamp is lit, you know you have a short circuit and can start looking for an open magnetic switch.

In practice, the relay and battery are both housed in the same enclosure. Usually the enclosure is metal and requires a key to open. Figure 38-B shows the wiring scheme. Two wires are run to every sensor, then the two wires are brought back to the control box. In effect, you must run four wires throughout the protective loop: two feed and two return. DON'T TAKE SHORTCUTS. Four conductor wire is widely

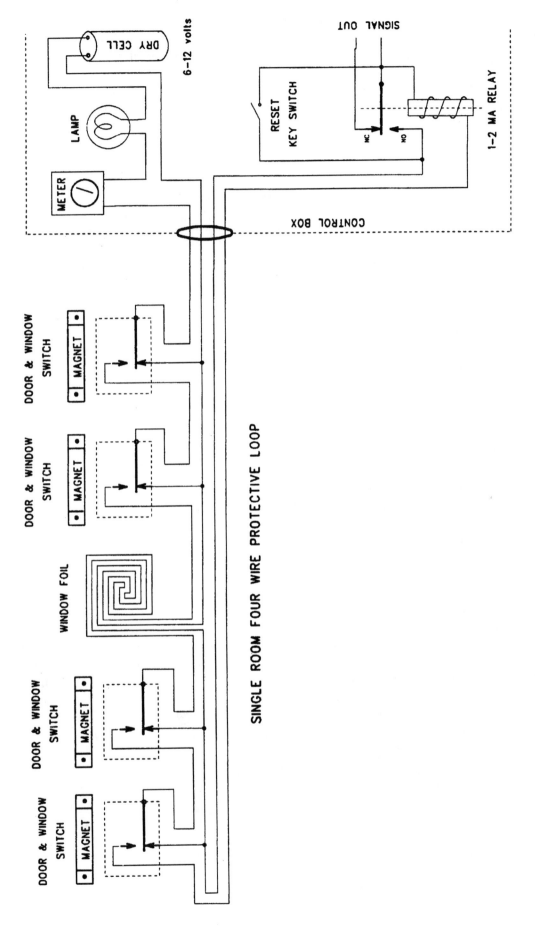

Figure 38-B

SINGLE ROOM FOUR WIRE PROTECTIVE LOOP

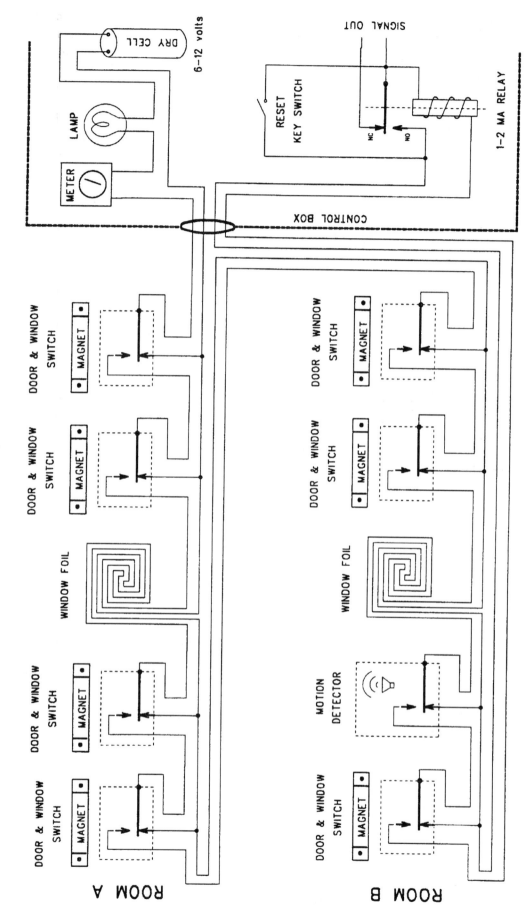

Figure 38-C

available and inexpensive. A would-be thief will find it hard to identify and defeat a four wire protective loop.

Several more items have been added to the control box. A switch is included to "set" the alarm. This might be a key switch on the frontof the enclosure, or a manual reset tab on the relay contacts.

A meter is in series with the battery. The meter gives you better information about a faulty protective loop. If the ammeter reads 0, then you have an open circuit (window foil may be cut). If the meter reads full scale, then you have a short circuit (a switch is not thrown, or the maid bumped the four conductor cable while cleaning, thereby crimping and shorting the wires). The meter should display the same current every day. If one day you observe an unusual reading, it might indicate a dirty contact or loose connection.

Figure 38-C illustrates how two or more rooms should be wired. Each room should be wired separately and then connected together. Note the motion detector included in one room's protective loop.

In my home, 12 sets of cables are routed to my alarm's control box. At the box, each cable is carefully labeled. The two returns from one cable are soldered to the two feeds of the next. I solder everything. When the system does not set up, I have a lot less places to consider for the cause.

Figure 38-D shows how to interface the burglar alarm's protective circuit to a computer. Relays generate back-EMF. You must protect your computer from possible damage. The safest method is to use an optocoupler. A second battery supplies current for the optocoupler's emitter LED. Q1 is wired as an inverter. The optocoupler's active high data bit is inverted by Q1. Q1's active low output is routed to the parallel printer port's ACK line at pin 10.

Software

Program listings UL_BA.BAS, UL_BA.C, and UL_BA.PAS demonstrate how your computer can monitor a burglar alarm system. The printer port's ACK line, pin 10, is held at an inactive low logic level by the burglar alarm interface. The software keeps reading the printer port's base + 2 data byte. When the ACK line moves from inactive low to active high, the "ALERT............" message is displayed. Replace the alert message with your software code.

The circut can activate a TSR hardware interrupt such as that described in Application 29. The interrupt is activated when the ACK line's logic goes from inactive low to active high.

Installing a hardware interrupt TSR will free your computer to do other things but jump into action

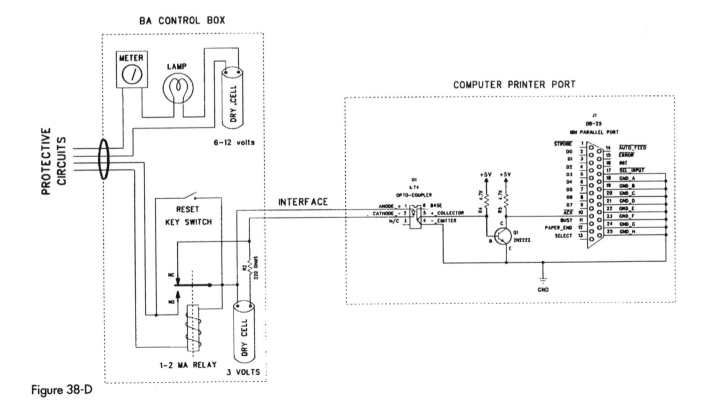

Figure 38-D

when an alarm condition develops. Since the ACK line is also the pin used by the printer port for hardware interrupts, no hardware modifications are needed when adding TSR software code. Refer to Application 29 for software details..

All the hallway lights in my three story house use "X10" controllers, similar to the ones sold by Radio Shack and Heathkit. The computer controls an X-10 computer/module controller from the serial port. The computer is also interfaced to my home's six station wireless intercom. A TSR is activated by a burglar alarm interfaced to the printer port. When activated, the computer flashes all the hallway lights and repeatedly "speaks" through my home's six station wireless intercom saying; " ALERT, ALERT, AN INTRUDER IS IN THE HOUSE. POLICE AND ALARM SERVICE HAVE BEEN NOTIFIED." Oh yes, my outdoor floodlights are also X10-controlled. If your were an intruder and heard sirens wailing, voices yelling, and lights flashing, what would you do?

BASIC Source Code Listing

```
100  REM FILE: UL_BA.BAS
110  REM
120  REM  Wait for parallel printer port's ACK line, pin 10, at BASE + 1, to go
130  REM  to an active low, then run burglar alarm code.
140  REM
150  D6 = 64
160  InputBits = BYTE
170  LptPortAddress = WORD
180  REM
190  LptPortAddress = 888: REM 888 = Graphics Card's printer port,
200  REM                            use 632 for IBM's 3ed parallel port address
210  REM                            and 956 for Monochrome Card's printer port
220  REM
230  LOCATE 1, 10
240  PRINT "waiting for alarm condition     "
250  InputBits = PORT[LptPortAddress + 1]: REM   read Base + 1 data bits
260  IF Input_Bits AND D6 <> 0 THEN GOTO 360
270  REM BEGIN
280     CLS
290     LOCATE1, 10
300     PRINT " ALERT, ALARM CONDITION EXISTS";
310     PRINT(CHR$(7)); :PRINT(CHR$(7)); PRINT(CHR$(7));
320     IF (INP(LptPortAddress + 1) AND D6) <> D6 THEN GOTO 320
330     LOCATE 1, 12
340     PRINT "alarm condition cleared        "
350  IF INKEY$ = "" THEN GOTO 220: REM press any key to exit
360  END
```

Pascal Source Code Listing

```
Program UL_BA;
{
 Wait for parallel printer port's ACK line, pin 10, at BASE + 1, to go
 to an active low, then run burglar alarm code.
}
USES CRT;
CONST D6 = 64;
VAR        Input_Bits : BYTE;
     Lpt_Port_Address : WORD;
```

```
BEGIN { main }
Lpt_Port_Address := 888; { 888 = Graphics Card's printer port,              }
                         { use 632 for IBM's 3ed parallel port address      }
                         { and 956 for Monochrome Card's printer port       }
   REPEAT
   GOTOXY(1,10);
   WRITELN('waiting for alarm condition  ');
   Input_Bits := PORT[Lpt_Port_Address + 1]; { read Base + 1 data bits      }
   IF Input_Bits AND D6 = 0 THEN             { "D6 is at active low?        }
     BEGIN
     ClrScr;
     GoToXY(1,10);
     WRITELN(' ALERT, ALARM CONDITION EXISTS' );
     WRITE(CHAR(7)); WRITE(CHAR(7)); WRITE(CHAR(7));
     REPEAT UNTIL (PORT[Lpt_Port_Address + 1] AND D6) = D6;
     GOTOXY(1,12);
     WRITELN('alarm condition cleared        ');
     END; { if }
   UNTIL KEYPRESSED;                         { press any key to exit        }
END.  { main }
```

C Source Code Listing

```
/*                         Program UL_BA

Wait for parallel printer port's ACK line, pin 10, at BASE + 1, to go
to an active low, then run burglar alarm code.
*/

#include <dos.h>
#include <stdio.h>
#include <conio.h>
#include <stdlib.h>
#include <string.h>
#include <bios.h>
#include "My_TPU.h"

const int D6 = 64;
unsigned char Input_Bits;
unsigned int Lpt_Port_Address, Lpt_Num;

void main()
{
 Lpt_Num = Select_Printer_Port();
 Lpt_Port_Address = Init_Printer_Port(Lpt_Num);
 clrscr();
 do
 {
  gotoxy(1,10);
  printf("waiting for alarm condition  \n");
  Input_Bits = inport(Lpt_Port_Address + 1); // read Base + 1 data bits
  if((Input_Bits & D6) == 0)                 //D6 is at active low?
  {
```

```c
    clrscr();
    gotoxy(1,10);
    printf("ALERT, ALARM CONDITION EXISTS \n");
    printf("%c  %c  %c  ",7,7,7);
    while((inport(Lpt_Port_Address + 1) & D6) == D6);
    gotoxy(1,12);
    printf("alarm condition cleared         \n");
    }
}while(!kbhit());                         // press any key to exit                    }
}
```

Converting a Voltage to a Binary Value

Circuit Theory

The real world is analog—not digital. Things such as temperature, the speed of an object, weights, etc., are all measured in units that are essentially continuous and assume an infinite number of values. For a computer to monitor conditions in the real world, you need a device that can read an infinitely changing variable and convert the value to a binary number. Fortunately, most real world analog sensors are designed to output a voltage or resistance proportional to the sensor's status. This greatly simplifies our conversion task.

A true workhorse analog to digital converter (ADC) IC is the ADC-0804 from Analog Devices. It converts an analog voltage between 0 and 5 volts to a binary value between 0 and 255. With the addition of a few resistors, it can be transformed into a multi-range multimeter able to read voltage, current, and resistance.

Figure 39 shows an ADC-0804 interfaced to an IBM parallel printer port. The 10K resistor and 150 pF capacitor form an RC network used by an on-chip oscillator. The network receives pulsed energy form pin 19. The RC's output is read at pin 4. The ADC-0804 requires a reference voltage. The 5 volt supply is input to Vref at pin 9. For more precision measurements, you can add a reference voltage to REF_IN/2. The reference voltage must be half of the maximum input voltage. Since the maximum input voltage of the ADC-0804 is 5 volts, the maximum reference voltage is 2.5 volts. The ADC-0804 contains an internal resistor network to supply Ref/2 with a 2.5 volt reference. However, you can provide an external referance voltage if your application requires it. Figure 39 includes a variable resistor for analog zero offset, and another variable resistor to adjust Ref/2.

The ADC-0804 reads the difference between the analog ground and the reference voltage, doubles the value, and divides the value into 256 parts. That means

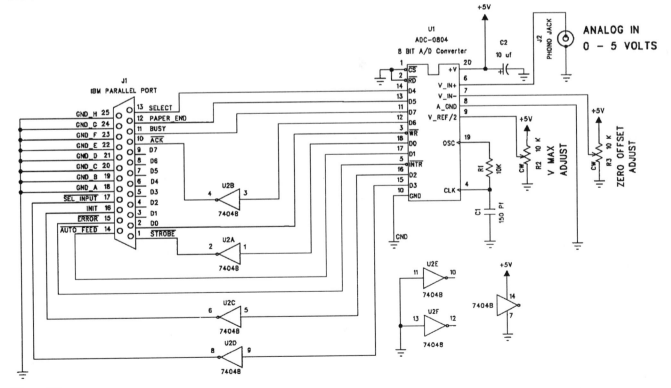

Figure 39

you can adjust the ADC-0804 to divide a small analog input voltage into 256 parts.

The 10 µF capacitor connected to pin 20 provides added supply voltage filtering. The manufacturer's data manual strongly recommends inclusion of this capacitor.

An IBM parallel printer port uses hardware logic to invert the STROBE, AUTO-FEED, SELECT, and BUSY input signals. In Figure 39, four sections of a 7404 octal buffer invert these signals on their way to the parallel port. The result: all received bits are interpreted as active high. The addition of a 15¢ IC reduces software complexity. Again, reinforcing my credo: solder is the best software!

Each time the 7404's write line, WR, is pulsed low, conversion data can be read from the tri-state output buffer. When the WR line is returned to its inactive high state, a new conversion is started. No conversion takes place while the WR line is low. That means the data on D0 - D7 will not change (is stable) while the WR line is low.

Software

On the IBM printer port, the BUSY, ACK, PAPER-END, and SELECT signals are read from the port's (base + 1) address. The SELECT-INPUT, INITIAL-IZE, AUTO-FEED, AND STROBE signals are read from the (base + 2) address. Listings ADC_0804.PAS and ADC_0804.C will do the following:

- set the WR line LOW
- read data from (base +1) and (Base + 2)
- set the WR line HIGH, to start a new ADC-0804 conversion
- extract the high nibble from (Base + 1) data
- extract the low nibble from (Base + 2) data
- merge the high and low nibbles
- display the resulting data byte
- repeat the whole process

It takes the computer longer to digest and display the data than it takes the ADC-0804 to do a voltage comparison. Therefore, with the provided software, the computer is never waiting for a conversion. The ADC-0804 computes the difference between the reference voltage and the analog ground. It then doubles the value, and divides that value into 256 parts. It then compares the input voltage to the reference and outputs a number representing the division closest to the reference voltage. Assume the reference voltage is 5 volts. If the input voltage is 5 volts, the ADC-0804 will output 255, if the input voltage is 2.5 volts, the ADC-0804 would output 127, and if the input voltage were 1.25 volts, the ADC-0804 would output 64. Listing ADC_DEMO.PAS is a demonstration program showing how the ADC-0804 typically operates.

Pascal Source Code Listing

```
PROGRAM Adc_0804;
  { Uses the parallel printer port to input analog data converted to        }
  {  8 bit binary by an ADC-0804 Analog / Digital, ( A/D ), converter IC     }

USES DOS, CRT;

CONST    Wr = $01;                { D0, at Base Address = Write line         }

VAR  Lpt_Num, Lpt_Port_Address : WORD;
        RD, New_Value, Old_Value : INTEGER;
                        Volts : REAL;
          Lo_Nibble, Hi_Nibble : BYTE;

PROCEDURE Read_Data( VAR Lo_Nibble, Hi_Nibble : BYTE);
BEGIN
{ pull-up all Base + 2, open collector output pins, BEFORE read instruction }
PORT[Lpt_Port_Address + 2] := $04; { 00000100 since D1, 2, & 3 are inverted }
Lo_Nibble := PORT[Lpt_Port_Address + 2];
Hi_Nibble := PORT[Lpt_Port_Address + 1];
END; { read data }

PROCEDURE Start_Conversion;
```

```
{ ADC-0804 will start new conversion each time  WR line is strobed         }
BEGIN
Port[Lpt_Port_Address] := WR; { while software digest the current data      }
Port[Lpt_Port_Address] := 0;  { Strobe 0804 WR line to start new conversion }
Port[Lpt_Port_Address] := WR; { while software digests the current data     }
END; { start next conversion }

PROCEDURE Digest_Data(VAR Lo_Nibble, Hi_Nibble : BYTE);
BEGIN
Lo_Nibble := Lo_Nibble AND $0F;
Hi_Nibble := Hi_Nibble AND $F0;
RD := Hi_Nibble OR Lo_Nibble;
New_Value := RD;
END; { digest data }

PROCEDURE Print_Results;
{ display the hi nibble, lo nibble, raw data, and scaled voltage value }
BEGIN
GoToXY(1,10); { go to first position of the tenth line                  }
Writeln('High Nibble = ',Hi_Nibble:3, ';        Low Nibble = ',Lo_Nibble:3);
Volts := RD * 5 / 255;
Writeln; write('Raw Value = ',RD:3,';        Volts = ',Volts:5:2);
Old_Value := New_Value;
END; { print results }

BEGIN { main }
Lpt_Port_Address := 632;   { MGA = 956, CGA = 888, and 3ed port = 632 }
New_Value := 0; Old_Value := 1;
Start_Conversion;
ClrScr;
  REPEAT
  Read_Data(Lo_Nibble, Hi_Nibble);
  Start_Conversion;
  Digest_Data(Lo_Nibble, Hi_Nibble);
    { only waist time going to the screen if reading has changed }
  IF New_Value <> Old_Value THEN  Print_Results;
  UNTIL KEYPRESSED;
END. { main, ADC_0804 }
```

C Source Code Listing

```c
/*                      PROGRAM Adc_0804
          Code conversion by Eugene Klein
     Uses the parallel printer port to input analog data converted to
     8 bit binary by an ADC-0804 Analog / Digital, ( A/D ), converter IC.
  */

#include <dos.h>
#include <stdio.h>
#include <conio.h>
#include <stdlib.h>
#include <string.h>
#include <bios.h>
#include "My_TPU.h"

const int Wr = 0x01;                    // D0, at Base Address = Write line.
unsigned char  Lpt_Num, Lo_Nibble, Hi_Nibble;
```

```c
unsigned int LPTx;
int  RD, New_Value, Old_Value;
float  Volts;

void Read_Data(void)
{
 // Pull-up all Base + 2, open collector output pins, BEFORE read instruction.
 outport(LPTx + 2,0x04); // 00000100 since D1, 2, & 3 are inverted.
 Lo_Nibble = inport(LPTx + 2);
 Hi_Nibble = inport(LPTx + 1);
}



void Start_Conversion(void)
 // ADC-0804 will start new conversion each time  WR line is strobed.
{
 outport(LPTx,Wr); // While software digest the current data.
 outport(LPTx,0);   // Strobe 0804 WR line to start new conversion.
 outport(LPTx,Wr); // While software digests the current data.
}

void Digest_Data(void)
{
 Lo_Nibble = Lo_Nibble & 0x0F;
 Hi_Nibble = Hi_Nibble & 0xF0;
 RD = Hi_Nibble | Lo_Nibble;
 New_Value = RD;
}

void Print_Results(void)
// Display the hi nibble, lo nibble, raw data and scaled voltage value.
{
 gotoxy(1,10); // Go to first position of the tenth line.                        }
 printf("High Nibble = %3i;        Low Nibble = %3i\n",Hi_Nibble,Lo_Nibble);
 Volts = ((float)RD * 5) / 255;
 printf("\nRaw Value = %3i;            Volts = %5.2f",RD,Volts);
 Old_Value = New_Value;
}

void  main()
{
 Lpt_Num = Select_Printer_Port();
 LPTx = Init_Printer_Port(Lpt_Num);
 New_Value = 0;
 Old_Value = 1;
 Start_Conversion();
   clrscr();
 do
 {
  Read_Data();
  Start_Conversion();
  Digest_Data();
    // Only waist time going to the screen if reading has changed.
  if(New_Value != Old_Value)
   Print_Results();
 }while(!kbhit());
}
```

```pascal
PROGRAM Adc_Demo;
{ Utilize the parallel printer port to input analog data converted to    }
{ 8 bit binary by an ADC-0804 analog / digital converter IC              }
{ Display readings in large letters                                      }

USES DOS, CRT, My_TPU;

TYPE Char_Design = Array[1..8] of BYTE;
     String80    = String[80];

CONST   Wr = $01;               { D0, Base = Write line          }

VAR Lo_Nibble, Hi_Nibble, Temp, X : BYTE;
        Lpt_Num, Lpt_Port_Address : WORD;
     Code, N, E, Whole, Remainder : INTEGER;
             Old_Value, New_Value : REAL;
                       A,B, St : String80;

PROCEDURE Print_Large_Letters(St : String80);
{ Create large letters by reading each pixel in character table and make it }
{   a character, 5 by 8 pixels                                              }
{ Turbo Pascal ToolBoox, 2ed Edition, Sybex Pub. by Frank Dutton, Pagbe 253 }
VAR Table    : ARRAY[0..255] OF Char_Design ABSOLUTE $F000:$FA6E;
    Ord_Ch, n, E, I, Col, Row, code : integer;
                             ch : CHAR;
                           temp : String[80];

PROCEDURE Lg_Char(Col, Row, To_Print, Fill_Char : INTEGER);
 { display large characters }
VAR  X, Y, E, I : INTEGER;
      Pattern    : Char_Design;
BEGIN
Pattern := Table[To_Print];
For X := 1 to 8 DO
  For Y := 1 to 8 DO
     BEGIN
     GoToXY((Col-1) + 8 - Y, ( Row - 1) + X);
     If ( Odd( Pattern[X] Shr Y)) THEN Write(Chr(Fill_Char));
     END; { for y }
END;   { large character }

BEGIN { print large letters }
Col := 10; Row := 4;
FOR I := 1 to  6  DO
   BEGIN
   IF St[i] IN ['0'..'9','.'] THEN Ord_Ch := ORD(st[i]) ELSE Ord_Ch := 32;
   lg_Char(Col, Row, Ord_Ch , Ord_Ch);
   Col := Col + 8;
   END; { for i }
END; { print large letters }

BEGIN { main,  adc demo }
Select_Printer_Port(Lpt_Num, Lpt_Port_Address);
Init_Printer_Port(Lpt_Num, Lpt_Port_Address);
```

```pascal
ClrScr; Cursor_Off; Old_Value := 0;
     { initialize A/D chip }
Port[Lpt_Port_Address] := WR;
Port[Lpt_Port_Address] := 0;
Port[Lpt_Port_Address] := WR;
DELAY(10);    { stay within A/D chip timing parameters }

REPEAT
{ read data }
{ pull-up all Base + 2, open collector, pins BEFORE a read instruction      }
  PORT[Lpt_Port_Address + 2] := $04; { 00000100, allow for inverted pins     }
  Lo_Nibble := PORT[Lpt_Port_Address + 2];  { get D0 - D3  bits              }
  Hi_Nibble := PORT[Lpt_Port_Address + 1];  { get D4 - D7  bits              }
{ strobe ADC-0804 to start new conversion }
  Port[Lpt_Port_Address] := WR; { while software digest the current data     }
  Port[Lpt_Port_Address] := 0;  { Strobe 0804 WR line to start new conversion }
  Port[Lpt_Port_Address] := WR; { while software digests the current data    }
{ digest data }
  Lo_Nibble := Lo_Nibble AND $0F; { extract the meaningful bits, 0 - 3        }
  Hi_Nibble := Hi_Nibble AND $F0; { extract the meaningful bits, 4 - 7        }
  X := Hi_Nibble OR Lo_Nibble;  { put all high bits in one byte               }
{ print results }
New_Value := ( X * 5 ) / 255;    { convert byte to a voltage between 0 and 5  }
IF New_Value <> Old_Value THEN   { only update if value has changed           }
  BEGIN
  gotoxy(1,15);
  Writeln('High Nibble = ',Hi_Nibble:3, ';       Low Nibble = ',Lo_Nibble:3);
  writeln;
  writeln('    D7     D6     D5     D4     D3     D2     D1     D0');
  N := 128;
  FOR E := 1 to 8 DO
    BEGIN
    WRITE((X AND N):6);
    N := N DIV 2;
    END; { for }
  WRITELN; WRITELN;
  WRITE('The A/D binary value is ',X:4);
  Whole := X * 5 DIV 255;
  Remainder := X * 5 MOD 255;
  Str(Whole:3,A);
  Str(Remainder:2,B);
  St := A + '.' + B;
  WRITELN(';     Voltage = ', St, ' volts');
  FOR E := 1 to 8 DO
    BEGIN
    GoToXY(1, 3 + E);
    WRITE('
    END; { for E }
  Print_Large_Letters(St);
  Old_Value := New_Value;
  END; { if }
UNTIL KEYPRESSED;
END. { main, adc demo }
```

Analog Sensors

Circuit Theory

This section presents a varied collection of analog sensors to be used with the ADC described in Application 39.

Figure 40-A shows a pressure/vacuum sensor built around the Motorola MPX2100 pressure/vacuum sensor. This device will respond either to pressure placed upon (such as by contact with another object) or to a drop in air pressure.

Figure 40-B shows temperature sensors built around the LM34 and LM35 ICs from National Semiconductor. The LM34 senses the temperature in Fahrenheit while the LM35 senses temperature in Centigrade (Celsius). The output of both devices is 10 mV for each degree in Fahreneheit or Centigrade. The range of the LM34 is –50° to +300° F while that of the LM35 is –55° to +150° C. These devices are self-contained; no external thermocouple or other measuring device is needed,

A frequency to voltage converter is a circuit whose output voltage varies in accordance with the frequency variations of an input signal. Figure 40-C shows such a circuit built around National Semiconductor's LM131 voltage to frequency converter IC. That's not a misprint—the LM131 is designed primarily for voltage to frequency conversion applications, but can be configured to handle frequency to voltage conversion. The input can be a pulse train or square wave of 3 volts or greater amplitude, and the output voltage is equal to:

*input frequency * 2.09 volts * (RL/RS) * (RT * CT)*

Figure 40-D shows another frequency to voltage converter. This circuit uses the LM2907 from National Semiconductor, a frequency to voltage conversion IC designed for use in tachometers and motor control circuits. The output of the circuit in Figure 40-D will increase at roughly the rate of one volt for each 67 Hz of input frequency.

The signals from these and similar sensors may need amplification and conditioning before being fed to an analog to digital converter. A useful and versatile circuit for such a purpose can be found on pages 32 to 40 of the February, 1993 issue of *The Computer Applications Journal*. This circuit, developed by Steve Ciarcia, offers a gain of up to 10.

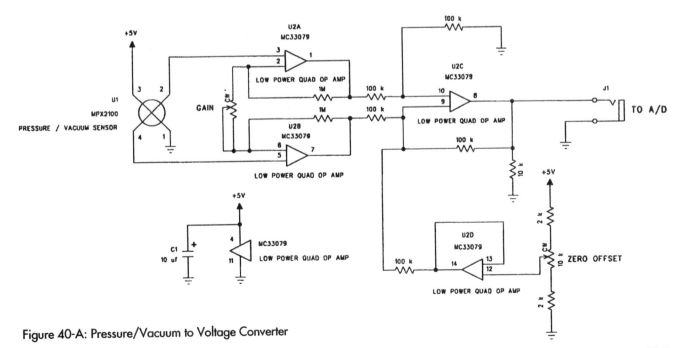

Figure 40-A: Pressure/Vacuum to Voltage Converter

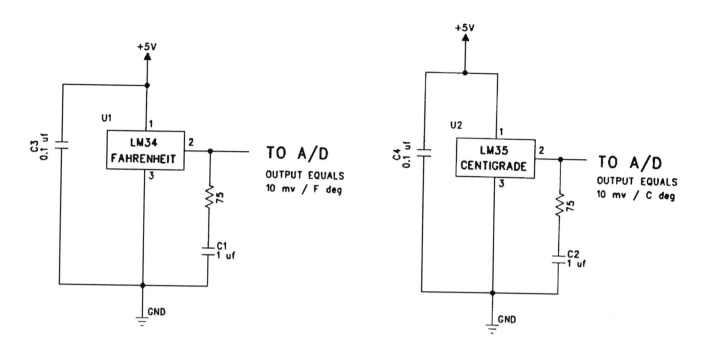

Figure 40-B: Temperature to Voltage Converter

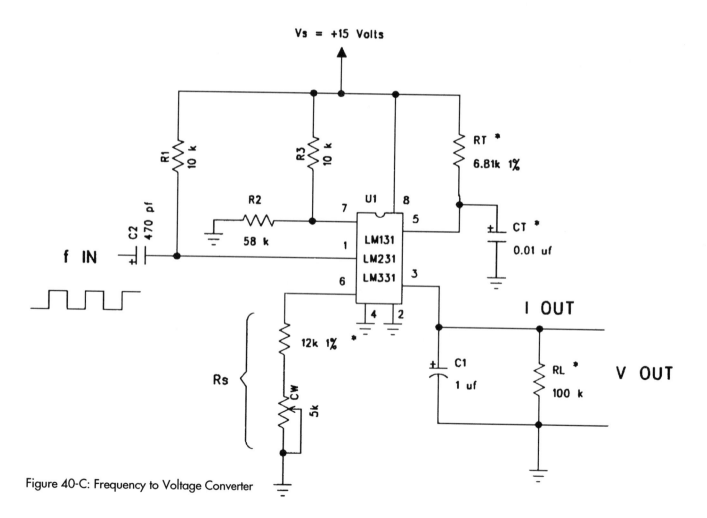

Figure 40-C: Frequency to Voltage Converter

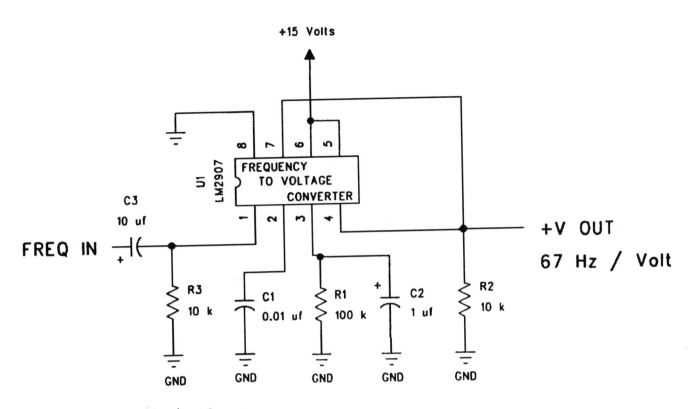

Figure 40-D: Frequency to Voltage Converter

Serial Analog to Digital Conversion

Circuit Theory

The ADC-0804-based analog to digital converter circuit described in Application 39 has parallel output. This means all eight bits are output simultaneously on different lines. This is the fastest method of data transfer. Serial output means each bit is sent on the same line, one bit after the other. Though serial data transfer is much slower than parallel data transfer, there are times when it may offer a practical design solution. Serial links need only four wires for interconnection while parallel links require eleven. If sensors must be opto-isolated from your microprocessor, then a serial link simplifies the process. It takes a lot less parts and space to isolate four wires than eleven. The final project will use less printed circuit board space and probably cost less.

The TLC548 is a CMOS 8-bit analog to digital converter IC with serial control. The TLC548 has an internal clock running at about 4 MHz. Using this internal clock, it can make very fast conversions because it uses 8-bit switched capacitor successive approximation ADC technology. It takes only 17 μsec per conversion, which translates into 45,500 8-bit conversions per second.

The TLC548 requires a reference voltage between 2.5 and Vcc volts for linear operation. The TLC548 divides the reference voltage into 256 parts. The analog input voltage is matched to the nearest reference voltage division. The result is placed in an output buffer for serial transmission. Think of the reference voltage as a "gain" control. You can adjust the full scale reading by adjusting the reference voltage. A Zener diode in series with a resistor can be used for a calibrated voltage divider.

The output is controlled by an external clock pulse, I/O_CLK. The I/O_CLK pulses have no effect on internal data conversion operations. Their only job is to tell the TLC548 when to put the next data bit, D_OUT, on the data line. Since it is CMOS, the TLC548 is well suited for battery powered data logging. The data sheets say this chip can drive two TTL loads. Therefore, the TLC548 can be directly interfaced to a TTL logic parallel printer port.

Figure 41-A shows the simplicity of interfacing the TLC548 to a parallel printer port. R2 and R4 form a voltage divider. The output, tapped at the wiper blade of R2, is the reference voltage input for +REF, pin 1. The input analog voltage can vary between 0

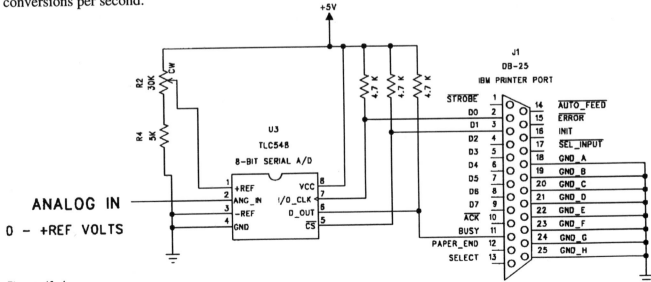

Figure 41-A

volts and +REF. The TLC548 sends 8-bit conversions, serially, one bit at a time, from D_out, pin 6.

Figure 41-B shows how to opto-isolate a TLC548. The HCPL-2211 is designed to accept a CMOS logic signal for input. The HCPL-2211's input LED needs only 1.6 ma. for proper operation. It is designed for 5MB signal rates, well above the TLC548's highest output rate. Input and output logic have beed designed to parallel Figure 41-A operation. Thus, the same software will correctly control both Figure 41-A and Figure 41-B.

Software

Program listings AD_SER.PAS and AD_SER.C, show how to input data from a TLC548. The software follows the following steps:

1) Chip Select, CS, is brought to an inactive high.

2) I/O_CLOCK is brought to an inactive low.

3) CS is brought to an active low. As the CS line goes from high to low, the most significant bit (MSB), D8, from the previous conversion is placed on the serial output line, D_OUT.

4) A "mark time" clock pulse is sent (I/O_CLK is set high, then low).

5) Seven more clock pulses are sent. On each trailing clock pulse transition, from high to low, the next data bit is placed on the serial output line, D_OUT (D6, D5, D4, D3, D2, D1, and finally D0).

6) On the same trailing transition that places data bit 4, (D4), on the serial output line, (D_OUT), the TLC548 starts the next data conversion.

The delay loops are not needed on my slow running AT. However, time delay may become an issue when operating from a high power 486 or Pentium machine. If your machine is "slow," then the delay loop code can be removed.

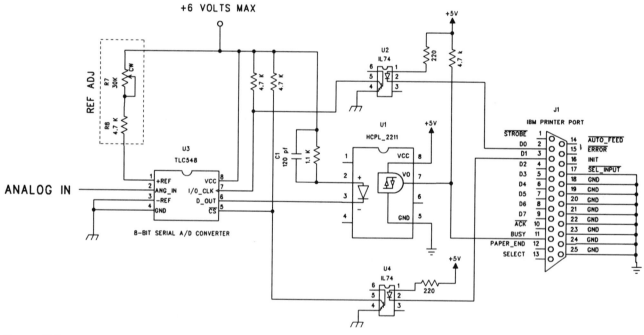

Figure 41-B

Pascal Source Code Listing

```pascal
PROGRAM AD_SER;    { -=[ input analog data from a serial A/D, the TLC548  }
USES CRT, DOS;
VAR               Lpt_Num : INTEGER;
        Lpt_Port_Address : WORD;

PROCEDURE Select_Printer_Port(VAR Num : INTEGER; VAR Lpt_Port_Address : WORD);
  {  Ask user which printer port to use.  Check to make sure      }
  {  that printer port is available.  Function returns port        }
  {  address of selected printer port.                             }
  { The Programmer's PC Sourcebook, MicroSoft Press, 1991, Page 7-75,  }
  { Compute's Mapping the IBM PC, Compute Books, 1985, page 234        }
CONST Base_Address = 1024;  { base address for IBM printer ports }
VAR               Temp, Offset : INTEGER;
                          Ch : CHAR;
BEGIN
REPEAT
ClrScr; WRITELN; WRITELN; WRITELN;
WRITELN; WRITE('Do you want to use LPT 1, 2, or 3: ');
  REPEAT
  Read(Num);
  IF Num IN [1..3] THEN BEGIN END
    ELSE BEGIN
          WRITE(CHAR(7)); WRITELN;
          WRITE('You must enter a number; 1, 2, or 3: ');
          END;
    UNTIL Num IN [1..3];

Offset := (2 * Num) + 6; { 8 = LPT1, 10 = LPT2, and 12 = LPT3 }
  IF Offset = 0 THEN
    BEGIN
    WRITELN;
    WRITELN('Port selected is not installed on this machine.');
    WRITELN; WRITELN('PRESS ANY KEY TO CONTINUE:');
    REPEAT UNTIL KEYPRESSED; Ch := Readkey;
    END
  ELSE Lpt_Port_Address := MemW[0: Base_Address + Offset];
UNTIL Offset <> 0;
END; { find lpt1 }

PROCEDURE Run_TLC548(Lpt_Port_Address : WORD);
CONST t = 1;            { value for time delay, will vary with computer model }
{
  Use printer port, base address, bit D0, for Clock, CLK.
  Use printer port, base address, bit D1, for Chip Select, CS.
  Use printer port, base address + 1, bit D7, for serial data input.
}
    (* sub *) PROCEDURE Init_Port;

            { -Set CLK, at printer port D0, LOW, and Set CS,
                at printer port D1, to INACTIVE HIGH.
              -Delay, so chip can digest the instruction
            }
            BEGIN
```

```
                    PORT[Lpt_Port_Address] := 2;   { 00000010 }
                    DELAY(t);
                    PORT[Lpt_Port_Address] := 0;  { set CS and CLK low  }
                    DELAY(T);
                    END; { sub, init port }

    (* sub *)  PROCEDURE Start_up;
                    {
                       chip counts two clock ticks before outputing data
                    }
                    BEGIN
                    PORT[Lpt_Port_Address] := 0;  { set CS and CLK low  }
                    DELAY(t);
                    PORT[Lpt_Port_Address] := 1;  { set CLK high }
                    DELAY(t);
                    PORT[Lpt_Port_Address] := 0;  { set CLK low  }
                    DELAY(t);
                    END;

    (* sub *)  PROCEDURE Strobe_CLK;
                    {
                       each clock strobe puts next data bit on D_out, pin 6
                    }
                    BEGIN
                    PORT[Lpt_Port_Address] := 0;  { set CLK low  }
                    DELAY(t);
                    PORT[Lpt_Port_Address] := 1;  { set CLK high }
                    DELAY(t);
                    PORT[Lpt_Port_Address] := 0;  { set CLK low  }
                    DELAY(t);
                    END;

    (* sub *)  PROCEDURE Input_Data;
                    {
                       input serial data bits and display value as they are read in
                    }
                    VAR Data, Mask, Bite : BYTE;
                                      Ch : CHAR;
                    BEGIN
                    Mask := 128;  { bit value for printer port, base + 1, D7 }
                      REPEAT
                      Start_up;
                      GOTOXY(1,5);
                      WRITELN('BIT  VALUE'); WRITELN;

{ input D7 }        PORT[Lpt_Port_Address] := 0;  { set CS LOW, CLK LOW }
                    DELAY(t);
                    Bite := ( PORT[Lpt_Port_Address + 1]);
{ process }         IF (Bite AND Mask ) <> Mask THEN Data := 128 ELSE Data := 0;
{ display }         WRITELN('D7:  ', ((data AND 128) ):3);

{ input D6 }        Strobe_CLK;
                    Bite := ( PORT[Lpt_Port_Address + 1] );
{ process }         IF (Bite AND Mask ) <> Mask THEN Data := Data OR 64;
{ display }         WRITELN('D6:  ', ((data AND 64) ):3);
                    Strobe_CLK;
```

```
{ input D5 }    Strobe_CLK;
                Bite :=  ( PORT[Lpt_Port_Address + 1] );
{ process }     IF (Bite AND Mask ) <> Mask THEN Data := Data OR 32;
{ display }     WRITELN('D5:  ', ((data AND 32) ):3);

{ input D4 }    Strobe_CLK;
                Bite :=  ( PORT[Lpt_Port_Address + 1] );
{ process }     IF (Bite AND Mask ) <> Mask THEN Data := Data OR 16;
{ display }     WRITELN('D4:  ', ((data AND 16) ):3);

{ input D3 }    Strobe_CLK;
                Bite :=  ( PORT[Lpt_Port_Address + 1] );
{ process }     IF (Bite AND Mask ) <> Mask THEN Data := Data OR 8;
{ display }     WRITELN('D3:  ', ((data AND 8) ):3);

{ input D2 }    Strobe_CLK;
{ input D2 }    Bite :=  ( PORT[Lpt_Port_Address + 1] );
{ process }     IF (Bite AND Mask ) <> Mask THEN Data := Data OR 4;
{ display }     WRITELN('D2:  ', ((data AND 4) ):3);

{ input D1 }    Strobe_CLK;
                Bite :=  ( PORT[Lpt_Port_Address + 1] );
{ process }     IF (Bite AND Mask ) <> Mask THEN Data := Data OR 2;
{ display }     WRITELN('D1:  ', ((data AND 2) ):3);

{ input D0 }    Strobe_CLK;
                Bite :=  ( PORT[Lpt_Port_Address + 1] ) ;
{ process D0 }  IF (Bite AND Mask ) <> Mask THEN Data := Data OR 1;
{ display D0 }  WRITELN('D0:  ', ((data AND 1) ):3);

                WRITELN; WRITELN; WRITELN('Data = ',Data:3);
                IF KeyPressed THEN Ch := ReadKey;
                UNTIL ORD(Ch) = 27;                    { press ESC to end program }
            END; { input data }

BEGIN { main }
Init_Port;
Input_Data;
END; {  main, run TLC548 }

BEGIN { main }
Select_Printer_Port(Lpt_Num, Lpt_Port_Address);
ClrScr;
Run_TLC548(Lpt_Port_Address);
END.
```

C Source Code Listing

```
/*                    PROGRAM AD_SER
          Code conversion by Eugene Klein
*/

#include <dos.h>
#include <stdio.h>
#include <conio.h>
#include <stdlib.h>
```

```c
#include <string.h>
#include <bios.h>
#include "My_TPU.h"

/*
   Input 8-bit analog conversion from T.I.'s TLC548 serial A/D Converter
   via your IBM / IBM clone parallel printer port.
*/



float Volts;
const int T = 30;              // Time delay in milliseconds.
unsigned char Chip_Select; //D1 = Base Address, Printer Port Pin 3; inactive high
signal.
unsigned char Clock;          // D0 = Base Address, Printer Port Pin 2, active high signal.
unsigned char Data_In;        // D7 of Base Address + 1 = BUSY line; Pin 11 on printer
card,
                 //    used to input serial data.
unsigned char Output_Data, Lpt_Num;

int Input_Data_Byte;
unsigned int Temp, LPTx;

unsigned int Input_Data_Bit( unsigned int Temp, int  Bit_Value)
{
 unsigned char T;
 // input data bit
 outport(LPTx,0);           // Chip_Select and Clock set to 0.
 delay(T);
 // set Chip Select, D1, LOW,  and Clock, D0, high.
 delay(T);
 outport(LPTx,1);           // Chip_Select and Clock set to 0.
 // Read data bit.
 delay(T);
 Temp = inport(LPTx + 1);
 Temp &= Bit_Value;
 // Set Clock, D0, low.
 outport(LPTx,0);           //  Clock set to 0.
 delay(T);
 return(Temp);
}

void main()
{
 // Select the printer port that the A/D converter is connected to.
 Lpt_Num = Select_Printer_Port();
 LPTx = Init_Printer_Port(Lpt_Num);
 // Initialize A/D converter I/O pins: Chip_Select = HIGH, Clock = Low.
 clrscr();
 do
 {
  Chip_Select = 2; // 00000010; set CS to inactive high.
  Clock = 0;
  Output_Data = Clock + Chip_Select;  // Default settings for clock and CS.
  outport(LPTx,Output_Data);          // Set default settings on printer port.
  delay(T);                           // Let A/C chip digest that information.
  // Set Chip_Select to Active Low, still keeping Clock low.
```

```
// Data conversion is placed in tri-state buffer.
// MSB of previous conversion is placed on output data line.
Clock = 0; Chip_Select = 0;
Output_Data = Clock + Chip_Select;
outport(LPTx,Output_Data);
delay(T);
// Read MSB from data line.
Temp = inport(LPTx + 1) & 128 ;    // Value now in Temp is 0 or 128.
Input_Data_Byte = Temp;
gotoxy(5,8); printf("%4i",Temp);
// Read D6.
Temp = Input_Data_Bit( Temp, 64);
Input_Data_Byte = Input_Data_Byte | Temp;
printf("%4i",Temp);
// Read D5.
Temp = Input_Data_Bit( Temp, 32);
Input_Data_Byte = Input_Data_Byte | Temp;
printf("%4i",Temp);
// Read D4,
// with this clock pulse, the TLC548 starts another conversion.
// Current value remains in tri-state buffer.
Temp = Input_Data_Bit( Temp, 16);
Input_Data_Byte = Input_Data_Byte | Temp;
printf("%4i",Temp);
// Read D3.
Temp = Input_Data_Bit( Temp, 8);
Input_Data_Byte = Input_Data_Byte | Temp;
printf("%4i",Temp);
// Read D2.
Temp = Input_Data_Bit( Temp, 4);
Input_Data_Byte = Input_Data_Byte | Temp;
printf("%4i",Temp);
// Read D1.
Temp = Input_Data_Bit( Temp, 2);
Input_Data_Byte = Input_Data_Byte | Temp;
printf("%4i",Temp);
// Read D0.
Temp = Input_Data_Bit( Temp, 1);
Input_Data_Byte = Input_Data_Byte | Temp;
printf("%4i",Temp);
// Display Result.
gotoxy(5,10);
printf("Input_Data_Byte = %5i",Input_Data_Byte);
Volts = ((float)Input_Data_Byte * 5) / 256;
printf(";     Voltage = %5.2f",Volts);
}while(!kbhit());
}
```

Multiplexed 8-Channel, 8-Bit Analog to Digital Converter

Circuit Theory

The ADC-0809 ADC chip from Analog Devices contains eight analog inputs lines, IN0 through IN7. Each input line can convert a 0 to 5 volt analog input signal to a binary number between 0 and 255. There is actually only one analog to digital converter on the chip. The eight inputs operate like an receptionist's telephone switchboard. You select which input you want from address lines AD0 through AD2. Next, you tell the chip to read the address lines by sending a strobe signal to pin 6, the START conversion line. The ADC-0809 permits a single 8-bit port (like your PC's printer port) to monitor eight analog signals, making it ideal for instrumentation monitoring applications.

After the strobe signal is received, the ADC-0809 does an analog to digital conversion of the selected input. The digital output is transferred to a tri-state buffer. The use of a tri-state-buffer means the chip can share data lines with other ICs. Only when the OUTPUT ENABLE line (OE, pin 9) is high will the data lines be "electrically" connected to the data bus.

The circuit in Figure 42 uses the 5 volt supply voltage for a reference. If your application requires it, you could increase the chip's accuracy by providing a precision 5 volt reference for +REF. Printer port circuitry provides inverting buffers for control lines STROBE, AUTO-FEED, SELECT-INPUT, and BUSY. On a printer, these lines are kept at inactive high logic levels. The computer provides buffers that invert these signals so its software is kept to a minimum. To keep OUR software to a minimum, four sections of a 7404 octal inverting buffer are used to invert the inverted logic. The result: when any ADC-0809 data line is high, the software "sees" a logic high.

It should be noted that the SELECT-INPUT, INITIALIZE, AUTO-FEED, and STROBE lines of base + 2 have open collector outputs. Before you can read from these pins, you must first set the four pins to a logic high. The ADC-0809 requires an external oscillator for proper operation. The Analog Devices data manual recommends a frequency of about 500 kHz. The crystal scillator, OSC1, is input to the ADC-0809 at pin 10 (the CLK input pin).

Software

The programs ADC_0809.PAS and ADC_0809.PAS.C ask the user to instruct the program with which printer port to use. Next, the program repeatedly reads the data at each input. If the value has changed from the last reading, then the new value is displayed on the screen. It takes time to write to the screen. There is no reason to waste time updating a display that has not changed. If the value has not changed, the program immediately reads the next analog input value without updating the screen. The user presses any keyboard key to exit the program.

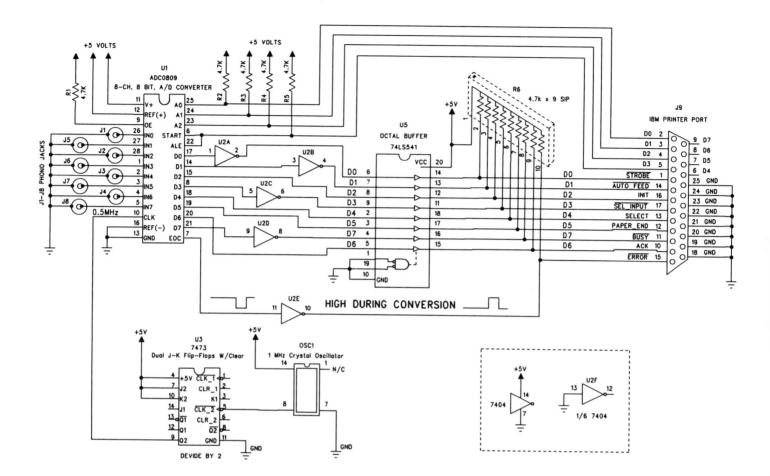

Figure 42-A

Pascal Source Code Listing

```
PROGRAM Adc_0809;
{
  Operate a multiplexed eight chanel A/D converter from a standard
  Centronic Parallel Printer Port.
}

USES CRT, DOS, My_Tpu;

CONST
  { input linex, BASE + 2 }
  D0 = 1;     { STROBE line line, base + 2, pin 1 on Cen. Par. Con. = D0    }
  D1 = 2;     { AUTO-FEED line, base + 2, pin 14 on Cen. Par. Con. = D1     }
  D2 = 4;     { INITIALIZE line, base + 2, pin 31 on Cen. Par. Con. = D2    }
  D3 = 8;     { SELECT-INPUT line, base + 2, pin 36 on Cen. Par. Con. = D3  }
  { input lines, BASE + 1 }
  D4 = 16;    { SELECT line, base + 1, pin 13, on Cen. Par. Con. = D4       }
  D5 = 32;    { PAPER-END line, base + 1, pin 12 on Cen. Par. Con. = D5     }
```

```
      D6 = 64;   { ACK line, base + 1, pin 10 on Cen. Par. Con. = D6       }
      D7 = 64;   { BUSY line, base + 1, pin 11 on Cen. Par. Con. = D7      }

      OE = 32;   { D5, base address,  pin 7 on Cen. Par. Connector        }
{ NOTE: pin numbers are for 36 pin Centronics Parallel Connector          }
   Max_Channels = 7; { max number of channels used on ADC-0809            }

       VAR                          E : INTEGER;
                                   Ch : CHAR;
        Lpt_Num, Lpt_Port_Address : WORD;
                                 Data : BYTE;
                                 Regs : REGISTERS;


PROCEDURE Start_Conversion(E : INTEGER; Lpt_Port_Address : WORD);
                       { pulse Start Conversion line, of selected channel E,   }
CONST Strobe = 8;      { data bit D3 is used to send 'start conversion' pulse }
VAR Pulse : BYTE;
  BEGIN { start }
  If E > Max_Channels THEN E := 0;
  Pulse := E OR Strobe;
  Port[Lpt_Port_Address] := E;       { select channel           }
  Port[Lpt_Port_Address] := Pulse;  { strobe start line HIGH }
  Port[Lpt_Port_Address] := E;       { strobe start line LOW  }
  END;  { start }



PROCEDURE Read_ADC0809( E : INTEGER; Lpt_Port_Address : WORD; VAR Data : BYTE);
VAR  Temp1, Temp2, Carry : BYTE;
     High_Nibble, Low_Nibble : BYTE;
BEGIN { read 0809 }
 { read A/D data }
Port[Lpt_Port_Address] := E OR OE; { turn on tri-state output            }
 { set all pins HIGH so you can read from base + 2 }
Port[Lpt_Port_Address + 2] := Port[Lpt_Port_Address + 2] OR $0F;
delay(50); { allow ADC-0809 time to digest instruction                  }
Low_Nibble :=  Port[Lpt_Port_Address + 2];
High_Nibble := Port[Lpt_Port_Address + 1];
Port[Lpt_Port_Address] := E; { turn off tri-state output                }
Start_Conversion(E + 1, Lpt_Port_Address); { give A/D time for next conversion }
 { digest raw data }
High_Nibble := High_Nibble AND $F0;     { HEX F0 = 11110000              }
Low_Nibble := Low_Nibble AND  $0F;      { HEX 0F = 00001111              }
Data := High_Nibble OR Low_Nibble;
END;  { read 0809  }

PROCEDURE Display_Value(E : INTEGER; Data : BYTE);
VAR L, S, T, U  : INTEGER;

BEGIN { display }
U := 1; S := 1; L := 3;
GOTOXY(1,E*3 + L);
WRITE( 'CHANNEL #',E, ':      D7    D6    D5    D4    D3    D2    D1    D0');
  REPEAT
  IF Data AND S = S THEN T := S ELSE  T := 0;
  GOTOXY(64 - (U * 6),E * 3 + L + 1); WRITE(T:3);
  S := S + S; U := U + 1;
  UNTIL U > 8;
```

```
    GOTOXY(1,E*3 + L + 1); WRITE(DATA:3,' dec        =');
    END; { display }


BEGIN { main }

Select_Printer_Port(Lpt_Num, Lpt_Port_Address); { in My_Tpu }
Cursor_Off; ClrScr;
 WRITELN('                 -=[ ADC-0809 MULTIPLEXED A/D CONVERTER ]=-                    ');

  REPEAT
  Start_Conversion(0, Lpt_Port_Address);
  FOR E := 0 TO Max_Channels  DO
    BEGIN { for e }
    Read_ADC0809(E, Lpt_Port_Address, Data );
    Display_Value(E, Data);
    IF KeyPressed THEN Ch := ReadKey;  { check for request to exit           }
    END; { for e }
  UNTIL ORD(Ch) = 27;                           { pressing ESC exits program          }

ClrScr;
END.  { main }
```

C Source Code Listing

```
/*                         PROGRAM Adc_0809
             Code conversion by Eugene Klein


   Operate a multiplexed eight channel A/D converter from a standard
   Centronic Parallel Printer Port.
*/


#include <dos.h>
#include <stdio.h>
#include <conio.h>
#include <stdlib.h>
#include <string.h>
#include <bios.h>
#include "My_TPU.h"



const unsigned char ESC = 0x1B;        //Escape

  // input lines, BASE + 2
const int   D0 = 1;      // STROBE , base + 2, pin 1 on Cen. Par. Con. = D0
const int   D1 = 2;      // AUTO-FEED line, base + 2, pin 14 on Cen. Par. Con. = D1
const int   D2 = 4;      // INITIALIZE line, base + 2, pin 31 on Cen. Par. Con. = D2
const int   D3 = 8;      // SELECT-INPUT line, base + 2, pin 36 on Cen. Par. Con. = D3
  // input lines, BASE + 1
const int   D4 = 16;     // SELECT line, base + 1, pin 13, on Cen. Par. Con. = D4
const int   D5 = 32;     // PAPER-END line, base + 1, pin 12 on Cen. Par. Con. = D5
const int   D6 = 64;     // ACK line, base + 1, pin 10 on Cen. Par. Con. = D6
const int   D7 = 64;     // BUSY line, base + 1, pin 11 on Cen. Par. Con. = D7

const int   OE = 32;     // D5, base address,  pin 7 on Cen. Par. Connector
   // NOTE: pin numbers are for 36 pin Centronics Parallel Connector
```

```c
const int Max_Channels = 7; // max number of channels used on ADC-0809

int     E;
char    Ch;
unsigned int LPTx;
unsigned char Data, Lpt_Num;
union REGS Regs;

void Start_Conversion(int E, unsigned int LPTx)
    // Pulse Start Conversion line, of selected channel E.
{
 const int     Strobe = 8; // Data bit D3 is used to send 'start conversion' pulse.
 unsigned char Pulse;
 if (E > Max_Channels)
   E = 0;
 Pulse = E | Strobe;
 outport(LPTx,E);      // Select channel.
 outport(LPTx,Pulse); // Strobe start line HIGH.
 outport(LPTx,E);      // Strobe start line LOW.
}


void Read_ADC0809(int E, unsigned int LPTx)
{
 unsigned char Temp1, Temp2, Carry;
 unsigned char High_Nibble, Low_Nibble;
 //Read A/D data.
 outport(LPTx,(E | OE)); // Turn on tri-state output.
 // Set all pins HIGH so you can read from base + 2.
 outport(LPTx + 2,inport((LPTx + 2) | 0x04));
 delay(50);   // Allow ADC-0809 time to digest instruction.
 Low_Nibble =  inport(LPTx + 2);
 High_Nibble =inport(LPTx + 1);
 outport(LPTx,E); // Turn off tri-state output.
 Start_Conversion(E+1,LPTx); // Give A/D time for next conversion.
 // digest raw data
 High_Nibble = High_Nibble & 0xF0;        // HEX F0 = 11110000
 Low_Nibble = Low_Nibble & 0x0F;          // HEX 0F = 00001111
 Data = High_Nibble | Low_Nibble;
}


void Display_Value(int E, unsigned char Data)
{
 int L, S, T, U;
 U = 1; S = 1; L = 3;
 gotoxy(1,(E*3) + L);
 printf("CHANNEL # %i:       D7    D6    D5    D4    D3    D2    D1    D0",E);
 do
 {
  if ((Data & S) == S)
    T = S;
   else
    T = 0;
   gotoxy(64 - (U * 6),E * 3 + L + 1); printf("%3i",T);
   S = S + S; U = U + 1;
  }while(U<=8);
  gotoxy(1,E*3 + L + 1); printf("%3i dec      =",Data);
}
```

```c
void main()
{
 Lpt_Num = Select_Printer_Port();
 LPTx = Init_Printer_Port(Lpt_Num);
 Cursor_Off(); clrscr();
 printf("              -=[ ADC-0809 MULTIPLEXED A/D CONVERTER ]=-              \n");
 do
 {
  Start_Conversion(0,LPTx);
  for(E = 0;E <= Max_Channels;E++)
  {
   Read_ADC0809(E, LPTx);
   Display_Value(E,Data);
   if(kbhit())
     Ch = getch();           // Check for request to exit.
  }
 }while(Ch != ESC);          // Pressing ESC exits program.
 clrscr();
}
```

Notes on Stepping Motors

Most of the following discussion is limited to the most popular motor type: the 4-coil stepping motor. I have seen 3-coil and 5 coil steppers, but the 4-coil version is the one most often used in book and magazine projects. Stepping motors are the easiest type of motor control possible from your computer. Your computer sends TTL out the parallel printer port. The signals are amplified by driver circuits, which in turn power the motor's coils.

During power-up, you monitor limit switches to initialize the motor shaft's position. Stepping motors are popular because, after initialization, they do not require any feedback circuit to monitor the shaft's position. The computer signals tell the motor where to go. Unless your load is too big for your motor, the shaft will be where it was told to be.

Stepping motor drivers are designed to satisfy the stepping motor's large current and voltage appetite. In addition, drivers insulate the computer from inductive load back-EMF. Energy stored by the motor's coils, in magnetic fields, can "backfire," shooting thousands of volts back to the computer's frail integrated circuits. These undesirable high voltage spikes are called back-EMF. Driver circuits must contain circuitry designed to stop back-EMF energy from entering the computer.

WARNING: When current is flowing in a stepping motor coil, a large electromagnetic field is created around the coil. When power is removed, the energy in the coil must go somewhere. If the path of least resistance is the computer's printer cable, say good-bye to your PC. The point is this: generating and controlling high coil current is not enough. Your circuits must provide back-EMF protection for your computer. If you are in doubt, use optocoupler devices to provide isolation.

Engineers have developed a variety of methods for controlling 4-coil stepping motors. Some methods are more efficient than others. Higher efficiency has a price tag. Efficient motor configurations usually require more hardware. Stepping motors abound with four, five, six, and eight leads. Each was designed to operate from different control logic.

Though we talk about a stepping motor having only four windings, the truth is a little more complicated. Each coil is actually made up of many series connected windings positioned in a circle. The small windings are arranged in sequence, one from A followed by one from B, followed by one from C, finally followed by one from D.

Inertia

Stepping motors must never drive a load approaching the motor's torque rating. The motor may skip a step and all successive movements will be in error. Once turning, load inertia plays a critical role. Quickly stopping the motor may force the load to behave like a flywheel, forcing the stepping motor past its rest position. The solution to this problem is to continually turn the load at a slow speed, or *ramp* the motor's speed. Ramping means the motor's speed starts off slowly and gradually increases to its maximum RPM. This speed continues until the end of the movement is approaoched. Then the speed is ramped down to the original value RPM value before stopping. Trial and error testing with your stepping motor and load will reveal a good ramping algorithm. Industrial stepping motors use ramping to achieve 3000 RPMs (10,000 full steps per second!). Without ramping, the start/stop range is between 200 to 500 RPMs.

Torque/Speed

Six and eight wire stepping motors can be operated in the bipolar configuration. Bipolar operation makes the most efficient use of stepping motors because all four windings are always energized. For bipolar operation, the four coils are connected into groups of two. Eight wire stepping motors allow the coils to be arranged in series or parallel groups. Six wire stepping motors can only be configured for series bipolar operation.

When power is applied to a coil, the coil generates a magnetic field. It takes time to build up the magnetic field. As the frequency of the driver pulses increases, a speed is reached where the coil is never fully energized. At that speed or higher, the stepping motor never develops its maximum torque. Maximum torque at varying speeds is dependent on how a stepping motor is wired into a circuit. Series and parallel coil groups yield different performance curves.

Series Operation

All stepping motors are rated for current through a single coil. If two coils are connected in series, the drive current must travel through twice as many winding turns. For the same current, this doubles the "amp-turns" and produces a similar increase in torque.

Doubling the number of winding turns also means you have increased the inductance by a factor of 4. This means the torque will drop off much more quickly as speed is increased. Therefore, series configured motors are most useful in low speed applications. Both six and eight wire stepping motors can be configured for series bipolar operation. Connecting two windings in series will double the total resistance and the current rating is reduced by a factor of 1.4. Thus, a series connected bipolar stepping motor with coils rated at 5 amps can now be operated from a 3.5 amp driver.

Parallel Operation

Connecting two coils of an 8-wire stepping motor in parallel allows the current to divide itself between the two coils. This does not change the effective number of turns and the inductance remains the same. Two windings in parallel cut the total resistanc ein half. The total current may now be increased by a factor of 1.4, or 40%. Thus, a parallel connected bipolar stepping motor with coils rated at 5 amps can now be operated from a 7 amp driver.

When compared to series bipolar operation, parallel bipolar operation provides less torque at low speeds and higher torque at high speeds. The torque is more uniform at high and low speeds. In general, parallel operation is preferred for high shaft power and a flatter torque curve. Series operation is preferred for low speed, high torque applications.

Binary Control of Stepping Motors

It is possible to control stepping motors with two-bit data. Figure A shows how this is done with a 5-wire stepping motor. Each winding of the motor is energized in sequence. Binary numbers 0, 1, 2, and 3 are input to one section of the 74F539 via A0 and A1. The output of U2 (the 74F539) is four data lines, 00, 01, 02, and 03. The 74F539 keeps all output lines low but one. That line is pulled to an active logic high based on the binary input at A0 and A1. U1, the ULN2803, inverts and amplifies each input. Since one of the four inputs is high, only one of the four outputs will be low. That output will sink the coil current to ground. When the PC sequentially generates numbers 0, 1, 2, and 3, stepping motor coils A, B, C, and D are energized in sequence. The data is latched into the 74F539 by the printer port's strobe line. The process is automatic when you use Pascal's WRITELN statement or BASIC's LPRINT statement.

Resistor R helps reduce back-EMF and permits higher operating speeds. It is common to use a value down to $1/7$ of the coil's resistance. For example, if you find a stepping motor rated at 3.5 volts, it was probably designed to operate from 12 to 24 volts with an appropriate low resistance, high wattage resistance in series with the coil. This wiring scheme works, but it is very inefficient.

Resistors R9 and R10 are pull-up resistors for the ACK and ERROR lines. By tying the ACK and ERROR lines to logic high while securing the BUSY and PAPER-END lines to logic low, the PC is fooled into thinking it is connected to an on-line printer ready to receive data. This means BASIC's LPRINT and Pascal's WRITE statements can easily output data.

A maximum of four stepping motors can be simultaneously controlled from one printer port. Since data remains latched in the printer port's data buffer until new data is received, the stepping motor will maintain its position even if the software "goes away" to do something else. Listings BINARY.PAS, BINARY.C, and BINARY.BAS can be used to control the circuit in Figure A; these listings are not given here but are included on the disk accompanying this book.

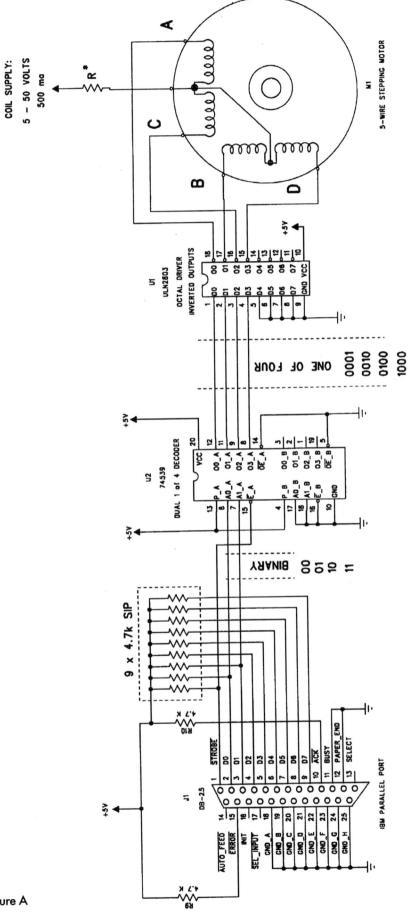

Figure A

PAGE 206, FIGURE A2

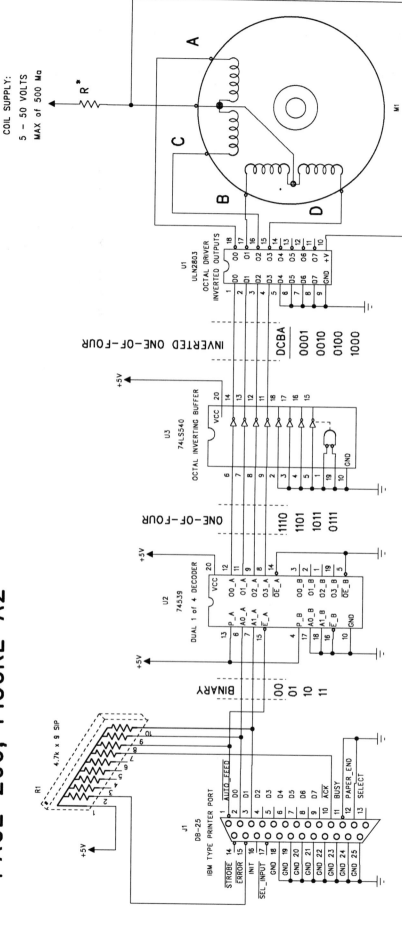

EFFICIENT 2-BIT CONTROL LOGIC FOR 5-WIRE, SINGLE PHASE, STEPPING MOTOR

TWO DATA BIT CONTROL, EACH WINDING IS ENERGIZED IN SEQUENCE

* R HELPS COUNTERACT COIL'S BACK-EMF

R VALUES DOWN TO 1/7 OF COIL RESISTANCE ARE COMMON

Crystal Oscillator Circuits

Some of the applications in this book require oscillator signal sources. The author has found quartz crystal oscillators to be very reliable and time effective—just select a device with the desired frequency and plug it in. When power is applied, they work. I call that quick and efficient design. The only drawback of quartz crystal oscillators is cost. A quartz crystal oscillator costs about four times the price of a crystal and related gate logic.

You might want to try to "roll your own" oscillators. Figure B gives a sampling of crystal oscillators using various logic gates. There is no "best" way to construct a crystal oscillator. The purpose of this section is to show you various methods that use different logic gates. I have found that any gate logic oscillator requires tweaking with an oscilloscope for proper operation. If you are not willing to spend time fine tuning your circuit, stick with a well engineered quartz crystal oscillator.

QUARTZ CRYSTAL OSCILLATOR

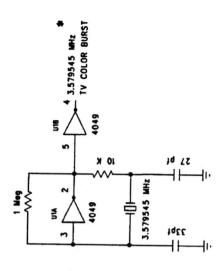

COSTS A LITTLE MORE, BUT ALWAYS WORKS

CRYSTAL OSCILLATOR

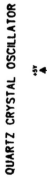

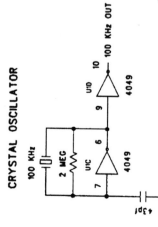

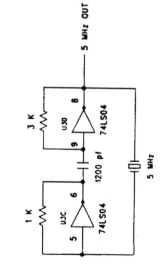

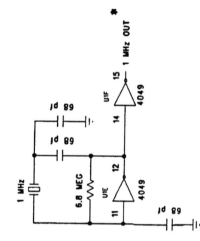

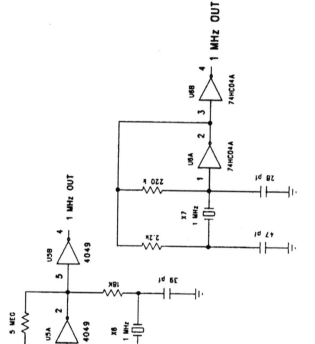

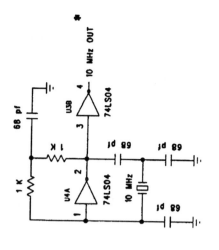

Figure B

Interfacing to the Serial Port

There may be times when you need to convert serial data to parallel form or parallel data to serial form. The circuit in Figure C lets you do this. The heart of the circuit is an AY-1015A. This chip is actually two completely independent devices housed in a common plastic case. One device converts serial to parallel, the other parallel to serial. It has two

independent clock inputs. The AY-5-8116 dual baud rate generator can supply independent clock pulses to each. The output of the AY-1015A is TTL logic. If you intend to use the chip with a standard RS232 serial interface, you must add the MAX232 inverter. The MAX232 inverts the TTL logic voltage levels to RS232 levels and vice-versa. Program listing SERIAL.BAS demonstrates how to input serial data via an IBM type serial port.

Here's a practical application of this circuit. I had the opportunity of working on Trenton State's 1993 entry in the Tour De Sol. Each year students design, construct, and drive an electrically powered vehicle in this seven day endurance race. Most of the students involved in the project use the experience as part of their senior project. An advisor-approved senior project is required of all engineering students for graduation.

While on my teaching sabbatical, I asked if I could join the team. I was accepted as part of the instrumentation design group. Using many of the concepts in this book, we designed panel mounted instruments to monitor the electric motor's current and voltage, engine RPM, battery compartment temperature, and distance traveled via a digital odometer.

We also wanted to log all sensor values. A laptop was installed inside the dash. All the sensors were routed to a DAC0808, which was interfaced to the laptop's printer port.

Two weeks before the race, the Department of Energy sent every entrant a panel mounting LCD power meter. The unit displays real time voltage and current usage and total power consumed. In addition, a cable allowed the data to be interfaced to a serial port. The program in listing SERIAL.BAS is the software I wrote to read and display the serial data.

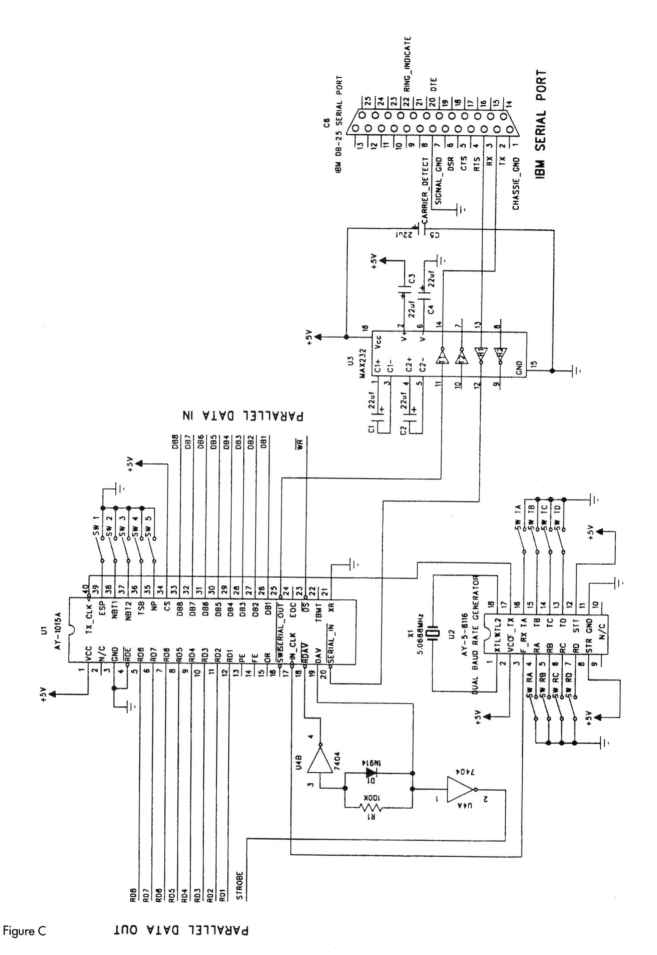

Figure C

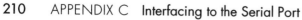

BASIC Source Code Listing

```
' SAVE'A:\BAS\SERIAL.BAS
' Serial I/O written in QBasic

' MS-DOS QBasic Programmer's Reference, Bob Arnson, MicroSoft Pub, Pg 403,412
' Digital Communications, David Schwaderer, Wiley Press 1984, Pg 166-218
' Mastering Serial Communications, Pete Gofton, Sybex Pub. 1986, Pg 202-216

' Open a communication port
' The next line dose the following: Open COM1, Baud = 9600, No parity,
' 8 data bits, 1 stop bit, send and receive binary data, disable Data Carrier
' Detect (DCD) time out, wait 0 seconds for a Clear To Send (CTS) time out,
' wait 0 seconds for Data Set Ready (DSR) time out, suppress Request to Send
' (RTS) detection, set receive data buffer to 1024 bytes, set transmit data
' buffer to 1024 bytes, access COM1 Port as file #1.


OPEN "COM1:9600,N,8,1,BIN,CD 0,CS 0,DS 0,RS,RB 1024,TB 1024" FOR RANDOM AS #1
DO  '  -=[ input characters ]=-
  IF NOT EOF(1) THEN
    PRINT INPUT$(LOC(1), #1)
  END IF
'      -=[ transmit characters ]=-
' MS-DOS QBasic Programmer's Ref, Pg 217
Char$ = INKEY$ 'scan keyboaard for character, return with or without character
IF Char$ <> "" THEN
    DO
    Ordinal% = ASC(Char$)
      IF Ordinal% > 31 THEN
        PRINT Char$;
      ELSEIF (Ordinal% = 13) OR (Ordinal% = 12) THEN PRINT
      END IF
    PRINT #1, Char$
    LOOP UNTIL Char$ <> ""
END IF
LOOP UNTIL Ordinal% = 27
END 'serial. bas
```

The Game Port

This book has focused on how to interface devices to the parallel printer port. Most IBM type computers are also equipped with a game port. The game port can input up to four analog values along with bit logic from four switches.

The game port is very slow. Each analog input is the wiper arm of a variable pot. The game port uses the pot as part of a simple RC timer circuit. The programmer must set the RC timer and then repeatedly check a memory address to see when the internal capacitor is charged. Different computers run at different operating speeds. The software to read joystick positions must be adjusted for each machine. Software can get messy, and applications are limited. (This is a glowing example of where Apple had a better hardware design.)

Figure D shows a diagram for connections to the game port. One of the pins on the game port's DB-15 connector plug can source a five volt supply. Normally, I never power an external device from the computer's power supply. The chance of smoking the computer is not worth the risk! However, used correctly, the game port can have some advantages. If you have a noninductive, low power, completely enclosed application that can operate from the game port's limited I/O functions, then give it a try.

The listings GAMEPORT.PAS and GAMEPORT.C demonstrate how to input analog and digital I/O data to the game port of any IBM type machine. The value of Max_Count will vary according to your machine's clock speed. Input is slow on every machine regardless of clock speed. The programs repeatedly read joystick and button positions. The user exits the program by pressing the ESC key.

The listings AT_GAME.PAS and AT_GAME.C demonstrate a more efficient method of using the game port of AT or higher type machines. Beginning with the IBM PC AT, code was added to the ROM BIOS that reads and records a game port's status. The AT_GAME program uses this BIOS call to get information about the game port. First the program checks to make sure a game port is installed. If a game port is installed, the program repeatedly reads the joysticks' and buttons' positions. The user exits the program by pressing the keyboard's ESC key.

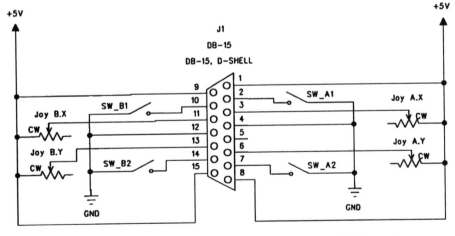

Joystick B   **Joystick A**

Figure D

213

Listing GAMEPORT.PAS

```pascal
PROGRAM GamePort;
{
  Relatively fast input of joystick port info for your application.
  Originally written for IBM XT / XT clone machines.  With the AT and
  higher machines, you can use BIOS interrupts to read the joysticks.
  However, I find this version more than adequate for my needs.
  Written in Borland's Turbo Pascal 6.0.

  REF: IBM PC Joystick Control Using Turbo Pascal by James P. McAdems,
       BYTE Mag., October 1985, Page 143-144.
}
USES DOS, CRT;

CONST Joy_Port_Address = $201; { game port base address }

VAR         I : INTEGER;
         Temp : BYTE;
           Ch : CHAR;
    Max_Count : INTEGER;        { Delay time needed for my AT clone machine }
                                { Adjust this value for your machine.       }


    FUNCTION Button_Pressed(Which_One : CHAR) : BOOLEAN;
     { return true if selected button is pressed }
    VAR Mask : BYTE;
    BEGIN
    IF NOT (Which_One IN ['A'..'D']) THEN Which_One := 'A';
    CASE Which_One OF
       'A' : Mask := 16;
       'B' : Mask := 32;
       'C' : Mask := 64;
       'D' : Mask := 128;
       END; { case }
    Button_Pressed := (PORT[Joy_Port_Address] AND Mask) = 0;
    END; { button pressed }

FUNCTION Joystick_Position(Which_One : CHAR) : INTEGER;
{
  Returns a number based on a joystick's position.  Values will
  vary depending on your joystick.  You can 'tweak' the program's
  performance by:

  Function returns 0 for out of range or uninstalled joystick polling.

       1) Changing value of Max_Count,
       2) Using larger capacitors on game card
}

VAR Counter : INTEGER;
    Mask : BYTE;

LABEL READ;
BEGIN
```

```
IF NOT (Which_One IN ['A'..'D']) THEN Which_One := 'A';
CASE Which_One OF
  'A' : Mask := 1;
  'B' : Mask := 2;
  'C' : Mask := 4;
  'D' : Mask := 8;
  END; { case }

{
  The Inline Code below causes the CX register to count down from Max_Count
  toward zero.  When CX reaches zero, or when the one-shot on the game
  adapter times out, the looping stops and counter is loaded with the
  active count.  Max_Count should be chosen so that CX never reaches 0,
  then the usable range ofthe joystick is not compromised.
}
                ASM
                MOV CX,Max_Count        {  Init down counter                }
                MOV DX,Joy_Port_Address {  load joystick port address       }
                MOV AH,Mask { [BP] } {  Mask of selected one_shot           }
                OUT DX,AL               {  Start the one shots              }
          READ: IN AL,DX                {  Read the one shots               }
                TEST AL,AH              {  Check selected one-shot          }
                LOOPNZ READ             {  Repeat until timed out           }
                MOV Counter,CX {  Make CX available to Turbo Pascal }
                END; { asm }
IF Counter = 0
  THEN Joystick_Position := 0
    ELSE Joystick_Position := Max_Count - Counter;
END;   { function joystick position }

PROCEDURE Process_Key_Press(VAR Ch : CHAR);
BEGIN
Ch := ReadKey;
IF CH IN ['J','j'] THEN
  BEGIN
  gotoxy(1,20); WRITE('Count now reads: ',Max_Count,';  Enter new value: ');
  ReadLn(Max_Count);
  gotoxy(1,20);
  WRITE('Count now reads: ',Max_Count,'                          ');
  END; { if }
END; { process key press }

BEGIN { main, GamePort }
ClrScr; Ch := ' ';
Max_Count := 2000;          { Delay time needed by my AT clone machine }
                            { Adjust this value for your machine.      }
REPEAT
gotoxy(1,24); write('Max_Count = ',Max_count,':   Press "J" to change');
GOTOXY(1,5);    { get joystick #1 info }
WRITE(Joystick_Position('A'):5, Joystick_Position('B'):5);
IF Button_Pressed('A') THEN WRITE('PRES':5) ELSE WRITE('UP':5);
IF Button_Pressed('B') THEN WRITE('PRES':5) ELSE WRITE('UP':5);
GOTOXY(1,7);    { get joystick #2 info }
WRITE(Joystick_Position('C'):5, Joystick_Position('D'):5);
IF Button_Pressed('C') THEN WRITE('PRES':5) ELSE WRITE('UP':5);
IF Button_Pressed('D') THEN WRITE('PRES':5) ELSE WRITE('UP':5);
```

```
If KeyPressed THEN Process_Key_Press(ch);
UNTIL ORD(Ch) = 27;
END. { main GamePort }
```

Listing GAMEPORT.C

```
/*                        PROGRAM GamePort
                     Code conversion by Eugene Klein

   Relatively fast input of joystick port info for your application.
   Originally written for IBM XT / XT clone machines.  With the AT and
   higher machines, you can use BIOS interrupts to read the joysticks.
   However, I find this version more than adequate for my needs.
   Written in Borland's Turbo Pascal 6.0.

    REF: IBM PC Joystick Control Using Turbo Pascal by James P. McAdems,
         BYTE Mag., October 1985, Page 143-144.
   */


#include <dos.h>
#include <stdio.h>
#include <conio.h>
#include <stdlib.h>
#include <string.h>
#include <bios.h>
#include "My_TPU.h"

const int ESC = 0x1b;
int Joy_Port_Address = 0x201; // game port base address
int I;
unsigned char Temp;
char Ch;
int   Max_Count = 2000;       // Delay time needed for my AT clone machine
                 // Adjust this value for your machine.



int Button_Pressed(char Which_One)
{
 // return true if selected button is pressed
 unsigned char Mask;
 if(Which_One  < 'A' && Which_One > 'D')
  Which_One = 'A';
 switch (Which_One)
 {
  case 'A':
   Mask = 16;
   break;
  case 'B':
   Mask = 32;
   break;
  case 'C':
   Mask = 64;
   break;
  case 'D':
   Mask = 128;
   break;
```

```
   default:
    Mask = 0;
  }
 return(inport(Joy_Port_Address) & Mask);
}

int Joystick_Position(char Which_One)
{
 /*
   Returns a number based on a joystick's position.  Values will
   vary depending on your joystick.  You can 'tweak' the program's
   performance by:


   Function returns 0 for out of range or uninstalled joystick polling.

        1) Changing value of Max_Count,
        2) Using larger capacitors on game card
 */

 int Counter;
 unsigned char Mask;


 if(Which_One <'A'& Which_One > 'D')
  Which_One = 'A';
 switch(Which_One)
 {
  case 'A':
   Mask = 1;
   break;
  case 'B':
   Mask = 2;
   break;
  case 'C':
   Mask = 4;
   break;
  case 'D':
   Mask = 8;
  default:
   Mask = 0;
 }

 /*
   The Inline Code below causes the CX register to count down from Max_Count
   toward zero.  When CX reaches zero, or when the one-shot on the game
   adapter times out, the looping stops and counter is loaded with the
   active count.  Max_Count should be chosen so that CX never reaches 0,
   then the usable range ofthe joystick is not compromised.
 */
        asm {
           MOV CX,Max_Count      //  Init down counter
           MOV DX,Joy_Port_Address
                    //  load joystick port address
           MOV AH,Mask           // [BP]
                                 //  Mask of selected one_shot
           OUT DX,AL             //  Start the one shots
```

```
            }
          READ:
          asm {
              IN AL,DX                // Read the one shots
              TEST AL,AH              // Check selected one-shot
              LOOPNZ READ             // Repeat until timed out
              MOV Counter,CX //  Make CX available to Turbo Pascal
            }
 if(Counter == 0)
  return(0);
 else
  return(Max_Count - Counter);
}


char Process_Key_Press(void)
{
 Ch = getch();
 if(Ch=='J'|| Ch=='j')
 {
  gotoxy(1,20); printf("Count now reads: %i;   Enter new value: ",Max_Count);
  scanf("%i",&Max_Count);
  gotoxy(1,20);
  printf("Count now reads: %i                                     ",Max_Count);
 }
 return(Ch);
}


void main()    // main, GamePort
{
 clrscr(); Ch = ' ';
 do
 {
  gotoxy(1,24); printf("Max_Count = %i:   Press \"J\" to change'",Max_Count);
  gotoxy(1,5);    // get joystick #1 info
  printf("%5i  %5i",Joystick_Position('A'), Joystick_Position('B'));
  if(Button_Pressed('A'))
   printf(" PRES");
  else
   printf("   UP");
  if(Button_Pressed('B'))
   printf(" PRES");
  else
   printf("   UP");
  gotoxy(1,7);    // get joystick #2 info
  printf("%5i  %5i",Joystick_Position('C'), Joystick_Position('D'));
  if(Button_Pressed('C'))
   printf(" PRES");
  else
   printf("   UP");
  if(Button_Pressed('D'))
   printf(" PRES");
  else
   printf("   UP");
  if(kbhit())
    Ch = Process_Key_Press();
 }while(Ch != ESC);
}
```

Listing AT_GAME.PAS

```pascal
PROGRAM AT_Game;
{
  Read joystick status.  Uses Bios calls added to AT bios.  This routine
  will not work on XT machines.

  REF: PC System Programming for Developers, Abacus Pub. 1989, Page 753

  INTERRUPT 15H, FUNCTION 84H, SUB-FUNCTION 0
  Reads status of joystick switches interfaced to a PC ( AT and higher ) IF
    a game port and switches are present.

  Read joystick info.  Uses BIOS Interrupt 15H
  INPUT:      AH = 84H
              DX = 0
  OUTPUT:     IF Carry Flag = 1 then no game port is installed
              IF Carry Flag = 0 then game port is installed
              AL = switch settings
                 If bit 7 = 0 then first joystick's button 'A' is enabled
                 If bit 6 = 0 then first joystick's button 'B' is enabled
                 If bit 5 = 0 then second joystick's button 'A' is enabled
                 If bit 4 = 0 then second joystick's button 'B' is enabled
  NOTES:      Sub Function 1 reads joystick positions

  INTERRUPT 15H, FUNCTION 84H, SUB-FUNCTION 1
  Reads position of joysticks interfaced to a PC ( AT and higher ) if game
  port and joysticks are present.

  INPUT:      AH = 84H
              DX = 1
  OUTPUT:     IF Carry Flag = 1 then no game port is installed
              IF Carry Flag = 0 then game port is installed
              AX contains X-Position of first joystick
              BX contains Y-Position of first Joystick
              CX contains X-Position of second Joystick
              DX contains Y-Position of second Joystick

              FLAGS Register =
                    BIT: 15 14 13 12 11 10  9  8  7  6  5  4  3  2  1  0
                    FUNCTION:  -  -  -  -  O  D  I  T  S  Z  -  A  -  P  -  C
}

USES DOS, CRT;
VAR Regs : REGISTERS;
    Ch   : BYTE;
    Bit  : WORD;

  (* sub *) PROCEDURE Process_Joysticks;

  BEGIN
  Ch := 32;
  REPEAT
  REGS.AH := $84;        { get joystick positions     }
  Regs.DX := $01;
  INTR($15,Regs);
```

```
        gotoxy(1,5);              { display stick position      }
        WRITE(Regs.AX:7, Regs.BX:9, Regs.CX:16, Regs.DX:10);

        REGS.AH := $84;          { get joystick button values }
        Regs.DX := $00;
        INTR($15,Regs);
        GOTOXY(1,8);
                                 { display button position      }
        IF (REGS.AL AND 16) <> 16 THEN WRITE(' ON':6) ELSE WRITE('OFF':6);
        IF (REGS.AL AND 32) <> 32 THEN WRITE(' ON':13) ELSE WRITE('OFF':13);
        IF (REGS.AL AND 64) <> 64 THEN WRITE(' ON':16) ELSE WRITE('OFF':16);
        IF (REGS.AL AND 128) <> 128 THEN WRITE(' ON':10) ELSE WRITE('OFF':10);

        IF KeyPressed THEN BEGIN Ch := ORD(ReadKey); END;
        UNTIL ch = 27;
        END; { process joystick }

BEGIN
ClrScr; Ch := 32;
WITH Regs DO
  BEGIN
  AH := $84;
  DX := $00;
  INTR($15,Regs);
  Bit := FLAGS AND $0001;
  IF Bit <> 0 THEN             { is game board installed }
    BEGIN
    WRITELN;
    WRITELN('NO GAME CARD IS INSTALLED ON THIS MACHINE'); WRITELN;
    WRITELN('PRESS ANY KEY TO CONTINUE '); READLN;
    HALT;
    END { if }
  ELSE
    BEGIN
    GOTOXY(1,3);
    WRITELN('          JOYSTICK A                    JOYSTICK B ');
    WRITE('    x-pos     y-pos             x-pos      y-pos');
    gotoxy(1,7); WRITE(' Button-A      Button-B       Button-A       Button-B');
    GOTOXY(5,24); WRITE(' Press ESC to exit');
    END; { else }
  Process_Joysticks;
  END; { with regs. }
END.
```

Listing AT_GAME.C

```
/*                     PROGRAM AT_Game
              Code conversion by Eugene Klein

Read joystick status.  Uses Bios calls added to AT bios.  This routine
will not work on XT machines.

REF: PC System Programming for Developers, Abacus Pub. 1989, Page 753

INTERRUPT 15H, FUNCTION 84H, SUB-FUNCTION 0
Reads status of joystick switches interfaced to a PC ( AT and higher ) IF
```

```
                a game port and switches are present.

        Read joystick info.   Uses BIOS Interrupt 15H
        INPUT:      AH = 84H
                    DX = 0
        OUTPUT:     IF Carry Flag = 1 then no game port is installed
                    IF Carry Flag = 0 then game port is installed
                    AL = switch settings
                       If bit 7 = 0 then first joystick's button 'A' is enabled
                       If bit 6 = 0 then first joystick's button 'B' is enabled
                       If bit 5 = 0 then second joystick's button 'A' is enabled
                       If bit 4 = 0 then second joystick's button 'B' is enabled
        NOTES:      Sub Function 1 reads joystick positions

        INTERRUPT 15H, FUNCTION 84H, SUB-FUNCTION 1
        Reads position of joysticks interfaced to a PC ( AT and higher ) if game
        port and joysticks are present.

        INPUT:      AH = 84H
                    DX = 1
        OUTPUT:     IF Carry Flag = 1 then no game port is installed
                    IF Carry Flag = 0 then game port is installed
                    AX contains X-Position of first joystick
                    BX contains Y-Position of first Joystick
                    CX contains X-Position of second Joystick
                    DX contains Y-Position of second Joystick

                    FLAGS Register =
                          BIT: 15 14 13 12 11 10  9  8  7  6  5  4  3  2  1  0
                      FUNCTION:  -  -  -  -  O  D  I  T  S  Z  -  A  -  P  -  C
*/

#include <dos.h>
#include <stdio.h>
#include <conio.h>
#include <stdlib.h>
#include <string.h>
#include <bios.h>
#include "My_TPU.h"


union REGS Regs;
unsigned char Ch;
unsigned int Bit;
unsigned char ESC = 0x1B;

void Process_Joysticks(void)
{
 Ch = 32;
 do
 {
  Regs.h.ah = 0x84;        // Get joystick positions.
  Regs.x.dx = 0x01;
  int86(0x15,&Regs,&Regs);
  gotoxy(1,5);             // Display stick position.
  printf("%7x%9x%16x%10x",Regs.x.ax, Regs.x.bx, Regs.x.cx, Regs.x.dx);
```

```c
  Regs.h.ah = 0x84;        // Get joystick button values.
  Regs.x.dx = 0x00;
  int86(0x15,&Regs,&Regs);
  gotoxy(1,8);
                    // Display button position.
  if((Regs.h.al & 16) != 16)
   printf("     ON");
  else
   printf("    OFF");
  if((Regs.h.al & 32) != 32)
   printf("           ON");
  else
   printf("           OFF");
  if((Regs.h.al & 64) != 64)
   printf("              ON");
  else
   printf("              OFF");
  if((Regs.h.al & 128) != 128)
   printf("             ON");
  else
   printf("             OFF");

  if(kbhit())
   Ch = getch();
 }while(Ch != ESC);
}


void main()
{
 clrscr(); Ch = 32;
 Regs.h.ah = 0x84;
 Regs.x.dx = 0x00;
 int86(0x15,&Regs,&Regs);
 Bit = Regs.x.flags & 0x0001;
 if(Bit != 0)
 {          // Is game board installed?
  printf("\n\nNO GAME CARD IS INSTALLED ON THIS MACHINE\n\n");
  printf("PRESS ANY KEY TO CONTINUE ");
  getch();
  exit(0);
 }
 else
 {
  gotoxy(1,3);
  printf("        JOYSTICK A                JOYSTICK B \n");
  printf("   x-pos    y-pos          x-pos    y-pos");
  gotoxy(1,7); printf(" Button-A    Button-B      Button-A    Button-B");
  gotoxy(5,24); printf(" Press ESC to exit");
 }
 Process_Joysticks();
}
```

Bidirectional Printer Port Adapter

I have found the parallel printer port a great way to prototype circuit designs. After construction, and debugging, many designs are then moved to an embedded controller like the Intel 8031. However, on occasion I have found one drawback. Many ICs are designed to use the same 8-bit bus for input and output. The parallel port uses some pins for input, some for output, and still others for both. I wanted a small "black box" that provided one end to plug into the parallel port and provided an 8-bit I/O port, with control lines out the other end. The circuit in Figure E was the result.

Output from Figure E is taken at the terminal block, J2. The terminal block supports 8-bit data I/O, via D0 - D7, and four control lines, A0 - A2 and RD/WR. Determining which parallel port pins should be used for input, and which for output is controlled by software.

Four data bits at address base + 1 input terminal block data bits D4 - D7. Four data bits at address base output terminal block data bits D0 to D3. Four data bits at address base + 1 input terminal block data bits D4 - D7. The 74LS242 selects which set of four printer port data lines will be used based on the logic level of base address D3. D3 is uses as a Read /Write control line. Base address D0 - D3 provide three address line for J2.

The software listings BI_PRN.PAS and BI_PRN.C demonstrate how to software control the circuit in Figure E. The code is well documented and should be easy to follow.

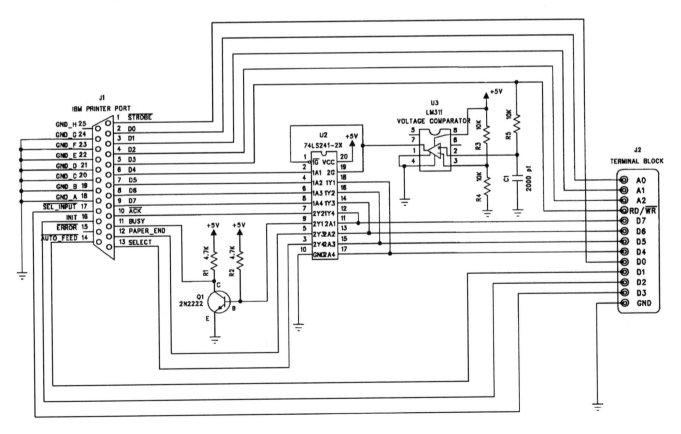

Figure E

Pascal Source Code Listing

```pascal
PROGRAM Bi_PRN;
  {
    Test program for Universal Adapter which converts a standard IBM parallel
    printer port into a true I/O  device with 8 bi-directional data bits and 4
    control lines.
  }
  USES CRT, My_tpu;
  CONST T = 130;
  VAR Num : INTEGER;
      A, E : BYTE;
      LPTx : WORD;
        Ch : CHAR;


PROCEDURE Send_Data( E : Byte);
CONST  Write_Bit = $00;                { D3, the Read / Write bit, is set LOW            }
VAR Lo_Nibble, Hi_Nibble : BYTE;

BEGIN { send data }
Port[LPTx] := Write_Bit;              { Write_Bit on 74LS241 is set HIGH              }
Lo_Nibble := E AND $0F;              { low nibble of byte  goes to BASE + 2 address }
Lo_Nibble := Lo_Nibble XOR $0B; { invert inverted pins, 0000 1011 = $0B hex   }
(* Hi_Nibble := (E AND $F0); *) { hi nibble of byte goes to BASE address       }
Hi_Nibble := (E AND $0F) * 16; { just to watch  display in hex                }
Port[lptx] := Hi_Nibble OR Write_Bit; { put high nibble on data lines          }
                                     { keep write bit active                }
PORT[LPTX + 2 ] := Lo_Nibble;   { put lo-nibble data on D4 to D7 data lines   }
delay(T);                             { slow process down so I can observe LEDs      }
END;   { send data }


PROCEDURE Input_Data;
VAR Lo_Nibble, Hi_Nibble, Temp, Data_Byte : BYTE;

BEGIN   { input data }
Ch := ' ';
  REPEAT
  Port[lptx] := $08;          { set R/W line for READ                        }
  PORT[LPTx + 2] := $04;   { 0000 0100,    init all pull-up resistors   }
{ -=[ input data byte ]=- }
  Lo_Nibble := PORT[LPTx + 2];       { read low nibble                    }
  Temp := Port[LPtx + 1];           { read high nibble                   }
{ -=[ process HI nibble ]=- }
  Hi_Nibble := Temp AND $80;         { extract D7                          }
  Temp := Temp AND $38;             { extract remaining three bits       }
  Temp := Temp * 2;                 { shift these bits to left one place }
  Hi_Nibble := Temp OR Hi_Nibble; { recombine bits of nibble           }
  Hi_Nibble := Hi_Nibble XOR $70; { invert inverted logic bits         }
{ process LO nibble }
  Lo_Nibble := Lo_Nibble AND $0F; { extract data bits                  }
  Lo_Nibble := Lo_Nibble xor $04; { invert inverted printer port logic }
{ display data }
  GoToXY(10,8);
  WRITE('Hi_Nibble = ', Hi_Nibble:3, ';      Lo Nibble = ', Lo_Nibble:2);
  Data_Byte := Hi_Nibble OR Lo_Nibble;  { combined hi and lo nibbles    }
  gotoxy(10,15); write('Input byte = ',Data_Byte:3);
  IF KEYPRESSED THEN CH := READKEY; { press any key to exit              }
  UNTIL ORD(Ch) = 27;
END;    { input data }


BEGIN  { Bi Printer Port Adapter }
```

```pascal
LPTx := Find_Lpt(Num);
Ch := ' ';
  REPEAT
{ set eight data bits high in binary order                                        }
  FOR E := 0 to 32 DO Send_Data(E);
{  set control bits high in binary sequence, ten times                            }
  FOR  A := 1 TO 10 DO
    BEGIN { for a }
    E := 1;
      REPEAT
      PORT[LPTx] := E AND $0F;
      delay(T) ;
      E := E + E;
      UNTIL (E > 8);
  END; { for a }
IF Keypressed THEN Ch := ReadKey;
UNTIL ORD(Ch) = 27;
Input_Data;
END.   { Bi Printer Port Adaptor }
```

C Source Code Listing

```c
/*                    PROGRAM Universal_Adaptor
                  Code conversion by Eugene Klein


    Test program for Universal Adaptor which converts a standard IBM parallel
    printer port into a true I/O  device with 8 bidirectional data bits and 4
    control lines.
 */


#include <dos.h>
#include <stdio.h>
#include <conio.h>
#include <stdlib.h>
#include <string.h>
#include <bios.h>
#include "My_TPU.h"


const int T = 130, ESC = 0x1B;     // ESC is escape character
int Num, E;
unsigned char A, Lpt_Num;
unsigned int LPTx;
char  Ch;

void Send_Data(unsigned char E)
{
  const int  Write_Bit = 0x00;              // D3, the Read / Write bit, is set LOW
  unsigned char Lo_Nibble, Hi_Nibble;

  outport(LPTx,Write_Bit);        //Write_Bit on 74LS241 is set HIGH
  Lo_Nibble = E & 0x0F;           //Low nibble of byte  goes to BASE + 2 address
  Lo_Nibble ^= 0x0B;              //Invert inverted pins, 0000 1011 = 0x0B hex
  /* Hi_Nibble := (E & 0xF0); */  //High nibble of byte goes to BASE address     }
  Hi_Nibble = (E & 0x0F) * 16;    //Just to watch  display in hex
  outport(LPTx, Hi_Nibble | Write_Bit); //Put high nibble on data lines          }
                    //Keep write bit active                  }
  outport(LPTx + 2,Lo_Nibble);    //Put lo-nibble data on D4 to D7 data lines     }
  delay(T);                       //Slow process down so I can observe LEDs        }
}
```

```c
void Input_Data(void)
{
 unsigned char Lo_Nibble, Hi_Nibble, Temp, Data_Byte;

 Ch = ' ';
 do
 {
  outport(LPTx,0x08);              // Set R/W line for READ
  outport(LPTx + 2,0x04);          // 0000 0100,   init all pull-up resistors
//-=[ input data byte ]=-
  Lo_Nibble =inport(LPTx + 2);     // Read low nibble
  Temp = inport(LPTx+ 1);          // Read high nibble
//-=[ process HI nibble ]=-
  Hi_Nibble = Temp & 0x80;         // Extract D7
  Temp &= 0x38;                    // Extract remaining three bits
  Temp *= 2;                       // Shift these bits to left one place
  Hi_Nibble |= Temp;               // Recombine bits of nibble
  Hi_Nibble ^= 0x70;               // Invert inverted logic bits
//process LO nibble
  Lo_Nibble &= 0x0F;               // Extract data bits
  Lo_Nibble ^= 0x04;               // Invert inverted printer port logic
//display data
  gotoxy(10,8);
  printf("Hi_Nibble = %3i Lo Nibble = %3i;",Hi_Nibble,Lo_Nibble);
  Data_Byte = Hi_Nibble | Lo_Nibble;   // combined hi and lo nibbles
  gotoxy(10,15); printf("Input byte = %3i",Data_Byte);
  if(kbhit())
   Ch = getch(); // press any key to exit
 }while(Ch != ESC);
}

void main()
{
 unsigned char Lpt_Num;

 Lpt_Num = Select_Printer_Port();
 LPTx = Init_Printer_Port(Lpt_Num);
 Ch = ' ';
 do
 {
  // set eight data bits high in binary order
  for(E = 0;E<= 32;E++)
    Send_Data(E);
  //set control bits high in binary sequence, ten times
  for(A=1;A<=10;A++)
  {
   E = 1;
   do
   {
    outport(LPTx,E & 0x0F);
    delay(T) ;
    E++;
   }while(E<=8);
  }
  if(kbhit())
   Ch = getch();
 }while(Ch != ESC);
 Input_Data();
}
```

Expanding the Parallel Port to 24-Bit Input/Output

The standard IBM type parallel printer port can be expanded to input or output 24 bits of data. The trick is to multiplex the data lines with tri-state buffers, some latches, and some glue logic. You could design a custom I/O port interface or use a reliable workhorse like Intel's 8255. Figure F shows a 24-bit "expander" circuit using the 8255.

The 8255 parallel interface adapter (PIA) is designed to take an 8-bit I/O and expand it into three 8-bit I/O ports. The operation theory of the 8255 is well beyond the scope of this book; there are entire books devoted to using this single IC. The 8255 supports three input/output ports, A, B, and C. You send the chip a control word that tells the 8255 whether a port should input or output 8-bit data (port C can also be configured as two independent 4-bit I/O nibbles). Once a port is set up, you can not change the port's function without resetting it, which would erases all data bits. Each port has a tri-state output buffer. Data sent to a port is latched. The ports have no input buffers. Data to be input must be stable during a computer read operation.

The listings PIA_8255.PAS and PIA_8255.C configure the 8255 to output 8-bit data on ports A and B while inputting 8-bit data through port C. The program continues until the keyboard ESC key is pressed.

To get you started, here are three examples of how you might use an expanded parallel printer port:

- If you were to wire two Figure F circuits to two printer ports, the ports could be configured into a 24x24 matrix, yielding 576 unique connection points. That arrangement could monitor a lot of model train layout points!

- Another application would use an 8255 to multiplex many input and output devices. Use port A as an 8-bit output data bus and port B as an 8-bit input data bus. Port C would then be free to provide three address lines and a strobe line for each data bus. Each group of three port C address lines could control eight input or eight output devices. That's sixteen 8-bit devices controlled from a single IBM type parallel printer port!

- A third application would be to allow an 8-bit data port to interface with 16-bit processors. Port A and port B could be used for 16-bit data I/O while port C would be used for processor control line I/O.

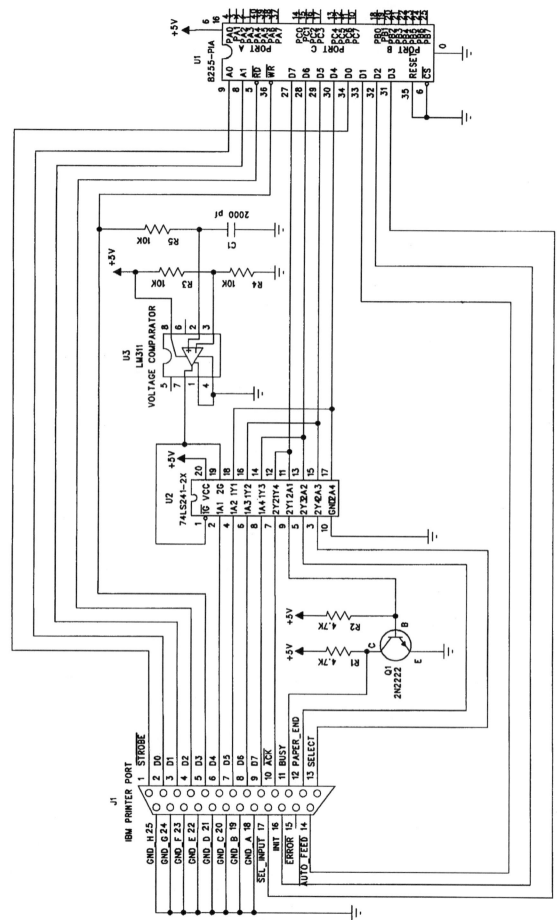

Pascal Source Code Listing

```pascal
PROGRAM PIA_8255; { Intel 8255 Parallel Interface Adapter }
{ Demonstrate 8255's operation form a parallel printer port.  program outputs
  data to 8255 Ports 1 and  2, while reading data form Port 3.  This IC
  expands a parallel printer port into a three byte I/O port.
}
USES CRT, PRINTER, My_TPU;

TYPE    Data_Type = ARRAY[0..16] OF BYTE;

CONST   A0 = 1; { Bit 1 = D0, STROBE at Base-Address + 2              }
        A1 = 2; { Bit 2 = D1, AUTO-FEED at Base-Address + 2           }
        RD = 4; { Bit 3 = D2, *INITIALIZE at Base-Address + 2         }
        WR = 8; { Bit 4 = D3, *SELECT-INPUT at Base-Address + 2       }
                { NOTE: an asterisk, (*),   denotes inactive high logic }
    T : BYTE = 5;


VAR  A, E, X, Port_Number, Control_Byte, Data_Byte, Control_Lines  : BYTE;
                          Base_Addr_LO_Nibble, Base_Addr_HI_Nibble : BYTE;
                                              Lptx, Data_Word : WORD;
                                                        Num : INTEGER;
                                          Inverted_Logic  : Data_Type;
                                              Ch : CHAR;


PROCEDURE Generate_Data(VAR Inverted_Logic : Data_Type);
{ makes "look-up" table for Base + 2's inverted signals on D0, D1, and D3  }
{ faster than doing repetitive logic conversions for all new data          }
VAR Count, Temp, D0, D1, D2, D3 : BYTE;
BEGIN
Count := 0;
FOR D3 := 1 DOWNTO 0 DO         { D3 of Base + 2 is inverted          }
  FOR D2 := 0 TO 1 DO           { D2 of Base + 2 is NOT inverted      }
    FOR D1 := 1 DOWNTO 0 DO     { D1 of Base + 2 is inverted          }
      FOR D0 := 1 DOWNTO 0 DO   { D0 of Base + 2 is inverted          }
        BEGIN
        Temp := (8 * D3) + ( 4 * D2) + ( 2 * D1 ) + D0;
        Inverted_Logic[Count] := Temp;
        Count := Count + 1;
        END;
END; { generate data }


PROCEDURE Send_Control_Word(Control_BYTE : BYTE);
{ issues control byte to the 8255.  Tells the 8255 the Mode, which ports   }
{ are inputs, and which parts are outputs.                                 }
VAR Temp : BYTE;
BEGIN
Base_Addr_LO_Nibble := $0F;                  { Initialize Control Lines, 0000 1111 }
PORT[LPTx] := Base_Addr_LO_Nibble;
Base_Addr_HI_Nibble := Control_Byte AND $F0;    { HI nibble of control byte }
PORT[LPTx] := Base_Addr_HI_Nibble OR Base_Addr_LO_Nibble;
Temp := Control_Byte AND $0F;                { LO nibble of control byte }
Temp := Inverted_Logic[Temp];
PORT[LPTx + 2] := Temp;
PORT[LPTx] := PORT[LPTx] AND $F7; { 1111 0111, set Write Line to active LOW   }
delay(T);      { the LM311 RC network forces the use of a prolonged WR signal }
PORT[LPTx] := PORT[LPTx] OR $08; {  0000 1000, set Write Line to inactive HIGH }
END;
```

```
PROCEDURE Send_Data(Data_Byte, Port_Number : Byte);
{ Send Data_Byte to Port [ Port_Number ]                                    }
VAR Temp : BYTE;
BEGIN
Base_Addr_LO_Nibble := $0C OR Port_Number;b { Initialize Control Lines,00001100 }
PORT[LPTx] := Base_Addr_LO_Nibble;
PORT[LPTx] := ( Data_Byte AND $F0 ) OR Base_Addr_LO_Nibble;
Temp := Data_Byte AND $0F;
Temp := Inverted_Logic[Temp];
PORT[LPTx + 2] := Temp;
PORT[LPTx] := PORT[LPTx] AND $F7; { 1111 0111, set Write Line to active LOW    }
delay(T);       { the LM311 RC network forces the use of a prolonged WR signal  }
PORT[LPTx] := PORT[LPTx] OR $08;  { 0000 1000, set Write Line to inactive HIGH }
END;

PROCEDURE Output_Data;
  { Generate data to set each pin of Port 1, and Port 2, HIGH in sequence      }
VAR Ct : BYTE;
BEGIN { output data }
For A := 0 to 1 dO
  BEGIN
  Ct := 1;
  FOR E := 1 TO 8 DO
    BEGIN
    Send_Data(Ct, A); Ct := Ct + Ct; IF KeyPressed Then Exit;
    END; { for e }
  Ct := 0; Send_Data(Ct, A);
  END; { for a }
For A := 1 DOWNTO 0 DO
  BEGIN
  Ct := 128;
  FOR E := 1 TO 8 DO
    BEGIN
    Send_Data(Ct, A); Ct := Ct DIV 2; IF KeyPressed Then Exit;
    END; { for e }
  Ct := 0; Send_Data(Ct, A);
  END; { for a }
END; { output data }

PROCEDURE Input_Data(VAR Data_Byte : BYTE; Port_Number : BYTE);
{ Read data from selected port, invert inverted data on lines D0, D1, and D3 }
{ Return, via Data_Byte, a correct reading byte of data                      }
VAR Temp, TempB : BYTE;
BEGIN { input demo }
Base_Addr_LO_Nibble := $0C;  { Initialize Control Lines,        0000 1100 }
Base_Addr_LO_Nibble := $0C OR Port_Number; { select port for input        }
PORT[LPTx] := Base_Addr_LO_Nibble;                            {  0000 1101 }
PORT[LPTX] := PORT[LPTx] AND $0B;                 { Rd line = LOW;  0000 1001 }
PORT[LPTx + 2] := $04;                   { set all lines high for read;  0000 0100 }
Data_Byte := ( PORT[LPTx + 2] AND $0F );
Data_Byte := Data_Byte OR ( PORT[LPTx + 1] AND $F0);
PORT[LPTx] := Base_Addr_LO_Nibble;                { Rd line = HIGH;  0000 11xx }
  { invert inverted BASE + 2 data lines: D0, D1, and D3; }
Temp := Data_Byte AND $0F;
Temp := Inverted_Logic[Temp];
Data_Byte := (Data_Byte AND $F0 ) OR Temp;
END;   { input demo }
```

```
PROCEDURE Process_Speed_Request(VAR Ch : CHAR);
{
  Check for PAGE-UP, PAGE-DOWN, or ESC key pressing.
  Process PAGE-UP, and PAGE-DOWN  as request for faster or slower display
}
VAR Ch1, Ch2 : CHAR;
BEGIN
Ch1 := READKEY;
IF KEYPRESSED THEN Ch2 := READKEY;
If Ch1 IN ['9', '3', CHAR(27)] THEN Ch := Ch1
  ELSE IF Ch2 IN ['I', 'Q'] THEN Ch := Ch2;
CASE Ch OF
  '9', 'I' : { Go Faster }   IF T > 4 THEN   T := T - 3;
  '3', 'Q' : { Go Slower } IF T < 200 THEN   T := T + 3;
  CHAR(27) : EXIT;
  END; { case }
END; { process speed request }


BEGIN { main }
ClrScr;
LPTx := Find_Lpt(Num);   { in My_Tpu.TPU
Generate_Data(Inverted_Logic);
Send_Control_Word($89); { PORT 1 & 2 Output, PORT 3 Input,        1000 1001 }
X := 0;
  REPEAT
  Output_Data;
  Port_Number := 2;
  Input_Data(Data_Byte, Port_Number);
  If X <> Data_Byte THEN    { only print data if it differs from old data, x }
    BEGIN WRITELN('Data = ',Data_Byte); X := Data_Byte; END;
  IF KEYPRESSED THEN Process_Speed_Request(Ch);
  UNTIL ORD(Ch) = 27;                              { exit if ESC key was pressed }
END. { main }
```

C Source Code Listing

```c
/*         PROGRAM PIA_8255; { Intel 8255 Parallel Interface Adaptor }
           Code conversion by Eugene Klein

  Demonstrate 8255's operation form a parallel printer port.  Program outputs
  data to 8255 Ports 1 and  2, while reading data form Port 3.  This IC
  expands a parallel printer port into a three byte I/O port.
 */

#include <dos.h>
#include <stdio.h>
#include <conio.h>
#include <stdlib.h>
#include <string.h>
#include <bios.h>
#include "My_TPU.h"

const unsigned char ESC = 0x1B;

const unsigned char    A0 = 1; // Bit 1 = D0, STROBE at Base-Address + 2
```

```
const unsigned char    A1 = 2; // Bit 2 = D1, AUTO-FEED at Base-Address + 2
const unsigned char    RD = 4; // Bit 3 = D2, *INITIALIZE at Base-Address + 2
const unsigned char    WR = 8; // Bit 4 = D3, *SELECT-INPUT at Base-Address + 2
            // NOTE: an asterisk, (*),  denotes inactive high logic
unsigned char    T = 5, Port_Number;

unsigned char A, E, x, Control_Byte, Data_Byte, Control_Lines;
unsigned char Base_Addr_LO_Nibble, Base_Addr_HI_Nibble, Lpt_Num;
unsigned int LPTx, Data_Word;
int Num;
unsigned char Inverted_Logic[16];
char Ch;

void Generate_Data(void)
{
 // makes "look-up" table for Base + 2's inverted signals on D0, D1, and D3
 // faster than doing repetitive logic conversions for all new data
 int Count, Temp, D0, D1, D2, D3;
 Count = 0;
 for(D3=1;D3>=0;D3—)                    // D3 of Base + 2 is inverted
 {
  for(D2=0;D2<=1;D2++)                   // D2 of Base + 2 is NOT inverted
  {
   for(D1=1;D1>=0;D1—)                  // D1 of Base + 2 is inverted
   {
    for(D0=1;D0>=0;D0—)                 // D0 of Base + 2 is inverted
    {
     Temp = (8 * D3) + ( 4 * D2) + ( 2 * D1 ) + D0;
     Inverted_Logic[Count] = Temp;
     Count = Count + 1;
    }
   }
  }
 }
}


void Send_Control_Word(unsigned char Control_Byte)
{
 // issues control byte to the 8255.  Tells the 8255 the Mode, which ports
 // are inputs, and which parts are outputs.
 unsigned char Temp;

 Base_Addr_LO_Nibble = 0x0F;                    // Initialize Control Lines, 0000 1111
 outport(LPTx, Base_Addr_LO_Nibble);
 Base_Addr_HI_Nibble = Control_Byte & 0xF0;        // HI nibble of control byte
 outport(LPTx,Base_Addr_HI_Nibble | Base_Addr_LO_Nibble);
 Temp = Control_Byte & 0x0F;                       // LO nibble of control byte
 Temp = Inverted_Logic[Temp];
 outport(LPTx + 2,Temp);
 outport(LPTx,inport(LPTx) & 0xF7);
 // 1111 0111 set Write Line to active LOW
 delay(T);
 // the LM311 RC network forces the use of a prolonged WR signal
 outport(LPTx,inport(LPTx) | 0x08);
 //  0000 1000 set Write Line to inactive HIGH
}
```

```c
void Send_Data(unsigned char Data_Byte, unsigned char Port_Number)
{
 // Send Data_Byte to Port [ LPTx ]
 unsigned char Temp;

 Base_Addr_LO_Nibble = 0x0C | Port_Number; // Initialize Control Lines, 00001100
 outport(LPTx,Base_Addr_LO_Nibble);
 outport(LPTx,( Data_Byte & 0xF0 ) | Base_Addr_LO_Nibble);
 Temp = Data_Byte & 0x0F;
 Temp = Inverted_Logic[Temp];
 outport(LPTx + 2,Temp);
 outport(LPTx,inport(LPTx & 0xF7)); // 1111 0111, set Write Line to active LOW
 delay(T);      // the LM311 RC network forces the use of a prolonged WR signal
 outport(LPTx,inport(LPTx | 0x08));  // 0000 1000, set Write Line to inactive HIGH
}

void Output_Data(void)
{
 // Generate data to set each pin of Port 1, and Port 2, HIGH in sequence
 unsigned char Ct;

 for(A=0;A<=1;A++)
 {
  Ct = 1;
  for(E=1;E<=8;E++)
  {
   Send_Data(Ct, A); Ct = Ct + Ct;
   if(kbhit())
     exit(0);
  }
  Ct = 0; Send_Data(Ct, A);
 }
 for(A=1;A>0;A—)
 {
  Ct = 128;
  for(E=1;E<=8;E++)
  {
   Send_Data(Ct, A); Ct = Ct / 2;
   if(kbhit())
     exit(0);
  }
  Ct = 0; Send_Data(Ct, A);
 }
}

unsigned char Input_Data( unsigned char Port_Number)
{
 // Read data from selected port invert inverted data on lines D0 and D1 and D3
 // Return via Data_Byte a correct reading byte of data

 unsigned char Temp, TempB;

 Base_Addr_LO_Nibble = 0x0C; // Initialize Control Lines,          0000 1100
 Base_Addr_LO_Nibble = 0x0C | Port_Number; // select port for input
 outport(LPTx,Base_Addr_LO_Nibble);                         //  0000 1101
 outport(LPTx,inport(LPTx) & 0x0B);              // Rd line = LOW;  0000 1001
```

```c
  outport(LPTx + 2,0x04);                    // set all lines high for read;  0000 0100
  Data_Byte = ( inport(LPTx + 2) & 0x0F );
  Data_Byte = Data_Byte | ( inport(LPTx + 1) & 0xF0);
  outport(LPTx,Base_Addr_LO_Nibble);              // Rd line = HIGH;  0000 11xx
  // invert inverted BASE + 2 data lines: D0, D1, and D3;
  Temp = Data_Byte & 0x0F;
  Temp = Inverted_Logic[Temp];
  return((Data_Byte & 0xF0 ) | Temp);
}


void Process_Speed_Request(void)
{
 /*
  Check for PAGE-UP, PAGE-DOWN, or ESC key pressing.
  Process PAGE-UP, and PAGE-DOWN  as request for faster or slower display
 */

 char Ch1, Ch2;

 Ch1 = getch();
 if(kbhit())
  Ch2 = getch();
 if(Ch1=='9'|| Ch1=='3'|| Ch1==ESC)
  Ch = Ch1;
 else
 {
  if(Ch2=='I'|| Ch2=='Q')
   Ch = Ch2;
 }
 switch(Ch)
 {
  case '9':
   if(T > 4)
    T = T - 3;
   break;
  case 'I':     // Go Faster
   if(T > 4)
    T = T - 3;
   break;
  case '3':
   if(T < 200)
    T = T + 3;
   break;
  case 'Q':     // Go Slower
   if(T < 200)
    T = T + 3;
   break;
  case '\27':
   exit(0);
 }
}

void main()
{
 Lpt_Num = Select_Printer_Port();
 LPTx = Init_Printer_Port(Lpt_Num);
 clrscr();
 Generate_Data();
```

```
Send_Control_Word(0x89); // PORT 1 & 2 Output, PORT 3 Input,        1000 1001
X = 0;
do
{
 //Output_Data();
 Port_Number = 2;
 Data_Byte = Input_Data(Port_Number);
 if(X != Data_Byte)     // only print data if it differs from old data, x
 {
  printf("Data = %i\n",Data_Byte);
  X = Data_Byte;
 }
 if(kbhit())
  Process_Speed_Request();
}while(Ch != ESC);                              // exit if ESC key was pressed
}
```

Parallel Printer Port
Technical Reference Chart

The printer port used on IBM and compatible PCs is made up of four address locations, although the fourth address is not used. The top of the chart in this appendix identifies the port address for the three IBM/compatible printer ports. IBM also assigned 64 port addresses, starting at hex 300, for prototype board development. To the best of my knowledge, no commercial product uses those 64 addresses.

The BASE ADDRESS is used to transmit 8-bit data. All IBM type printer ports use this address to transmit data. Some laptop manufacturers have started making this address bidirectional. This allows for a very efficient data link between machines. The material in this book assumes your port is not bidirectional; you can use the material in this book with any IBM type printer port.

The BASE + 1 ADDRESS is used to control input signals. Bits D3 to D7 are used for input (D0 to D3 are not used). D6, the acknowledge line, can also be used for hardware interrupts. Applic. 29 demonstrates how to use this pin for a hardware-activated TSR.

The BASE + 2 ADDRESS is used to input or output control signals. Bits D0 to D3 are used for input/ output. Though initialized at system start-up for output, they can be easily programmed for input. Note that when used for input, the lines are open collector. D4 is used by software to set up the ACK line for hardware interrupt operation. If your printer port is bidirectional, D5 is a control line to tell the BASE address to input or output data.

A line over a pin's name indicates that the pin is internally wired for inactive high operation. Some printers using a Centronics type connector supply +5 volts at pin 18. This pin has no connection on an IBM/ compatible port.

The reference chart in this appendix illustrates conversion between IBM and Centronics connectors.

The pin assignments for the 36-pin Centronics parallel printer port are identified in the chart by "Cent." IBM and compatibles use a female DB-25 connector for the printer port. They are identified in the chart by "DB." The DB-25 connector is grounded on pins 19 through 25. The Centronics connector should be grounded on pins 16, 19 through 30, and 33.

If your hardware pulls the ACK and ERROR lines high with 4.7 Ω resistors while pulling the BUSY and PAPER-END low, the PC can be fooled into thinking it is connected to an on-line printer ready to receive data. Every computer language contains specific commands to "talk" to the LPT1 printer (for example, Pascal uses LST while BASIC uses LPRINT). If your application just outputs data, then this technique can simplify your code.

To under stand how your PC's printer port operates, I suggest that you construct the circuit in Figure G-1. Program listings TEST_PRN.BAS, TEST_PRN.PAS, and TEST_PRN.C show you how to input and output data from a parallel printer port. These listings are provided on the disk accompanying this book, but will not be given here.

Data (D0 to D7) is output through the BASE address. An additional four control bits, D0 to D3, are output from BASE + 2. Five data bits, D3 to D7, are input from BASE + 1.

I have found this circuit very useful in debugging my software. I can "see" what is going on by observing the LEDs or flipping the switches. Most programming language environments have a command for stepping through a program (for example, in QBASIC it is the F7 key). Using the "step" commands with the circuit in Figure G-1 helps keep debugging time to a minimum.

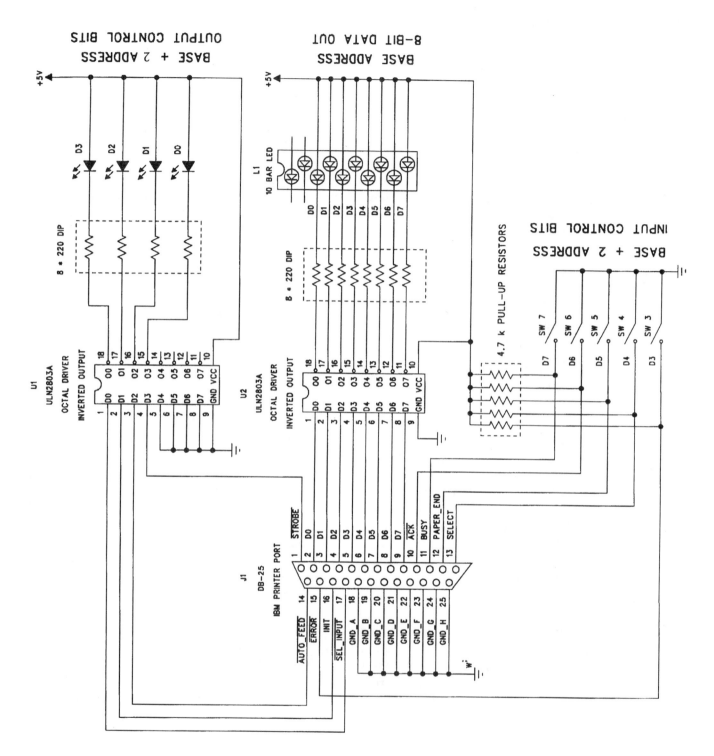

Figure G-1

IBM Parallel Printer Port Technical Reference Chart

	PORT	HEX BASE ADDRESS	DEC BASE ADDRESS	RANGE in HEX
MGA	Port A	3BCh	956	3BCh – 3BFh
CGA	Port B	378h	888	378h – 37Fh
PS/2	Port C	278h	632	278h – 27Fh
experimental		300h	768	300h – 340h

Port C is also the IBM XT, AT, & 386 machine's 3rd PRN port IBM allocated Hex 300h – 340h for prototype board development.

BASE ADDRESS

	D7	D6	D5	D4	D3	D2	D1	D0
	DATA	DATA	DATA	DATA	DATA	DATA	DATA	DATA
DB	9	8	7	6	5	4	3	2
Cent	9	8	7	6	5	4	3	2

Many laptops are now being shipped with D0 – D7 as bidirectional data bits.
This book assumes your printer port's data bits are NOT bidirectional.

BASE + 1

	in $\overline{BUSY}$	in ACK	in PAPER END	in SELECT	in $\overline{ERROR}$		
DB	11	10	12	13	15		
Cent	11	10	12	13	15		

The ACK pin is also used for a hardware interrupt.
NOTE: BUSY is internally hard wired for inactive high, ACK is internally hard wired for active high.

BASE + 2

				internal control IRQ ENABLE	in / out SELECT $\overline{INPUT}$	in / out INITIALIZE	in / out $\overline{AUTO\text{-}FEED}$	in / out $\overline{STROBE}$
DB					17	16	14	1
Cent					36	31	14	1

SELECT, INIT, AUTO-FEED, and STROBE outputs are OPEN COLLECTOR.
NOTES: DB: = DB-25 connector, CENT = Centronics 36 pin parallel port connector.
IRQ ENABLE: = software controls this bit to enable or disable interrupt operation of, D6, at base + 1.
Grounds on DB-25 connector: pins 18 to 25 on 36 pin Centronics connector: pins 16, 33, and 19 to 30.

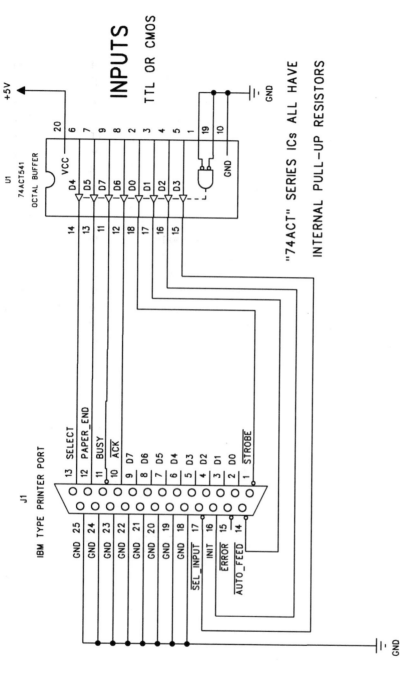

INPUTS

TTL OR CMOS

"74ACT" SERIES ICs ALL HAVE
INTERNAL PULL-UP RESISTORS

FIGURE G-2: BUFFERED 8-BIT DATA INPUTS

THIS IS THE SAFE WAY TO INPUT DATA VIA YOUR COMPUTER'S PRINTER PORT

Use Sw_IN.PAS, Sw_IN.C, or Sw_IN.BAS TO DISPLAY INPUT DATA

PAGE 240, FIGURE G-2

Gray Code/Binary Conversion Logic

Suppose you had a disk with binary numbers from 0 to 15 represented as punched holes. Phototransistors placed near one side of the disk are positioned to detect a light source from the opposite side. As the disk turns, binary numbers are detected and transmitted back to your computer. The disk stops turning and comes to rest right on the boundary between 7 and 8. What would the output be? Since the area between the number codes is a "never-never land," any bit might be high or low. Therefore, any combination of highs and lows are possible, and that means any number from 0 to 15 is possible.

That's not acceptable. What we need is a feedback system that would oscillate between 7 and 8 and only output a 7 or 8 when the disk was in "never-never land." That's what the Gray code was designed for.

The Gray code can, among other things, provide reliable position feedback of rotating and straight line movement. Like binary, Gray code consists of ones and zeros. However, with Gray code only one bit changes between adjacent numbers. The chart in Figure H compares binary and Gray code numbers between 0 and 15. The Gray code can be generated with any number of bits. Figure H also shows gate logic diagrams to convert a nibble of binary to Gray code or Gray code to binary.

Through observation and experimentation, I discovered that Gray code logic matches the control logic used for dual phase and bipolar stepping motors. I have not seen this concept documented anywhere else. Armed with this knowledge, you can simplify your stepping motor control software by adding a little inexpensive hardware "glue logic."

GRAY CODE TO BINARY

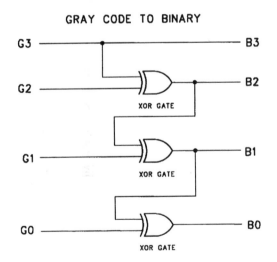

BINARY TO GRAY CODE

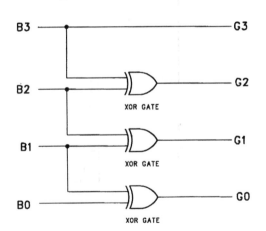

Figure H

TPU Units

A TPU unit is a collection of procedures that are used repeatedly. The procedures in MY_TPU.PAS and MY_TPU.C are used repeatedly throughout this book. Rather than include them with each application, they have been collected and grouped together in the following units.

MY_TPU.PAS Listing

```
UNIT My_TPU;
{ A TPU unit of procedures I repeatedly use                                  }
INTERFACE

USES CRT, DOS, GRAPH;

TYPE Set_Of_Char = Set Of CHAR;
     Digit_Type  = ARRAY[0..10,0..10] OF STRING[15];
     Line_Info_Type =
       RECORD
       X1, Y1, X2, Y2 : INTEGER;
       END; { line info type }

VAR  OK_Set                  : Set_Of_Char;
     Digit                   : Digit_Type;
     X, Y, Color, Xdir, Ydir : INTEGER;
     Lines                   : Line_Info_Type;

PROCEDURE Cursor_Off;
 { Hide the cursor.  Use BIOS interrupt $10, Function 1 to hide the curser  }
PROCEDURE Cursor_ON;
 { Determine the active vidio card.  This is not a trival task              }
PROCEDURE Clear_Kbd_Buffer;
 { Clear contents of keyboard buffer.                                       }
PROCEDURE Get_Character( OK_Set : Set_Of_Char; VAR Ch : CHAR);
 { Read a character from the keyboard.  Print the character's ASCII code at }
 { the cursor.  Return the ASCII code to program via variable Ch           }
PROCEDURE Select_Printer_Port(VAR Lpt_Num, Lpt_Port_Address : WORD);
 { check for valid port selection  ( 1, 2, or 3 )                          }
 { check that selected printer port is actually installed on machine       }
 { return port address from BIOS variable segment, ( Lpt_Port_Address )    }
PROCEDURE Find_Lpt1(VAR Lpt1_Base_Address : INTEGER);
 { find first printer port, LPT1 }
FUNCTION Find_LPTx(Num : INTEGER) : WORD;
 { return port address of printer port 1, 2, or 3, selected by variable Num. }
PROCEDURE Init_Printer_Port(Lpt_Num, Lpt_Port_Address : WORD);
 { Initilize selected printer port;                                        }
 { Tell ROM-BIOS service routine $17, function $01, to initilize the       }
 { selected printer port, Lpt_Num.                                         }
```

```
PROCEDURE Generate_Characters( Digit : Digit_Type );
  { generate large numbers from extended ASCII characters }

IMPLEMENTATION
VAR        Regs : REGISTERS;

PROCEDURE Clear_Kbd_Buffer;
  { Clear contents of keyboard buffer.                                        }
  { From PC Intern, by Michael Tischer, Abacus Press, 1992, page 462          }
BEGIN
INLINE ( $FA );                       { CLI: disable hardware interrupts      }
MemW[$40:$1A] := MemW[$40:$1C];       { No more characters in Buffer          }
INLINE ( $1B );                       { STI: enable hardware interrupts       }
END;

PROCEDURE Get_Character( OK_Set : Set_Of_Char; VAR Ch : CHAR);
{ Read a character from the keyboard.  Print the character's ASCII code at    }
{ the cursor.  Return the ASCII code to program via variable Ch               }
BEGIN
  REPEAT
  REPEAT UNTIL KEYPRESSED;
  Ch := ReadKey;
  IF ORD(Ch) = 0 THEN { it's an extended character code, between 128 and 255 }
    BEGIN
    Ch := ReadKey;
    Ch := CHAR(ORD(Ch) + 127);
    END;
  IF (Ch IN OK_Set) AND (Ch IN [CHAR(32)..CHAR(255)]) THEN WRITE(Ch);
  IF (Ch IN OK_Set) THEN BEGIN END ELSE WRITE(CHAR(7));
  UNTIL Ch IN OK_Set;
END; { get character }

PROCEDURE Select_Printer_Port(VAR Lpt_Num, Lpt_Port_Address : WORD);
VAR Ch : CHAR;
  { check for valid port selection  ( 1, 2, or 3 )                           }
  { check that selected printer port is actually installed on machine        }
  { return port address from BIOS variable segment, ( Lpt_Port_Address )     }
  {   $0408 contains port address of LPT1                                    }
  {   $040A contains port address of LPT2                                    }
  {   $040C contains port address of LPT3                                    }
  { The Programmer's PC Sourcebook, MicroSoft Press, 1991, Page 7-75,        }
  { Compute's Mapping the IBM PC, Compute Books, 1985, page 234              }

BEGIN
  REPEAT
  ClrScr; Ch := ' ';    Lpt_Port_Address := 0;
  GOTOXY(1,10); WRITE('Which printer port do you want to use, 1, 2, or 3? ');
  OK_Set := ['1'..'3'];
  Get_Character( OK_Set, Ch);
  Lpt_Num := ORD(Ch) - 48;
  Lpt_Port_Address := MemW[ 0: $0400 + 6 + ( Lpt_Num * 2 ) ];
  IF Lpt_Port_Address = 0 THEN
    BEGIN
    WRITELN;
    WRITELN('Port selected is not installed on this machine.');
    WRITELN; WRITELN('PRESS ANY KEY TO CONTINUE:');
```

```
      REPEAT UNTIL KEYPRESSED;      Ch := Readkey;
    END; { else }
  UNTIL Lpt_Port_Address <> 0;
END; { select printer port }


PROCEDURE Find_Lpt1(VAR Lpt1_Base_Address : INTEGER);
CONST Base_Address = 1024;      Offset = 8;
  { use 8 for LPT1, use 10 to find LPT2, and 12 to find LPT3 }
BEGIN
Lpt1_Base_Address := MemW[0: Base_Address + Offset];
END;


FUNCTION Find_LPTx(Num : INTEGER) : WORD;
{
return port address of printer port, 1, 2,  or 3, selected by variable Num.
From:
  Compute's Mapping The IBM PC & PCjr, Russ Cavies, Compute Books, 1985, P 234
  The Programmer's PC Source Book, 1991, Thom Hogan, Microsoft Press, Page 7-75
}
CONST Base_Address = 1024;  { base address for IBM printer ports }
VAR Offset : INTEGER;
BEGIN
Offset := (2 * Num) + 6; { 8 = LPT1, 10 = LPT2, and 12 = LPT3 }
Find_LPTX := MemW[0: Base_Address + Offset];
END; { find lpt1 }


PROCEDURE Init_Printer_Port(Lpt_Num, Lpt_Port_Address : WORD);
{ Initilize selected printer port;                                        }
{ Tell ROM-BIOS service routine $17, function $01, to initilize the selected }
{   printer port, Lpt_Num.                                                }
{ Referances:                                                             }
{ PC Interrupts, Addison-Wesley, 1991, page 3-31, &  Programmer's Reference }
{ Manual for IBM Personal Computers, Dow Jones Pub, 1986 Pub. Page 678    }
BEGIN
WITH Regs DO  { from Mastering Turbo Pascal 6, (c) 1991, Tom Swan, Page 889 }
  BEGIN
  AH := $01;      { function number }
  DX := Lpt_Num; { printer port number }
  END; { with }
INTR($17, Regs);
END; { init printer port }


PROCEDURE Cursor_Off;
{ Hide the cursor.  Actually, sets cursor off the screen                  }
{ Uses BIOS interrupt $10, Function 1 to hide the curser                  }
{ Restores the normal default cursor settings.                           }
{ Uses BIOS interrupt $10, Function 1 to hide the curser                  }
{ Turbo Pascal 6, Comp. Ref; Borland/Osborne Pub; Stephen. O'Brien, Page 416 }
{ PC Interrupts, Addison Wesley Pub. 1991, by Ralf Brown; Page 5-12       }
{ Programmer's Ref Man for IBM Per. Comp. Dow Jones Irwin Pub, 1986; P.522 }
{ Programming the IBM User Interface; Addison-Wesley 1989; Ben Ezzell; P.223 }

BEGIN
WITH Regs DO
  BEGIN
  ah := $01;  { set cursor shape            }
```

```
      ch := $20;   { hide cursor, starting row  }
      cl := $02;   { hide cursor, ending row    }
    END; { with }
INTR($10, Regs);
END; { cursor off }


PROCEDURE Cursor_ON;
{ Find out if a graphics card is being used.  Use apropreate procedure to   }
{ turn on the cursor. Hercules and MDA video cards are different from CGA    }
{ Turbo Pascal 6 System Programming, Abacus 1991, by Michal Tischer, Pg 414  }

TYPE Video_Cards = (MDA, CGA, HERC, EGA, VGA, Unknown );
     VioSaveBuf = ARRAY [$0000..$3FFF] OF BYTE;
     VSPtr = ^VioSaveBuf;
VAR                         Video_Card : Video_Cards;
                               Vio_Ptr : VSPtr;   { pointer to video RAM }
                              IN_Graphc : BOOLEAN;
                            Active_Mode : String[10];
                 Video_Mode, Scr_Lines : BYTE;
                             Vidio_Mode : BYTE;
               Graph_Driver, Graph_Mode : INTEGER;


PROCEDURE Graphics_Cursor_ON;
{ Uses BIOS interrupt $10, Function 1 to restore the normal cursor         }
{ Restores the normal default cursor setings to any color graphics card    }
{ Programming the IBM User Interface; Addison-Wesley, 1989; P.223           }
BEGIN
WITH Regs DO
  BEGIN
  ah := $01;
  ch := $06;
  cl := $07;
  END; { with }
INTR($10, Regs);
END; { graphics cursor on }


PROCEDURE Mono_Cursor_ON;
{ Uses BIOS interrupt $10, Function 1 to restore the normal cursor. Restores }
{ the normal default cursor to monochrome and Hercules graphics cards.       }
{ Programming the IBM User Interface; Addison-Wesley, 1989; P.223            }
BEGIN
WITH Regs DO
  BEGIN
  ah := $01;
  ch := $09;
  cl := $0A;
  END; { with }
 INTR($10, Regs);
END; { mono cursor on }


PROCEDURE Get_Video_Card;
{ Determine the active vidio card.  This is not a trival task                }
{ Turbo Pascal 6 System Programming, Abacus 1991, Michael Tischer,Pg 410-15 }
Const VGA_Vidio_Tab : ARRAY[0..12] OF Video_Cards =
                   (Unknown, MDA, CGA, Unknown, EGA, EGA,
                    Unknown, VGA, VGA, Unknown, CGA, CGA, CGA );
```

```
          Mono_Adr_Reg = $3b4;                        { monochrome card port address }
          Mono_Status = $3ba;               { monochrome card's status port address }
VAR   Regs : Registers;
         i : INTEGER;
      Status : BYTE;                                      { MDA-/ Hercules status port }

BEGIN
Video_Card := Unknown;
Regs.AH := $0F;                                  { Function to determine vidio mode }
INTR($10, Regs);
Video_Mode := Regs.AL and $7f;                               { store vidio mode }

Regs.AX :=$1a00;                              { Function to determine if only VGA }
INTR($10,Regs);
IF (Regs.AL = $1a) THEN                             { is function available? }
  BEGIN
  IF (Regs.BL <> $1a) THEN             { yes, VGA, code of current card in  BL }
    Video_Card := VGA_Vidio_Tab[Regs.BL]          { yes, get code from table }
  END
ELSE                                                { not VGA, is it an EGA ? }
  BEGIN
  Regs.AH := $12;                                        { call function $12 }
  Regs.BL := $10;                                        { sub function $10  }
  INTR($10, Regs);                                       { call video BIOS   }
  If (Regs.BL <> $10) THEN Video_Card := EGA;            { EGA  is installed }
  END; { else }
IF (Video_Card = Unknown) THEN                   { vidio card  still unknown? }
  IF   (MemW[$0040:$0063] = Mono_Adr_Reg ) THEN          { monochrome card ? }
    BEGIN                                         { yes, must be MDA or Hercules }
    { if card is Hercules, then bit 7 in CRT status register will change,   }
    { otherwise, the card is a monochrome display                          }
    Vio_Ptr := PTR($B000, $0000 );
    Status := PORT[Mono_Status] AND $80;               { read CRT status port }
    i := 0;
    WHILE ( PORT[Mono_Status] AND $80 = Status) AND (i < 32767) DO INC(I);
    IF ( I = 32767 ) THEN Video_Card := MDA ELSE Video_Card := Herc;
    END { if mem }
ELSE Video_Card := CGA;
END;

PROCEDURE Error_Message;
BEGIN
ClrScr;
WRITELN;
WRITELN('Unable to restore your cursor. ');
WRITELN('Your type of vidio display is "UNKNOWN" to this software');
WRITELN; WRITE('PRESS ANY KEY TO CONTINUE: ');READLN;
END; { case }

BEGIN { cursor on }
Get_Video_Card;
CASE Video_Card OF
        MDA, HERC : Mono_Cursor_ON;
    CGA, EGA, VGA : Graphics_Cursor_ON;
          UNKNOWN : Error_Message;
              END; { case }
```

```
END;  { cursor on }

PROCEDURE Generate_Characters( Digit : Digit_Type );
 { generate large numbers from extended ASCII characters }
BEGIN
DIGIT[0,1] := (' ÛÛÛÛÛÛ ');
DIGIT[0,2] := ('Ûß      ßÛ');
DIGIT[0,3] := ('Û        Û');
DIGIT[0,4] := ('Û        Û');
DIGIT[0,5] := ('Û        Û');
DIGIT[0,6] := ('Û        Û');
DIGIT[0,7] := ('Û        Û');
DIGIT[0,8] := ('ÛÛ      ÛÛ');
DIGIT[0,9] := (' ßÛÛÛÛÛß ');

DIGIT[1,1] := ('         Û');
DIGIT[1,2] := ('         Û');
DIGIT[1,3] := ('         Û');
DIGIT[1,4] := ('         Û');
DIGIT[1,5] := ('         Û');
DIGIT[1,6] := ('         Û');
DIGIT[1,7] := ('         Û');
DIGIT[1,8] := ('         Û');
DIGIT[1,9] := ('         Û');

DIGIT[2,1] := (' ÛÛÛÛÛÛ ');
DIGIT[2,2] := ('Ûß      ßÛ');
DIGIT[2,3] := ('         Û');
DIGIT[2,4] := ('       ÛÛ');
DIGIT[2,5] := (' ÛÛÛÛÛÛß ');
DIGIT[2,6] := ('Ûß        ');
DIGIT[2,7] := ('Û         ');
DIGIT[2,8] := ('Û         ');
DIGIT[2,9] := ('ÛÛÛÛÛÛÛÛÛÛ');

DIGIT[3,1] := (' ÛÛÛÛÛÛ ');
DIGIT[3,2] := ('Ûß      ßÛ');
DIGIT[3,3] := ('         Û');
DIGIT[3,4] := ('       ÛÛ');
DIGIT[3,5] := ('   ÛÛÛÛÛ ');
DIGIT[3,6] := ('         ßÛ');
DIGIT[3,7] := ('         Û');
DIGIT[3,8] := ('ÛÛ      ÛÛ');
DIGIT[3,9] := (' ßÛÛÛÛÛß ');

DIGIT[4,1] := ('Û        Û');
DIGIT[4,2] := ('Û        Û');
DIGIT[4,3] := ('Û        Û');
DIGIT[4,4] := ('Û        Û');
DIGIT[4,5] := ('ÛÛÛÛÛÛÛÛÛÛ');
DIGIT[4,6] := ('         Û');
DIGIT[4,7] := ('         Û');
DIGIT[4,8] := ('         Û');
DIGIT[4,9] := ('         Û');
write('5');
```

```pascal
  DIGIT[5,1] := ('ÛÛÛÛÛÛÛÛ');
  DIGIT[5,2] := ('Û        ');
  DIGIT[5,3] := ('Û        ');
  DIGIT[5,4] := ('ÛÛÛÛÛÛÛÜ ');
  DIGIT[5,5] := ('       ßÛ');
  DIGIT[5,6] := ('        Û');
  DIGIT[5,7] := ('        Û');
  DIGIT[5,8] := ('ÛÜ     ÜÛ');
  DIGIT[5,9] := (' ßÛÛÛÛÛß ');

  DIGIT[6,1] := (' ÜÛ      ');
  DIGIT[6,2] := ('ÛÜß      ');
  DIGIT[6,3] := ('Û        ');
  DIGIT[6,4] := ('ÛÜÛÛÛÛÛÜ ');
  DIGIT[6,5] := ('ÛÜß    ßÛ');
  DIGIT[6,6] := ('Û       Û');
  DIGIT[6,7] := ('Û       Û');
  DIGIT[6,8] := ('ÛÜ     ÜÛ');
  DIGIT[6,9] := (' ßÛÛÛÛÛß ');

  DIGIT[7,1] := ('ÛÛÛÛÛÛÛÛ');
  DIGIT[7,2] := ('        Û');
  DIGIT[7,3] := ('        Û');
  DIGIT[7,4] := ('        Û');
  DIGIT[7,5] := ('        Û');
  DIGIT[7,6] := ('        Û');
  DIGIT[7,7] := ('        Û');
  DIGIT[7,8] := ('        Û');
  DIGIT[7,9] := ('        Û');

  DIGIT[8,1] := (' ÜÛÛÛÛÛÜ ');
  DIGIT[8,2] := ('ÛÜß    ßÛ');
  DIGIT[8,3] := ('Û       Û');
  DIGIT[8,4] := ('ÛÜ     ÜÛ');
  DIGIT[8,5] := (' ÛÛÛÛÛÛ ');
  DIGIT[8,6] := ('ÛÜß    ßÛ');
  DIGIT[8,7] := ('Û       Û');
  DIGIT[8,8] := ('ÛÜ     ÜÛ');
  DIGIT[8,9] := (' ßÛÛÛÛÛß ');

  DIGIT[9,1] := (' ÜÛÛÛÛÛÜ ');
  DIGIT[9,2] := ('ÛÜß    ßÛ');
  DIGIT[9,3] := ('Û       Û');
  DIGIT[9,4] := ('ÛÜ     ÜÛ');
  DIGIT[9,5] := (' ßÛÛÛÛÛÛ');
  DIGIT[9,6] := ('        Û');
  DIGIT[9,7] := ('        Û');
  DIGIT[9,8] := ('        Û');
  DIGIT[9,9] := ('        Û');
END; { generate characters }

END. { my TPU }
```

```
/*                          UNIT My_TPU
                   Code conversion by Eugene Klein
             A TPU unit of procedures I repeatedly use
  */
union REGS regs;
struct Line_Info_Type
        {
      int X1;
      int Y1;
      int X2;
      int Y2;
        };


char OK_Set[15];
char Digit[10][10][15];
int X, Y, Color, Xdir, Ydir;
struct Line_Info_Type Lines;
unsigned int Lpt_Port_Address;


void Clear_Kbd_Buffer(void)
  // Clear contents of keyboard buffer.
  // From PC Intern, by Michael Tischer, Abacus Press, 1992, page 462
{
 disable();                     // disable hardware interrupts
 poke(0x40,0x1A,peek(0x40,0x1C));  // No more characters in Buffer
 enable();                      // enable hardware interrupts
}

int Get_Character( char OK_Set[15])
// Read a character from the keyboard.  Print the character's ASCII code at
// the cursor.  Return the ASCII code to program via variable Ch
{
 unsigned int Ch=0;
 unsigned int extended;
 char *ptr=0;
 while(!ptr)
 {
  while(!kbhit()){}
   Ch=getch();
  if(!Ch)
  {
   extended = getch();
   Ch=extended + 0x80;
  }
  ptr=strchr(OK_Set,Ch);
  if(ptr)
  {
   if((Ch >= 0x32) && (Ch <=0xff))
   printf("%c",Ch);
  }
  else
   printf("\a");
```

```c
    }
  return(Ch);
}


unsigned char Select_Printer_Port(void)
{
  // check for valid port selection  ( 1, 2, or 3 )
  // check that selected printer port is actually installed on machine
  // return port address from BIOS variable segment, ( Lpt_Port_Address )
  //   0x0408 contains port address of LPT1
  //   0x040A contains port address of LPT2
  //   0x040C contains port address of LPT3
  // The Programmer's PC Sourcebook, MicroSoft Press, 1991, Page 7-75,
  // Compute's Mapping the IBM PC, Compute Books, 1985, page 234

  char Ch;
  unsigned char Lpt_Num;

  do
  {
    char *OK_Set = "123";
    clrscr(); Lpt_Port_Address = 0;
    gotoxy(1,10); printf("Which printer port do you want to use, 1, 2, or 3? ");
    Ch=Get_Character( OK_Set);
    Lpt_Num = Ch - 48;
    Lpt_Port_Address = peek( 0, 0x0400 + 6 + ( Lpt_Num * 2 ) );
    if (Lpt_Port_Address == 0)
    {
      printf("\nPort selected is not installed on this machine.\n");
      printf("PRESS ANY KEY TO CONTINUE:");
      getch();
    }  // if address = 0
  }while(Lpt_Port_Address == 0);
  return(Lpt_Num);
}


unsigned int Init_Printer_Port(unsigned char Lpt_Num)
// Initialize selected printer port;
// Tell ROM-BIOS service routine $17, function $01, to initialize the selected
//   printer port, Lpt_Num.
// References:
// PC Interrupts, Addison-Wesley, 1991, page 3-31, &  Programmer's Reference
// Manual for IBM Personal Computers, Dow Jones Pub, 1986 Pub. Page 678
{
  regs.h.ah=0x01;          //function number
  regs.x.dx=Lpt_Num;       //port number
  int86(0x17,&regs,&regs);
  return( peek(0, 0x0400 + 6 + ( Lpt_Num * 2 )) );
}


void Cursor_Off(void)
// Hide the cursor.  Actually, sets cursor off the screen
// Uses BIOS interrupt $10, Function 1 to hide the curser
// Restores the normal default cursor settings.
// Uses BIOS interrupt $10, Function 1 to hide the curser
// Turbo Pascal 6, Comp. Ref; Borland/Osborne Pub; Stephen. O'Brien, Page 416
```

```
// PC Interrupts, Addison Wesley Pub. 1991, by Ralf Brown; Page 5-12
// Programmer's Ref Man for IBM Per. Comp. Dow Jones Irwin Pub, 1986; P.522
// Programming the IBM User Interface; Addison-Wesley 1989; Ben Ezzell; P.223

{
 regs.h.ah = 0x01;   // set cursor shape
 regs.h.ch = 0x20;   // hide cursor, starting row
 regs.h.cl = 0x02;   // hide cursor, ending row
 int86(0x10, &regs,&regs);
}


void Graphics_Cursor_ON(void)
// Uses BIOS interrupt $10, Function 1 to restore the normal cursor
// Restores the normal default cursor settings to any color graphics card
// Programming the IBM User Interface; Addison-Wesley, 1989; P.223
{
 regs.h.ah = 0x01;
 regs.h.ch = 0x06;
 regs.h.cl = 0x07;
 int86(0x10,&regs,&regs);
}


void Mono_Cursor_ON(void)
// Uses BIOS interrupt 0x10, Function 1 to restore the normal cursor. Restores
// the normal default cursor to monochrome and Hercules graphics cards.
// Programming the IBM User Interface; Addison-Wesley, 1989; P.223
{
 regs.h.ah = 0x01;
 regs.h.ch = 0x09;
 regs.h.cl = 0x0A;
 int86(0x10,&regs,&regs);
}


char *Get_Video_Card(void)
// Determine the active video card.  This is not a trivial task
// Turbo Pascal 6 System Programming, Abacus 1991, Michael Tischer,Pg 410-15
{
 char VGA_Vidio_Tab[13][8]  =
          {"Unknown","MDA","CGA","Unknown","EGA","EGA","Unknown",
           "VGA","VGA","Unknown","CGA","CGA","CGA"};
 unsigned int Mono_Adr_Reg = 0x3b4; // monochrome card port address
 unsigned int Mono_Status = 0x3ba;  // monochrome card's status port address
 unsigned int i;
 int status;                        // MDA-/ Hercules status port
 char Video_Card[10] ="Unknown";
 //int Video_Mode;

 regs.h.ah = 0x0F;                  // Function to determine vidio mode
 int86(0x10,&regs,&regs);
 //Video_Mode = regs.h.al && 0x7f;   // store vidio mode
 regs.x.ax = 0x1a00;               // Function to determine if only VGA
 int86(0x10,&regs,&regs);
 if(regs.h.al == 0x1a)             // is function available?
 {
  if(regs.h.bl != 0x1a)            // yes, VGA, code of current card in  BL }
    strcpy(Video_Card,VGA_Vidio_Tab[regs.h.bl]);    // yes, get code from table }
```

```c
  }
  else                                     // not VGA, is it an EGA ?
  {
   regs.h.ah = 0x12;                       // call function $12
   regs.h.bl = 0x10;                       // sub function $10
   int86(0x10,&regs,&regs);                // call video BIOS
   if(regs.h.bl != 0x10)
     strcpy(Video_Card,"EGA");             // EGA  is installed
  }
  if(!strcmp(Video_Card,"Unknown"))   // vidio card  still unknown?
  {
    if  (peek(0x0040,0x0063) == Mono_Adr_Reg ) // monochrome card ?
    {
     // yes, must be MDA or Hercules
     // if card is Hercules, then bit 7 in CRT status register will change,
     // otherwise, the card is a monochrome display
     status = inport(Mono_Status) && 0x80; // read CRT status port
     i = 0;
     while((inport(Mono_Status) && 0x80 == status) && (i++ <=32767))
     {
      if ( i == 32767 )
        strcpy(Video_Card,"MDA");
      else
        strcpy(Video_Card,"Herc");
     }
    }
  }
  else
    strcpy(Video_Card,"CGA");
  return(Video_Card);
}




void Error_Message(void)
{
 clrscr();
 printf("\nUnable to restore your cursor.\nYour type of vidio display is UNKNOWN to
this software");
 printf("\nPRESS ANY KEY TO CONTINUE:");
 getch();
}


void Generate_Characters( char DIGIT[8][9][10])
// generate large numbers from extended ASCII characters
{
 strcpy(DIGIT[0][1]," ÜÛÛÛÛÛÜ ");
 strcpy(DIGIT[0][2],"Ûß      ßÛ");
 strcpy(DIGIT[0][3],"Û        Û");
 strcpy(DIGIT[0][4],"Û        Û");
 strcpy(DIGIT[0][5],"Û        Û");
 strcpy(DIGIT[0][6],"Û        Û");
 strcpy(DIGIT[0][7],"Û        Û");
```

```
strcpy(DIGIT[0][8],"ÛÜ      ÜÛ");
strcpy(DIGIT[0][9]," ßÛÛÛÛÛß ");

strcpy(DIGIT[1][1],"         Û");
strcpy(DIGIT[1][2],"         Û");
strcpy(DIGIT[1][3],"         Û");
strcpy(DIGIT[1][4],"         Û");
strcpy(DIGIT[1][5],"         Û");
strcpy(DIGIT[1][6],"         Û");
strcpy(DIGIT[1][7],"         Û");
strcpy(DIGIT[1][8],"         Û");
strcpy(DIGIT[1][9],"         Û");

strcpy(DIGIT[2][1]," ÜÛÛÛÛÛÜ ");
strcpy(DIGIT[2][2],"Ûß      ßÛ");
strcpy(DIGIT[2][3],"         Û");
strcpy(DIGIT[2][4],"        ÜÛ");
strcpy(DIGIT[2][5]," ÜÛÛÛÛÛß ");
strcpy(DIGIT[2][6],"Ûß        ");
strcpy(DIGIT[2][7],"Û         ");
strcpy(DIGIT[2][8],"Û         ");
strcpy(DIGIT[2][9],"ÛÛÛÛÛÛÛÛÛ");

strcpy(DIGIT[3][1]," ÜÛÛÛÛÛÜ ");
strcpy(DIGIT[3][2],"Ûß      ßÛ");
strcpy(DIGIT[3][3],"         Û");
strcpy(DIGIT[3][4],"        ÜÛ");
strcpy(DIGIT[3][5],"   ÛÛÛÛÛÛ ");
strcpy(DIGIT[3][6],"        ßÛ");
strcpy(DIGIT[3][7],"         Û");
strcpy(DIGIT[3][8],"ÛÜ      ÜÛ");
strcpy(DIGIT[3][9]," ßÛÛÛÛÛß ");

strcpy(DIGIT[4][1],"Û        Û");
strcpy(DIGIT[4][2],"Û        Û");
strcpy(DIGIT[4][3],"Û        Û");
strcpy(DIGIT[4][4],"Û        Û");
strcpy(DIGIT[4][5],"ÛÛÛÛÛÛÛÛÛ");
strcpy(DIGIT[4][6],"         Û");
strcpy(DIGIT[4][7],"         Û");
strcpy(DIGIT[4][8],"         Û");
strcpy(DIGIT[4][9],"         Û");

strcpy(DIGIT[5][1],"ÛÛÛÛÛÛÛÛÛ");
strcpy(DIGIT[5][2],"Û         ");
strcpy(DIGIT[5][3],"Û         ");
strcpy(DIGIT[5][4],"ÛÛÛÛÛÛÛÜ ");
strcpy(DIGIT[5][5],"        ßÛ");
strcpy(DIGIT[5][6],"         Û");
strcpy(DIGIT[5][7],"         Û");
strcpy(DIGIT[5][8],"ÛÜ      ÜÛ");
strcpy(DIGIT[5][9]," ßÛÛÛÛÛß ");

strcpy(DIGIT[6][1]," ÜÛ       ");
strcpy(DIGIT[6][2],"Ûß        ");
strcpy(DIGIT[6][3],"Û         ");
```

```c
    strcpy(DIGIT[6][4],"ÛÜÛÛÛÛÛÜ ");
    strcpy(DIGIT[6][5],"Ûß    ßÛ");
    strcpy(DIGIT[6][6],"Û      Û");
    strcpy(DIGIT[6][7],"Û      Û");
    strcpy(DIGIT[6][8],"ÛÜ    ÜÛ");
    strcpy(DIGIT[6][9]," ßÛÛÛÛß ");

    strcpy(DIGIT[7][1],"ÛÛÛÛÛÛÛÛ");
    strcpy(DIGIT[7][2],"       Û");
    strcpy(DIGIT[7][3],"       Û");
    strcpy(DIGIT[7][4],"       Û");
    strcpy(DIGIT[7][5],"       Û");
    strcpy(DIGIT[7][6],"       Û");
    strcpy(DIGIT[7][7],"       Û");
    strcpy(DIGIT[7][8],"       Û");
    strcpy(DIGIT[7][9],"       Û");

    strcpy(DIGIT[8][1]," ÜÛÛÛÛÜ ");
    strcpy(DIGIT[8][2],"Ûß    ßÛ");
    strcpy(DIGIT[8][3],"Û      Û");
    strcpy(DIGIT[8][4],"ÛÜ    ÜÛ");
    strcpy(DIGIT[8][5]," ÛÛÛÛÛÛ ");
    strcpy(DIGIT[8][6],"Ûß    ßÛ");
    strcpy(DIGIT[8][7],"Û      Û");
    strcpy(DIGIT[8][8],"ÛÜ    ÜÛ");
    strcpy(DIGIT[8][9]," ßÛÛÛÛß ");

    strcpy(DIGIT[9][1]," ÜÛÛÛÛÜ ");
    strcpy(DIGIT[9][2],"Ûß    ßÛ");
    strcpy(DIGIT[9][3],"Û      Û");
    strcpy(DIGIT[9][4],"ÛÜ    ÜÛ");
    strcpy(DIGIT[9][5]," ßÛÛÛÛÛÛ");
    strcpy(DIGIT[9][6],"       Û");
    strcpy(DIGIT[9][7],"       Û");
    strcpy(DIGIT[9][8],"       Û");
    strcpy(DIGIT[9][9],"       Û");
}
```

IC CHIPS